Innovations and Advances in

Cognitive Behaviour Therapy

Edited by Danielle A. Einstein

First published in 2007 from a completed manuscript presented to
Australian Academic Press
32 Jeays Street
Bowen Hills Qld 4006
Australia
www.australianacademicpress.com.au

National Library of Australia
Cataloguing-in-Publication data:

Innovations and advances in cognitive-behaviour therapy.

1st ed.
Bibliography.
Includes index.
ISBN 9781875378777 (pbk.).

1. Cognitive therapy - Textbooks. I. Einstein, Danielle A.
II. Title.

616.89142

Editing and typesetting by Australian Academic Press, Brisbane.

Contents

CONTENTS

CONTENTS

Introduction

This book has been written for clinicians wishing to update their awareness and skills based on clinical research being conducted predominantly
in Australia and New Zealand. It explores innovations and cutting edge
developments in the way cognitive–behaviour therapy (CBT) is applied
across the full spectrum of psychopathology. Emphasis is placed on flexible modes of delivery and new directions in treatment modality. Chapters
discussing new treatments focus on the practical implementation of the
new treatment. Data-driven investigations are included when they reveal
advances in treatment or where research provides exciting information
for clinical practice. Authors have provided a clear description of new
treatment procedures. The book has combined a theoretical basis with
practical applicability for the experienced clinician.

Innovations and Advances in Cognitive–Behaviour Therapy is divided
into three parts. The first part examines innovative treatments for specific
presentations.

Chapter 1 presents a cognitive–behavioural treatment package for
music performance anxiety (MPA). The treatment developed by Tarrant
and Leatham incorporates a range of strategies in which clients (i) acquire
an understanding of the nature of MPA and its relationship with anxiety,
(ii) develop insight through examination of their personal performance
history, (iii) examine the role of personality contributions to MPA, (iv)
explore the role of technical and non-technical preparation prior to performance, (v) learn to discriminate alternate options of focus for their
attention during performance. The chapter is practical and detailed and the
authors describe an evaluation of the treatment. They have included a copy
of their measure 'the Music Performance Anxiety Scale' as an Appendix.

Chapter 2 is a practitioner guide for the treatment of Magical Ideation
(MI). This treatment was developed for use with individuals suffering
from obsessive–compulsive disorder (OCD) with high levels of magical

ideation. It is the first published description of the treatment package and the majority of materials (patient handouts and target articles) are provided. A review of the research program supporting the importance of addressing MI in the treatment of OCD is provided and pilot data supports implementation of the package within this population.

Chapter 3 provides a rationale for the use of mindfulness as a treatment for bipolar disorder. It is a more theoretical chapter. Ball, Corry and Mitchell describe rationales, precautions and techniques which, from their experience, are important in the application of mindfulness to clients with bipolar disorder.

Huxter's chapter (chapter 4) examines the Buddhist origins of mindfulness treatments. Given the explosion in evidence suggesting the use of mindfulness for treatment of recurrent depression, this perspective is valuable and enlightening. Huxter alerts clinicians of the need to be informed of the origins of mindfulness and provides an accessible description of its Buddhist roots.

Chapter 5 presents a new treatment of trauma-related nightmares for children. Encel and Dohnt have adapted imagery rehearsal therapy (IRT) for this population. They provide an introduction to IRT, a description of how to implement this therapy within the paediatric population, and information on where to find further resources for clinicians wishing to learn more about IRT with adults. As standard treatment of childhood trauma does not try to address nightmares, this chapter may be the first of its kind. It is extremely practical and detailed.

Woodcock, Milic and Johnson then describe the treatment of selective mutism in chapter 6. This comprehensive chapter reviews the literature, explains the theoretical basis of selective mutism and compares their program to alternative treatments. The authors have provided a detailed description of how to apply their intervention. They report data they have collected and provide case examples useful to any therapist wishing to commence treatment.

Reading about computer treatments is often less than exciting. However, the chapter written by Cunningham, Donovan and March is captivating. Their chapter thoroughly examines the issues arising in the development and delivery of computer- and Internet- based CBT for anxiety disorders in young people. They describe the issues that arose in developing two treatment programs ('The Cool Teens Program', developed at Macquarie University, and 'The BRAVE program', developed at The University of Queensland). They compare the ways that these two independent and eminent groups of clinical academics chose to handle each issue.

Chapter 8 is a useful starting point for any clinician wishing to expand their practice into work with an older population. Deborah Koder combines a review of the literature with her own clinical experience to impart practical advice on the implementation of CBT. She provides examples of how to adjust CBT for this population. Her reference list will be a useful resource for those wishing to further their knowledge in this area.

Merritt, Pervan and Sheady have written a practitioner guide for the implementation of acceptance and commitment therapy (ACT) for individuals suffering from chronic pain. These clinicians describe exercises and metaphors they have found useful from their work at Prince Alfred Hospital in Sydney with this notoriously difficult group to treat. Their description of the treatment explains miniature steps by which to break down behaviour therapy and introduce it in a palatable way to this population. Once again, information on where to find out more about ACT is provided throughout the chapter.

Shearsby, Walker and Steel have written a chapter about cognitive–behavioural treatment of psychosis that is both philosophical and helpful. It attempts to remove the myths behind what clinicians aim for in their treatment of psychosis. Their chapter is written from the perspective of a group that has conducted a randomised controlled trial (RCT) of two treatments for psychosis: cognitive therapy and coping strategy enhancement (the 'Voices and Beliefs Project'). They provide three case studies from which they draw lessons to assist clinicians wishing to work in this area.

The second part of the book presents results from treatment comparisons. Once again, the authors have provided a detailed description of the treatments and explanations of how these treatments represent advances on existing treatments.

Chapter 11 describes a trial conducted at the Black Dog Institute in which emotive techniques have been added to cognitive therapy in the treatment of bipolar disorder. In chapter 12, Maree Abbott provides an in depth description of her new package for the treatment of generalised anxiety disorder and presents initial results. In chapter 13, a new treatment focuses on engagement of eating disorders patients within an inpatient setting. It is not hard to envisage how aspects of motivational enhancement treatment could be attempted with a range of populations where there is reluctance to initiate change. Chapter 14 presents a RCT of cognitive processing therapy for assault victims with acute stress disorder. Chapter 15 presents the results of a RCT of MoodGYM (a computerised treatment for depression).

The final section focuses on clinical research being conducted throughout Australia. Prominent researchers were asked to describe their research where the questions under investigation have implications for understanding aetiology or treatment. For example, Hill and Touyz discuss their research into schema underlying eating disorders; Moulds and Kandris review their research examining the role of avoidance in depression; Parker reviews his research on modelling the depressive disorders; and Bryant, Sutherland and Guthrie present studies on the role of autobiographical memory in posttraumatic stress disorder (PTSD). In chapter 20, Ellis and Nixon examine the role of cognitive and social factors in the development of trauma responses within children. In chapter 21, Haarhoff examines the role of therapist schema in training and attitudes of intern cognitive therapists. From a clinician's perspective understanding and considering therapist schema seems to be a worthwhile goal within one's professional development. In the final chapter, Theiler and Bates investigate the significance of early childhood memories. They discuss the potential use of these within assessment and treatment.

Innovations and Advances in Cognitive–Behaviour Therapy is based on a select group of submissions to the national conference of the Australian Association for Cognitive Behaviour Therapy, held in Sydney (October, 2006). All submissions were reviewed and chapters were invited from research groups where it was clear that innovative clinical research had been, or was in the process of being, conducted. The authors were asked to write chapters with an emphasis on the 'how to' of the procedures being evaluated for each disorder. Of course, as scientist practitioners, the authors have provided concise reports of their data or, when the research was still in its infancy (e.g., case studies), have discussed how their research relates to the current literature. What has resulted is, in my view, a wonderful resource for clinicians wishing to know more about treatment in a range of areas. If a certain area arouses particular interest, the authors have provided a comprehensive review, treatment outlines (including experienced clinical suggestions), and references to allow readers to obtain further information.

Acknowledgment
I would like to thank the organising committee from the 19th National Conference of the Australian Association for Cognitive Behaviour Therapy. This book was produced independently of the conference, yet with the full support of the committee.

Danielle Einstein, PhD
Dr Danielle Einstein and Associates, Sydney, Australia

List of Contributors

Abbott, Maree	University of Sydney, Australia
Ball, Jillian	University of New South Wales, Black Dog Institute, Australia
Bates, Glen	Swinburne University of Technology, Australia
Bryant, Richard	University of New South Wales, Australia
Christensen, Helen	Centre for Mental Health Research, The Australian National University, Australia
Corry, Justine	University of New South Wales, Black Dog Institute, Australia
Cunningham, Michael J.	Macquarie University, Australia
Dean, Helen Y.	University of Sydney, Australia
Dohnt, Hayley K.	Flinders University, Australia
Donovan, Caroline L.	The University of Queensland, Australia
Einstein, Danielle A.	University of Sydney, Australia
Ellis, Alicia A.	Flinders University, Australia
Encel, Jason S.	Anxiety Disorders and Trauma Clinic, Adelaide, Australia
Gibson, Malcolm	The Australian National University, Australia
Griffiths, Kathy	Centre for Mental Health Research, The Australian National University, Australia
Guthrie, Rachel	University of New South Wales, Australia
Haarhoff, Beverly	Massey University, New Zealand
Hill, Sandi	University of Sydney, Australia
Huxter, Malcolm John	Private Practice and Lismore Mental Health Service, Australia
Johnson, Susan	Child and Family Team, Prince of Wales and Sydney Children's Hospitals, Australia
Kandris, Eva	University of New South Wales, Australia

Kang, Kanwal	The Australian National University, Australia
Koder, Deborah-Anne	James Cook University and Private Practice, Australia
Leatham, Janet	Massey University, New Zealand
March, Sonja	The University of Queensland, Australia
Menzies, Ross G.	University of Sydney, Australia
Merritt, Anthony	Pain Management Centre, Royal Prince Alfred Hospital and Camperdown Pain Management Centre, Eastern Suburbs Pain Clinic, Sydney, Australia
Milic, Maria	Adolescent and Family Unit/Selective Mutism Research Clinic, Redbank House, Sydney, Australia
Mitchell, Philip	University of New South Wales, Black Dog Institute, Australia
Moulds, Michelle	University of New South Wales, Australia
Nixon, Reginald D.V.	Flinders University, Australia
O'Kearney, Richard	The Australian National University, Canberra
Parker, Gordon	University of New South Wales, Australia
Pervan, Susan	Royal Prince Alfred Hospital Pain Management Centre, Sydney, Australia
Rieger, Elizabeth	University of Sydney, Australia
Sheady, Jo	Royal Prince Alfred Hospital Pain Management Centre, Sydney, Australia
Shearsby, Julia	Banks House, Bankstown Hospital, Sydney South West Area Health Service, Australia
Skillecorn, Ashleigh	University of New South Wales, Australia
Steel, Zachary	University of New South Wales and Centre for Population Mental Health Research, Liverpool Hospital, Sydney South West Area Health Service, Australia
Sutherland, Kylie	University of New South Wales, Australia
Tarrant, Ruth	Massey University, New Zealand
Theiler, Stephen	Swinburne University of Technology, Australia
Thornton, Christopher E.	Kiloh Centre, Prince of Wales Hospital, South Eastern Illawarra Area Health Service, Sydney, Australia
Touyz, Stephen W.	Peter Beumont Centre for Eating Disorders, Wesley Private Hospital, Sydney and University of Sydney, Australia

Walker, Peter	Kiloh Centre, Prince of Wales Hospital, South Eastern Illawarra Area Health Service, Sydney, Australia
Williamson, Paul	Flinders University, Australia
Woodcock, Elizabeth	Selective Mutism Clinic, Sydney, Australia

Innovative treatment for specific presentations

CHAPTER 1

A CBT-Based Therapy for Music Performance Anxiety

Ruth A. Tarrant and Janet M. Leathem

Any public performance whether it involves playing music, sport, public speaking, acting, or test-taking can be associated with fears that have the potential to detract from the quality and enjoyment of the performance. Frequency of performance does not necessarily reduce performance anxiety (PA) levels, and some performers who experience high and unpleasant levels abandon their careers (Powell, 2004; Wesner, Noyes, & Davis, 1990). Despite the potential impact of music performance anxiety (MPA) most musicians do not formally learn effective PA management strategies as part of their training. This chapter outlines current techniques used to manage PA, and introduces an intervention for MPA that could be adapted to assist in other performance arenas.

Drug Therapy

Because musicians generally perceive MPA to be a problem unrelated to other psychological difficulties, many self-medicate with sedatives, alcohol or illegal drugs (e.g., Valium, beta-blockers, cannabis; see Sataloff, Rosen, & Levy, 2000; Wilson, 1997). However, cerebral depressant substances can have side effects that are detrimental to performance (Wesner et al., 1990; Wilson, 1997).

Behaviour Therapy

According to Lehrer (1987), frequent exposure to performing — starting from the least to the most threatening performance situation — appears to be the most beneficial *behavioural* therapy for MPA. Regular relaxation techniques can reduce general autonomic arousal in people who tend to be 'uptight' or fearful (National Health Committee, 1998), thus can be helpful in the days, perhaps hours, leading up to an important performance.

Cognitive Therapy

Studies have found that negative self-talk is often associated with increases in PA (e.g., Lloyd-Elliot, 1991; Steptoe & Fidler, 1987), destructive thoughts undermining confidence and increasing self-doubt about ability to perform, even after many hours of focused practice. Cognitive therapy has assisted performers to become aware of and manage their thoughts (Kendrick, Craig, Lawson, & Davidson, 1982; Sweeney & Horan, 1982).

Cognitive–Behavioural Therapy

Closely linked to behaviour therapy, cognitive–behaviour therapy (CBT) has proven efficacy in anxiety management (see National Health Committee, 1998; Wilkinson, Moore, & Moore, 2000). Nagel, Himle and Papsdorf (1989) reported that following a CBT trial with a group of performance-anxious musicians, significant reductions were demonstrated in trait-anxiety and test-anxiety scores for the treatment group compared with a wait-listed control group. Clark and Agras (1991) found a significant difference between two groups that received CBT (CBT with placebo; CBT with the anxiolytic Buspirone) and two groups that did not receive CBT (Buspirone only; placebo only).

Other Therapies

Other therapies trialled for MPA, including psychodynamic therapy (Nagel, 1993), the Alexander technique (Valentine, Fitzgerald, Gorton, Hudson, & Symonds, 1995), and hypnotherapy (Stanton, 1994), have not been widely reported as effective.

In summary, while there is no current agreement on the most effective therapy for MPA (Brodsky, 1996), CBT has most support both in the literature and intuitively. In a prior exploratory study of MPA in a group of university student-musicians conducted by the present authors, some additional elements not typically included in CBT interventions were identified. These elements have received little or no attention in previous treatment studies for MPA and involve the roles of (a) anxiety as facilitating performance, (b) personal performance-history and its relationship to present performing, (c) impact of personality on performing, (d) importance of preparation (technical and non-technical), and (e) direction of attention while performing (referred to in terms of process versus outcome, a term adopted from the sport performance literature).

The intervention itself has its basis in the anxiety literature, specifically in performance anxiety studies, and in the findings of an earlier exploratory study conducted by the present authors. This study had identified four MPA symptom groups (physiological, cognitive, affective, and behavioural) and three broad groups of influential factors (personality factors, performing experience including preparation, and situational factors). It is the inclusion of components from all three categories of influential factors, plus exploration of the role played by MPA symptoms, that distinguishes this intervention from previous intervention approaches, most approaches having generally focused on a single or limited category of factors.

Data from previous MPA treatment studies have generally been analysed on a group basis only, often obscuring individual results. In the present study, individual results were investigated as well as group results. The group situation is the favoured context for CBT treatment reported in MPA studies to date, and the present study is also conducted in a group situation. Key advantages of the group situation include a supportive environment for performers who share common MPA problems, where individually appropriate strategies can be developed to manage MPA. An intervention for MPA based on CBT is described below.

Participants

Participants were volunteers recruited from the 140 students (40 classical/ 100 jazz) studying at the Conservatorium of Music at Massey University, Wellington, New Zealand. In total, twenty-five participants (14 males/11 females; 21 classical/4 jazz) began, and 14 completed the intervention (8 males/6 females; 13 classical/1 jazz) representing string, brass, woodwind and voice. Classical students (13 of 14 completions) were disproportionately represented, particularly considering their smaller representation in total student numbers at the conservatorium. This imbalance reflected the higher MPA scores in classical students compared with the jazz, in the exploratory study. In light of the conservatorium students' demanding schedules, attempts to recruit a control group for the present study were unsuccessful.

Measures

Measures selected for the present study were the Musicians Performance Anxiety Scale (M-PAS), the trait-anxiety scale (Form Y2) of the State–Trait Anxiety Inventory (STAI; Spielberger, 1983), and the neuroticism and extraversion scales of the Eysenck Personality Questionnaire — Revised Short Scale (EPQ-R Short Scale; Eysenck & Eysenck, 1996). Measures were administered at the beginning and end of the intervention, and at four-month follow-up. The purpose of the measures was to (a) demonstrate any change in MPA levels, as measured by the M-PAS scale, over time; and (b) show relationships between MPA, as measured by the M-PAS scale and personality variables. The M-PAS (see Appendix A) was developed, trialled and evaluated by the authors in a previous exploratory study.

Procedure

The intervention was conducted over six weekly sessions. Apart from an extra 10 minutes taken before Session One and after Session Six to complete pre- and post-questionnaires, sessions were kept to one hour to encourage participation and to minimise loss of participants. Participants met in groups of four to six. Apart from completing measures, sessions comprised the same components: a review of homework from the previous session; educational material; group discussion; group exercises; setting of personal application exercises (homework) and, in four of the sessions, relaxation exercises.

All six sessions included an examination of participants' thoughts and emotions in relation to the subtopics, encouraged constant exposure to performing with follow-up critical discussion, and four sessions included relaxation exercises. The rationale for, and description of, sessions is outlined below.

Intervention: Rationale and Description

Session 1 ■ Understanding Anxiety: A Psychoeducational Model

Participants learned about the psychoeducational model of the fight and flight response, with emphasis on the connection between cognitions, affect, behaviour and physiological symptoms. Further, they learned that anxiety has a *facilitative* role — increased arousal of anxiety is necessary to enable the heightened sensitivity, strength and mental focus required to perform well. Participants identified symptoms and indicators of anxiety in a case study of an anxious performer, and then examined their own anxiety symptoms and indicators. The relationship between thoughts, emotions, physiological responses and behaviours associated with anxiety was clearly established at this point in the intervention.

Session 2 ■ Examining Performance History: Reassessing Performance Criteria

Examining one's past performances can be helpful when developing strategies to manage or control future performances, but often, reasons for outcomes have been neither examined nor understood. It is important for performers to understand what has contributed to, or caused, a specific problem or outcome so they can bring into focus areas that need developing.

At times, performers link their performance expectations to someone else's technical skill (e.g., a recording artist's), rather than to their own level of development. Thus, performers can be disappointed when their performance outcomes do not meet their, unrealistic, goals. Linked to this, performers may downplay their own performance achievements. Alternatively, at times performers may be overconfident, taking on performances that are unlikely to be successful for them. If performers are continually dissatisfied with their performance, it is likely they are setting up inappropriate environments for their development. Therapeutic components in the present study addressed setting realistic, objective performance criteria and expectations. This component was inevitably tied to examining negative thoughts and feelings that can result in performers undermining their own confidence to perform; throughout the intervention, attention was drawn to rapid automatic thoughts that can contain errors that may otherwise be left unchallenged.

Thus it is critical that aspects of therapy are designed to motivate performers to examine their performance history to understand and learn from their experience. In the present study, participants examined the context of one or two of their most 'pleasant', and 'unpleasant' performing experiences. In this 'looking back' exercise (conducted part in session and part for homework), participants examined, for instance, their level of technical preparation; confidence at various, specific times prior to performing; familiarity with the particular performing environment; expectations; feelings; positive thoughts and their potential to build confidence; attention to the music while performing; perceived opinions of other people; and the extent and nature of negative thinking. The exercise was followed by participants composing balanced or alternative thoughts to replace negative thoughts.

Session 3 ■ Personality and Performance: Can Personality Influence Performing?

Participants were provided with broad information,[1] about their own trait-anxiety and extraversion scores (in relation to norm scores), based

---

1 Scores were categorised as *average, slightly above average*, and *slightly below average* on the following basis: *average* — within one *SD* of the mean score; *slightly above average* — at least one *SD* above the mean score; *slightly below average* — at least one *SD* below the mean score.

on a view that participants may better understand their own reactions to performing, and recognise the value of using particular strategies to manage their individual responses.

Feedback on neuroticism scores was not provided to students as it was believed that students might perceive neuroticism in pejorative terms, given the difference between everyday usage of the term and the psychological definition.

Generally, the higher an individual's trait-anxiety, the higher their state-anxiety when under stress (Spielberger, 1983). That is, trait-anxiety levels can often predict state-anxiety. However, individual state anxiety (e.g., MPA) can vary greatly, depending on a number of other factors. Although some anxiety-related factors will be important for everyone (e.g., preparation, confidence level), performers should be aware of what is particularly important for them individually. Alternatively, performers who tend to feel less anxious than most people may need to create some excitement around themselves to lift their arousal level a little, ready to perform — otherwise their performance could be dull and lifeless.

Extraverts generally enjoy attention from other people — including the attention they receive in performance situations. Introverts however, are less sociable, often tending to keep close control of their feelings and they are generally less interested in attracting attention to themselves. The more extraverted performer can build on their tendency to be outgoing and expressive, and enjoy the attention that comes with performing — although an extreme extravert may also need to take care not to become overconfident. The less extraverted performer may benefit from 'acting' in a more extraverted manner in instances where it is likely to enhance their ability to perform.

In Session 3, an exercise was included in anticipation of the typically more introverted, classical musicians who were expected to take part in the intervention; participants were encouraged to consider the idea of developing a greater willingness or 'freedom' to express themselves. They were encouraged to experiment with 'overacting' a verbal introduction to a piece to discover a style they were comfortable with. The authors considered this verbal rehearsal another way to assist in building stage confidence. For homework, in addition to keeping a thought record regarding performing, participants were urged to 'play like an extreme extravert', the aim again being to encourage participants to project themselves beyond their comfort zone, exploring some new expressive approaches that may help them feel more comfortable in performance situations. Interestingly, a number of participants indicated they had enjoyed the 'extreme extravert' exercises, experiencing a certain 'freedom' on those occasions.

Session 4 ■ Preparation: The Importance of Non-Technical Preparation

If an important performance has been pleasing for the performer, it is likely to have been because preparation was appropriate and adequate. The opposite is also true; it is not surprising that an unprepared performer should lack confidence, or perform poorly. However, many performers appear not to clearly link preparation with performing or performance outcomes. Preparation can be considered in terms of technical preparation and non-technical preparation. Technical preparation concerns the requirements for making the music, and non-technical preparation concerns matters such as selection of appropriate pieces to play, ability to concentrate under pressure, establishment of routines and rituals, experience and familiarity with similar performance environments, confidence, sufficient physical stamina for the demands of a particular performance, sufficient and realistic challenge to raise performance levels, expectations for the performance, planning to deal with the unexpected, or ability to manage anxiety. Non-technical preparation is just as critical as technical preparation, but often receives less attention.

In the group sessions, participants discussed various aspects of non-technical preparation, and how these related to their own more successful, and less successful performances. For example, even with a high level of technical ability, a performer who has not performed in front of a large audience can be distracted by the size of the occasion — and choke. In the sessions, attention was given to the routines and rituals that can be set in place and followed for important performances. The routines or rituals that precede a performance can provide the performer with a familiarity and confidence that says: 'I've been here before and I know what to do right now'. Participants were encouraged to consider the value of setting up routines that could assist in their preparation for important performances. A homework exercise concerned participants identifying gaps in their own non-technical preparation, and building their own list of preparation elements that 'worked' for them.

Session 5 ■ Direction of Attention: Process Versus Outcome

The direction of attention component of the therapy focused particularly on evaluation awareness, and examining process versus outcome performing. In a prior study conducted by the authors, student-musicians awareness of others evaluating them was one of the most marked causes of anxiety, both *before* performing and *while* performing. Music performance anxiety represents a 'fear of negative evaluation by other people' (Wilson, 1997, p. 231). However, the occasions when performers want to produce their most outstanding performances are the very occasions when they are most vulnerable and when some performers are most likely to be distracted.

The direction of attention component was designed to assist participants in developing strategies to help them focus exactly on what they were doing, and to deal with their thoughts about people evaluating them. Essentially, strategies centred around (a) directing attention away from evaluation concerns, and getting back to the content and requirements of performing; and (b) becoming aware of their own thoughts about people's opinions, and then examining thoughts for accuracy, relevance, and consequences.

Participants were encouraged to consider what they were thinking about prior to and, often, during the performance itself. They were asked to reflect on whether thoughts were about the *process* of playing/singing, or are whether they were about the *outcome* (i.e., result). Performers who direct attention to possible outcomes, will have reduced their mental capacity that should be available for the process of performing.

In this session, participants took part in an exercise that required divided attention. Attention had to be divided between completing five very simple mathematics tasks (achievable by an average 11-year-old) while simultaneously listening to a short story (duration: one minute). Participants were then asked to write a single word or phrase answer to five questions relating to the content of the story. Mathematics and comprehension answers were then scored. Although individual scores could remain confidential, participants were surprised how poorly they had done, and readily talked about this with the rest of the group. No one achieved 10/10; most scored under 5/10. This exercise proved to be a graphic illustration of how divided attention can result in compromised performance on task execution.

In therapy, participants were encouraged to discuss attention issues in relation to performing, to raise awareness of the critical nature of attention for the performer and, in particular, to consider where their own attention was directed while they were performing. Participants completed individual pie graph exercises where they estimated percentages of time spent on different types of thoughts that occurred while they were performing. Typical percentages included, for instance, 'What's my teacher thinking (30%)', 'I hope I don't get my timing wrong (10%)', 'Please let this be over (20%)', 'I hope I look all right (5%)', or 'I hope this is going well (10%)'. Although there were individual differences, the objective of the exercise was clearly illustrated: participants realised that no one was allocating 100% of their attention to the requirements of performing.

Participants considered strategies that would help them to focus on the process of performing, rather than allocating attention to outcome or peripheral issues. The process versus outcome approach to performance means staying in the present, moment by moment, until the task has been completed. But, to attend 100% to the process is a discipline that requires practice. Most people benefit from having directive self-statements that help them to focus back on the process when they start to think about outcome issues. Helpful, pithy phrases or sayings, with individual meaning for the performer, are created by the performer and are immediately available to him/her to help get back on track. In Session Five, and for homework, participants worked on developing personal sayings or slogans, often quirky, that they could subvocalise to refocus their wandering attention while performing.

Session 6 ■ Thoughts, Feelings and Performance: Confirming the Links
Throughout the intervention, attention was given to the relationship between what an individual was thinking and how they were feeling, as well as to how they were performing. In the final session, attention was drawn to how the body reports what the person is thinking and feeling. Participants discussed a diagram (adapted from Haider & Groll-Knapp, 1981) that depicted heart rate (via an electrocardiograph [ECG]) and mental activity (via an encephalogram [EEG]) as a horn player approached and performed a solo passage in an orchestral piece. Examination of the ECG and EEG demonstrated a shift in physiological indicators as the performer waited for the solo passage, and then moved to a more focused attention during the solo passage itself. The final session of the intervention also provided an opportunity for participants to draw together and record a summary of material that was personally relevant for them in terms of increasing their confidence and performance levels.

Results and Discussion
The MPA scores, as measured by the M-PAS, reduced from pretest to posttest to four-month follow-up, with the difference between pre-test and follow-up being statistically significant, $z = -2.167$, Sig (2-tailed), $p = .030$. The significant difference is likely to be explained by strategies learnt in therapy having been practised and applied over time. In terms of individual scores, of the 14 participants who completed the therapy, 11

reported decreased scores. Of the three that did not decrease, one participant reported consistent increases in trait-anxiety and neuroticism, suggesting (s)he may have experienced an elevated anxiety overall. However, the authors had no reason to exclude this participant from the analysis. The other two increases were small. An examination of individual pretest, posttest, and follow-up scores indicated the greatest reduction in scores was achieved by participants with the highest pretest scores. While it is possible that follow-up scores may represent a regression toward the mean, the qualitative data gathered at the end of the therapy would suggest otherwise: participants reported perceived benefits from the therapy.

The M-PAS scale, with a reliability coefficient (Cronbach's alpha) of .904, was again evaluated in the present study. Comparisons of the scale were consistent with the authors' previous study and with Spielberger's (1983) trait-anxiety scale ($r = .743, p = .001$), state and trait-anxiety being correlated at a similar rate (see Spielberger, 1983).

A slight reduction in trait-anxiety scores over time (*ns*) was consistent with the reduction in MPA (a state-anxiety), suggesting that MPA is associated with other types of anxiety. There was also a slight reduction in neuroticism over time (*ns*), perhaps suggesting a slight reduction in tension associated with performing. Extraversion scores remained relatively stable. Over the period of therapy and follow-up, it is not surprising there was reasonable consistency in the personality scores, personality being viewed as reasonably stable. However, relationships between personality and M-PAS scores were investigated in the present study so the M-PAS could be reassessed, and so relationships between MPA and personality could be re-examined. Consistent with previous studies, it appears that performers who report the highest levels of MPA also score highest on trait-anxiety (Cox & Kenardy, 1993; Craske & Craig, 1984) and, often, neuroticism (MacLeod, 1999; Steptoe & Fidler, 1987).

Of the participants who dropped out of therapy, time issues (including employment, childcare, and assessment deadlines) were cited as the reason. 'The loss of large numbers of subjects in intervention research is not at all rare' (Kazdin, 1994, p. 43). Most dropouts were in their first year at the Conservatorium, and they may have had the most difficulty managing time and university study. Further, participants knew they were taking part in a new, untrialled therapy, so perhaps there was little incentive to stay in the face of time demands. They may also have believed they could not be helped. All participants who began therapy ($N = 25$), provided pretest data before their first session, and those who dropped out did so after their first or, for two participants, second session. In the absence of being able to recruit a control group, the pretest data for all who began was compared with follow-up data for the completers. The difference in M-PAS scores was significant, $t(23) = 3.32$, $p < .01$, $\eta^2 = 0.32$, with a large effect size.

Conclusion

Ideally, participants would have performed within the group (not possible in the present study) and then discussed their performance experience. Instead, participants were asked to talk about their between session performance efforts when they came to therapy. In future deliveries of the intervention, the inclusion and discussion of live performance within sessions would likely add a most useful therapeutic component.

Like the present study, many previous studies have had small numbers of participants, but together such studies contribute to an increased understanding of MPA. The present intervention allowed an assessment of an until now untrialled approach to PA management that may shed some light on the way forward.

Looking beyond music performance, elements of PA investigated and trialled in the present study are likely to have implications across a range of other performance domains. Two issues of particular importance that have received little or no attention in the PA treatment literature to date are preparation, and the role of attention in high levels of performance. These performance elements, critically linked to PA, are often overlooked, especially by the less experienced performer. It is critical that PA therapies assist performers to understand and manage preparation concerns and, likewise, that attention issues are addressed. The concept of process versus outcome has direct and broad application to performance, and it is essential for PA management that performers develop the ability to focus on the present, disregarding any thoughts about future outcomes.

Three further issues requiring consideration in PA therapies are the facilitative role of anxiety; critical appraisal of past performing efforts, contexts and outcomes; and the possible impact of personality on performing. Finally, it appears that a conventional CBT approach can be broadened to include elements outlined in the present study, to expand performers' exploration and application of personally relevant strategies to assist in performance anxiety management.

References

Brodsky, W. (1996). Music performance anxiety reconceptualised: A critique of current research practices and findings. *Medical Problems of Performing Artists, 11,* 88–98.

Clark, D.B., & Agras, W.S. (1991). The assessment and treatment of performance anxiety in musicians. *American Journal of Psychiatry, 148*(5), 598–605.

Cox, W.J., & Kenardy, J. (1993). Performance anxiety, social phobia, and setting effects in instrumental music students. *Journal of Anxiety Disorders, 7*, 49–60.

Craske, M.G., & Craig, K.D. (1984). Musical performance anxiety: The three-systems model and self-efficacy theory. *Behavioural Research Therapy, 22*(3), 267–280.

Eysenck, H.J., & Eysenck, S.B.G. (1996). *Manual of the Eysenck Personality Scales (EPS Adult)*. London: Hodder & Stoughton.

Haider, M., & Groll-Knapp, E. (1981). Psychophysiological investigations into the stress experienced by musicians in a symphony orchestra. In M. Piperek (Ed.), *Stress and music: Medical, psychological, sociological, and legal strain factors in a symphony orchestra musician's profession* (pp. 15–34). Vienna, Austria: Wilhelm Braumuller.

Kazdin, A.E. (1994). Methodology, design, and evaluation. In A.E. Bergin & S.L. Garfield (Eds.). *Handbook of Psychotherapy and Behaviour Change* (4th ed.). (pp. 19–71). New York: John Wiley & Sons Inc.

Kendrick, M.J., Craig, K.D., Lawson, D.M., & Davidson, P.O. (1982). Cognitive and behavioural therapy for musical-performance anxiety. *Journal of Consulting and Clinical Psychology, 50*(3), 353–362.

Lehrer, P.M. (1987). A review of the approaches to the management of tension and stage fright in music performance. *Journal of Research in Music Education, 35*(3), 143–153.

Lloyd-Elliot, M. (1991). Witches, demons and devils: The enemies of auditions and how performing artists make friends with saboteurs. In G.D. Wilson (Ed.), *Psychology and performing arts* (pp. 211–217). Amsterdam: Swets & Zeitlinger Publishers.

MacLeod, C. (1999). Anxiety and anxiety disorders. In T. Dalgleish & M. Power (Eds.), *Handbook of cognition and emotion* (pp. 447–477). Chichester: John Wiley & Sons.

Nagel, J.J. (1993). Stage fright in musicians: A psychodynamic perspective. *Bulletin of the Menninger Clinic, 57*(4), 492–503.

Nagel, J.J., Himle, D.P., & Papsdorf, J.D. (1989). Cognitive-behavioural treatment of musical performance anxiety. *Psychology of Music, 17*, 12–21.

National Health Committee. (1998). *Guidelines for assessing and treating anxiety disorders*. Wellington, New Zealand: National Health Committee.

Powell, D.H. (2004). Treating individuals with debilitating performance anxiety: An introduction [In-Session issue]. *Journal of Clinical Psychology, 68*(8), 801–808.

Sataloff, R.T., Rosen, D.C., & Levy, S. (2000). Performance anxiety: What singing teachers should know. *Journal of Singing, 56*(5), 33–40.

Spielberger, C.D. (1983). *State-Trait Anxiety Inventory*. Redwood City, CA: Mind Garden.

Stanton, H.E. (1994). Reduction of performance anxiety in music students. *Australian Psychologist, 29*(2), 124–127.

Steptoe, A., & Fidler, H. (1987). Stage fright in orchestral musicians: A study of cognitive and behavioural strategies in performance anxiety. *British Journal of Psychology, 78*, 241–249.

Sweeney, G.A., & Horan, J.J. (1982). Separate and combined effects of cue-controlled relaxation and cognitive restructuring in the treatment of musical performance anxiety. *Journal of Counseling Psychology, 29*(5), 486–497.

Valentine, E., Fitzgerald, D., Gorton, T., Hudson, J., & Symonds, E. (1995). The effect of lessons in the Alexander technique on music performance in high and low stress situations. *Psychology of Music, 23*, 129–141.

Wesner, R.B., Noyes, R., & Davis, T.L. (1990). The occurrence of performance anxiety among musicians. *Journal of Affective Disorders, 18*, 177–185.

Wilkinson, G., Moore, B., & Moore, P. (2000). *Treating people with anxiety and stress: A practical guide for primary care.* Oxon, UK: Radcliffe Medical Press.

Wilson, G. (1997). Performance anxiety. In D.J. Hargreaves & A. North (Eds.), *The social psychology of music* (pp. 229–245). New York: Oxford University Press.

Appendix A
Musicians Performance Anxiety Scale (M-PAS)

Please circle the number that best answers how you feel or react in the situations described below.

	A little			A lot
Overall, how anxious do you usually feel while practising ....1 in a group	2	3	4	5
Overall, how anxious do you usually feel in a group-lesson..........1 with your teacher?	2	3	4	5
Overall, how anxious do you usually feel playing in a group ....1 in front of your musician-peers	2	3	4	5
Overall, how anxious do you usually feel playing in a group ....1 in front of *non-musician* friends?	2	3	4	5
Overall, how anxious do you usually feel playing in a group ......1 in anything where the performance is NOT formally judged?	2	3	4	5
Overall, how anxious do you usually feel in a lesson with ....1 only you and your teacher?	2	3	4	5
Overall, how anxious do you usually feel playing solo in..............1 front of your musician-peers?	2	3	4	5
Overall, how anxious do you usually feel playing solo in..............1 front of non-musician friends?	2	3	4	5
Overall, how anxious do you usually feel playing solo in any ......1 situation that is NOT formally judged?	2	3	4	5
Overall, how anxious do you usually feel playing any solo ....1 that IS formally judged?	2	3	4	5
Do you have trouble remembering *during* the performance? 1	2	3	4	5
Do you have trouble concentrating *during* the performance?......1	2	3	4	5
Do you feel detached from yourself or from the present ....1 *during* the performance?	2	3	4	5
Do you feel panicky *during* the performance? 1	2	3	4	5
Do you fear making mistakes *during* the performance? 1	2	3	4	5
Are you aware of people evaluating you *during* the ....1 performance?	2	3	4	5
Do you sweat *during* a performance?..1	2	3	4	5
Do you have shaky hands, voice, legs or diaphragm *during* ....1 a performance?	2	3	4	5

Appendix A (CONTINUED)
Musicians Performance Anxiety Scale (M-PAS)

Please circle the number that best answers how you feel or react in the situations described below.

	A little				A lot
Do you have a thumping or racing heart *during* a performance?	1	2	3	4	5
Do you have any noticeable changes in breathing *during* a performance?	1	2	3	4	5
Do you feel tight in the chest *during* a performance?	1	2	3	4	5
Do you get a dry mouth or have difficulty swallowing *during* a performance?	1	2	3	4	5
Do you feel sick in the stomach *before* a performance?	1	2	3	4	5
Do you feel the need to go to the toilet more than usual *before* a performance?	1	2	3	4	5
Do you have trouble sleeping *before* a performance?	1	2	3	4	5
Do you get tense muscles (e.g. shoulders or back) *before* a performance?	1	2	3	4	5

CHAPTER 2

The Treatment of Magical Ideation

Danielle A. Einstein and Ross G. Menzies

What is Magical Ideation?

Magic refers to the belief in the individual's power to cause some event. *Magical thinking* refers to a tendency to invoke a causal connection beneath the appearance of independent phenomena (Woolley, 1997). Magical thinking develops in childhood alongside an understanding of scientific principles (see further, Johnson & Harris, 1994). Theoretically, it is proposed that magical thinking is a primitive form of ontological belief, activated in situations of perceived danger. In obsessive–compulsive disorder (OCD) its presence is represented by rituals which defy scientific explanation, for example, the belief that the act of counting could prevent oneself or a close family member from experiencing a plane accident. Other examples include (a) the belief that tapping on a table would positively affect an interview, (b) the belief that one could balance the food in one's mouth and digestive system to prevent food poisoning, and (c) the idea that repeating a mantra would stop a person becoming pregnant. Magical thinking is apparent in rituals involving a specific fear of harm to oneself or others, compulsive checking and superstitious compulsions. The aim of this chapter is to provide therapists with material required to challenge magical thoughts when they appear in treatment.

Evidence Supporting the Role of Magical Ideation in OCD

Several studies have been conducted investigating the role of schizotypy and magical thinking in OCD (Basoglu et al., 1988; Einstein & Menzies, 2004a, 2004b, 2006; Jenike, Baer, Minichiello, Schwartz, & Carey, 1986). Norman, Davies, Malla, Cortese and Nicholson (1996) administered a composite of the Magical Ideation (MI; Eckblad & Chapman, 1983) and Perceptual Aberration (PA; Chapman, Chapman,

& Raulin, 1978) scales to a clinical sample. They observed that OC symptoms[1] were more closely related to the composite score (r = .60) than to either depression (r = .38) or anxiety (r = .42). Einstein and Menzies (2004b) administered the MI scale, the Lucky Behaviours and Lucky Beliefs Scales (Frost et al., 1993), the Thought Action Fusion-Revised scale (Shafran, Thordarson, & Rachman, 1996), the Padua Inventory (PI; Sanavio, 1988), and the Obsessive-Compulsive Inventory-Short Version (OCI-SV; Foa et al., 2002) to 60 obsessive–compulsive patients at a hospital clinic. Of all the measures, the MI scale was found to be the most strongly related to obsessive–compulsive symptoms (r = .69 with the PI; r = .50 with the OCI-SV). Large and significant relationships between MI scores and the measures of OCD were obtained even when alternative constructs (Lucky behaviours, Lucky beliefs, Thought Action Fusion-Revised scales) were held constant. No other variable remained significantly related to the Obsessive–Compulsive Inventory-Short Version when MI scores were held constant. These findings suggested that a general magical thinking tendency may underpin previous observed links between superstitiousness, thought action fusion and OCD severity (Einstein & Menzies, 2004b).

In a retrospective study, Jenike et al. (1986) examined 43 treatment-resistant obsessive–compulsives. They found that individuals with con-comitant schizotypal personality disorder had a high rate of treatment failure (7% improvement). In a study conducted at Westmead Hospital, 34 obsessive–compulsive patients completed the MI, the Maudsley Obsessional-Compulsive Inventory (MOCI; Hodgson & Rachman, 1977), the OCI-SV, and the PI, pre- and post cognitive–behavioural treatment (Einstein & Menzies, 2006b). Treatment did not address magical thinking. Obsessive–compulsive symptoms (as measured by the PI, the OCI-SV, and the MOCI) decreased significantly post treatment. Pretreatment MI scores significantly predicted response to treatment with correlations of –.53 (p < .002) for the OCI-SV and –.52 (p < .001) for the PI. Thus low levels of clinical improvement were associated with high levels of pretreatment magical thinking. The size of these correlations reveals that pretreatment magical thinking accounted for 25% of the variance in improvement across treatment. Thus high magical thinking (as indicated by scores on the MI scale) is an indicator of poor response to standard cognitive–behavioural treatment.

---

1   A composite of scores on the Maudsley Obsessional-Compulsive Inventory and Padua Inventory indicated obsessive–compulsive symptoms.

How to Conduct Magical Ideation Treatment

The essence of magical ideation treatment is teaching critical thought. This occurs through an analysis of the emotional reasons that permit contemplation of magical thoughts. The aim of treatment is to assist the individual to challenge and dismiss their magical thoughts through the use of analogies which they do not follow in their day-to-day lives. Clients consider emotional, cultural and political factors that draw others into the worlds of clairvoyance, astrology, spirit influences, telepathy, cults and other paranormal phenomena. Using examples, in which others suspend their judgment and endorse bizarre beliefs, provides distance and perspective for the client by removing the specific danger feared. Clients comment on the reasons that people may be persuaded to suspend critical thought and draw conclusions, which they then apply to their own magical thoughts. The issues brought up through the magical ideation treatment package include recognition of:

- a basic human desire for certainty
- the desire for control
- the normality of fear and reasons why others may wish to instil fear
- the ways in which others abuse fear
- the 'imagined' power that magical thoughts instil in the individual.

The magical ideation package is composed of eight elements. In this chapter, six of the eight elements will be described with handouts and the materials provided. Two elements have not been included due to impracticality and copyright limitations of reproducing the material. These were the cult video and the tarot card-reading website. Materials to examine paranormal phenomena are frequently available in the media. The observant therapist should be able to create additional activities from current affairs television programs and newspapers. Our package includes the following components:

- Astrology Today article
- Explanation of the origins of fire
- Horoscope Analysis
- Superstition Questionnaire
- The Carlos Hoax
- Report of UFO sighting
- Agon Shu cult video
- Guide for Tarot card readers.

Activity 1: Astrology Today Article

This article is reproduced with permission from the Australian Skeptics. It is an adaptation of an article written by Harry Edwards, first published in 1992 in *The Skeptic*. In the article, the author responds to an advertisement for free horoscope readings. He sends off six responses, under different names, and describes how the clairvoyant uses simple emotional ploys to sell worthless products. The handout below examines comprehension of the article and the messages that may be drawn from it. It is completed in consultation with the clinician, after reading the target article (see following page).

Astrology Today Handout

1. How many responses did Harry Edwards send to the advertisement in Astrology Today?
2. What does the phrase 'personal, private and confidential' printed on the outside of the letter suggest about its contents?
3. How does the astrologer instil fear and create a sense of need in the letter?
4. What is the purpose in the astrologer's offering the recipient a 'secret'?
5. What powers does the astrologer claim the crystal talisman possesses?
6. What is the size of the cheque that needs to be sent in order to receive a 'free Inca crystal'?
7. What was the real value of the crystal found to be by Professor Ian Plimer, Head of the School of Earth Sciences at Melbourne University?
8. Is it possible for a 'genuine' business to give away $109.00 worth of free gifts for $27.00?
9. What does this article make you think about written offers of personal astrological charts?

Activity 2: Explanation of the Origins of Fire

Three competing descriptions of the origins of fire were drawn from diverse cultural backgrounds (Ancient Egypt, a North African tribe, and the Australian Aborigines). This was contrasted with a history and description of fire based on the scientific paradigm of today. When reading through this exercise, the therapist should focus on the more civilised Ancient Egyptian culture in which gods were used to further the Pharaoh's power within the community. This contrasts with the more natural Aboriginal and Dahomean cultures, which appreciated the ecosystem and valued animals as cohabitants of their world. The accompanying handout encourages the client to contemplate how different explanations can all be correct (or incorrect) and yet have meaning for the individuals and the culture. One client who suffered from intrusive moral thoughts drew the following meaning from this exercise:

INVESTIGATION Summer 92 **the skeptic**

Astrology Today

Early in 1992 advertisements appeared in newspapers across Australia under the heading ASTROLOGY TODAY, offering free horoscopes. Because I believed that nothing is for free I decided to investigate the offer to look for a hidden trap. I decided to try and get my share of something for nothing and wrote six letters to the advertiser under six different names and six different addresses.

Back came a 1 metre long computer print-out horoscope containing a huge amount of meaningless information about the stars, together with a few ambiguous lines about each person. Each name and address received a similar printout.

So far, so good. Then a few weeks later, we all received a long 'personal, private and confidential' follow up letter from Mr Ray Hastings-Clarke, Astrology Today's Director of Astrological Research. The letters were identical in every respect, except for the date and the names and addresses.

The letters were so full of honesty, sincerity, warmth and concern for my well being and, by the time I finished reading the letter my faith in humanity was all but restored. Let me share some extracts with you:

I wrote to you some time ago about your very exciting horoscope and strongly recommended that you have a more fully detailed transit report plotted for you personally … you know Mr Edwards I have become so familiar with certain horoscopes of special promise such as your own *(and the other five?)* that I often feel as though I am reading the horoscope of a close friend, and I become quite concerned when I see either troublesome events on the horizon, or, perhaps even more importantly, wonderful opportunities that you may not yet have achieved *(Usual ploy — instil fear or create a need, then offer a solution or appeal to greed)* … planetary transits as favourable as yours *(and however many others received the same letter?)* only last a year or so at the most and I am very concerned that you may miss the bus on a once in a lifetime opportunity. *(Hurry or you'll miss out).* For this reason I have made a special effort to select for you a most powerful crystal talisman to give you that extra help. This talisman is my special free gift to you when you order your full horoscope. My recent re-examination of your chart has convinced me that the time is right to share with you a secret that has not only changed my life but has also given new vitality to the lives of a small group of others *(six out of six in my case, how lucky can you be?)* … I strongly feel that this secret will be of great benefit to you too.

I see that you are a person who deserves a better deal in life *(He's right there)* and I feel duty bound to leave no stone unturned in helping you to achieve the wonderful promise of your true astrological potential … and I am going to offer you that help right now.

The secret I want to share with you Mr Edwards *(Ms Williams, Mrs Brown, Mr Smith etc).* is the recently rediscovered crystal of the Incas *(and I didn't even know it was lost)*, a rare item *(so rare he can give them away by the bucketful)* of great good fortune previously only known to the ancient rulers of the great Inca Empire of golden magnificence.

These mystical crystals actually seemed to increase their owner's natural energy, giving them a special ability to succeed beyond their wildest dreams ...

Now modern scientific research has confirmed that the powers attributed to these crystals by the Inca are in fact not just superstitious mumbo-jumbo but do in fact have a very solid scientific base. *(Now there's some research I must have*

missed) University *(unnamed)* research published *(where?)* in 1990 confirmed that the Inca crystal gives off dynamic electromagnetic energy waves creating a strong force field that enhances the user's own natural ability to attract great good fortune to themselves *(I wrote and asked for the details of the research showing this and did not receive a reply).*

All you have to do is fill in the question-naire and a 3 page fully detailed horo-scope for a special price of $25 plus $2 postage (normally $37) and a free Inca crystal (usually $40) will be in your hands within two weeks.

I did not reply (under any of the six names). Three weeks later six identical 'personal, private and confidential' letters arrived from Mr Hastings Clarke stating that I (we) may lose my (our) specially selected free Inca Power Crystal(s) and increasing the free offer to include a Crystal pyramid of wealth (usually $35) a book of lucky lotto numbers (normally $18) and a book entitled 'The 5 minute Miracle, a secret that could change your life forever'. A whole $109 worth for only $27.

The letter said that you need to reply quickly before I have to return your crystal to Brazil where it will be lost to you forever.

That did it. I couldn't afford to miss a bargain like that, so order form completed, cheque signed and into the post. The date was May 30. The cheque was deposited on June 1. August 31 I received my horoscope and free gifts. The horoscope was a computer print out; the lucky lotto was a sheet of random numbers; the pyramid of wealth was a piece of red moulded substance (not a pyramid); the five minute miracle consisted of 1300 words about 'Creative visualisation' printed on five cards; and the mysterious Inca Crystal looked like a rough-cut piece of quartz.

However first impressions may be deceptive so I sent the 'crystal' and the 'pyramid' to Professor Ian Plimer, Head of the School of Earth Sciences at Melbourne University. His report:

Under a scanning microscope and an electron microprobe the $35 Pyramid of Wealth was shown to be costume jewellery, probably from Taiwan or Korea and valued, at most, at a few cents.

Being of quartz, the most common mineral on the surface of the Earth the origin of the 'Inca' crystal was difficult to determine. It was, however, an inferior specimen containing inclusions, and was deformed and fractured. Value: 'Less than an ice cream'.

Professor Plimer added that the superb museum specimens of quartz come from South America and are quite distinctive. Abundant supplies can also be found in NSW.■

There can be any number of interpretations that someone can give intrusive thoughts. Somebody's actions and intent are much more important than the spontaneous thought that has occurred. Religion and culture have a self-serving purpose, and influence one's interpretation of the thoughts that occur. They can lead to harsh judgements that have no true basis in the facts.

The client was encouraged to rote learn this interpretation as a part of treatment. St Clare, Menzies and Jones (2006) report that overlearning is an important part of treatment for OCD.

Fire Handout

1. In which stories is fire believed to be a gift to the people?
2. Why do you think that the ancient societies like the Egyptians involve Gods in their stories, while the North Africans and Aboriginal stories refer to animals?
3. Are the mystical beliefs of the Egyptians any different from contemporary beliefs about Lucky Numbers and the powers of crystals?
4. Can four fundamentally different explanations of the origins of fire be correct?
5. Which of the four explanations for the origin of fire do you think is correct?

FIRE TARGET ARTICLE

The Origins of Fire

Here are four stories that explain the origin of fire. They are from four different cultures: Aboriginal, a North African tribe (the Dahomean Legend), the Egyptians and the 21st century western scientific explanation.

Although these stories were from four different societies, times and cultures they were all created for the same purpose.

1. Egyptian Fire God

The Egyptians believed in several gods, a local god (based in the temple) and the great divinities of nature. By believing in many gods, the Ancient Egyptians created a religion focused on polytheism. The Egyptians believed in gods to explain things that they could not understand. If they came to an explanation about a thing they previously didn't understand, then that particular god lost status. It wasn't until a Pharaoh named Akhenaten that the sun God was considered to be all powerful. However it wasn't for purely religious reasons that Akhenaten wanted the people of Egypt to worship the Sun god. He saw that too much emphasis was being placed on the gods which took away some of the power of the Pharaoh. Akhenaten introduced a new version of the sun god in which he believed himself to be the direct link to this god. In this way he promoted the people of Egypt to worship the Pharaoh as a god. The Egyptians believed that it was the Sun god Ra-Atem who gave them the gift of fire.

Forty, J. (1996). *Ancient Egyptian mythology.* New Jersey: Chartwell Books Inc Quirke, S. (1992). *Ancient Egyptian religion.* London: British Museum Press.

2. Aboriginal Fire Discovery Myth

The story began when two women were fighting a group of snakes which had ambushed them. As the two women fought, one of the woman's fighting sticks broke into two pieces. Suddenly out of the broken fighting sticks, sparks and smoke emerged. A crow saw the unusual stick and flew down to grab it. Then two men saw the bird with the smoking stick and began to chase it and throw stones at it. This startled the bird, causing it to drop the smoking stick into a field of grass. The grass caught fire. This is how human's gained the gift of fire.

Reed, A.W. (1982). *Aboriginal myths, legends and fables.* Sydney: Reed Publishing.

3. Dahomean Fire Discovery Myth

The earth creatures wanted fire but it was protected by a great being named Agbakankan. Many animals like lion, elephant, panther and antelope tried to steal fire from Agbakankan, but they all failed. Tortoise offered to get fire for earth but he needed straw. Straw was also kept from earth. Another great being, Gede, guarded the straw. Many more animals tried to steal the straw from Gede, but like with fire, they all failed. Chameleon offered to get the straw. He crept into where Gede kept the straw and using his gift of camouflage stole a piece of straw from Gede and gave it to Tortoise. Tortoise crept into Agbakankan camp, where he protected fire and using straw he stole some fire and hid it inside his shell. Tortoise escaped from Agbakankan and brought the creatures on earth, fire.

Roth, S.L. (1988). *Fire came to the Earth People.* New York: St Martin's Press.

4. 21st Century Scientific Explanation

The scientific name for burning is combustion. Combustion occurs when oxygen from the air combines with material that is capable of burning. This reaction produces heat. When it takes place rapidly, we can see fire. Flames are a sign of combustion that occur when wood or paper combine with oxygen. For combustion to occur both oxygen and materials which are 'combustible' are needed. Some combustible materials that most people know are wood, coals and kerosene. One way of producing fire is by using matches. Modern matches were invented after the discovery of phosphorous. Phosphorous catches fire at a very low temperature. The first match was invented in 1681 when Robert Boyle dipped a small piece of wood (treated with sulphur) into a mixture of sulphur and phosphorous. The matches caught fire so easily that the invention could not be used. In 1844, the first safety matches were invented. These were made in Sweden and instead of putting all of the necessary chemicals into the match head; red phosphorous was painted into the striking surface of the container. These are the matches we know today.

Leokum, A. (1972). *Tell me why.* London: Odham Books.■

Activity 3: Horoscope Analysis

This activity relies on a horoscope from a recent magazine or newspaper. It should be composed at the time of treatment to ensure its direct relevance to the individual. A photocopy of the horoscope should be made. The headings (e.g., Taurus) should be removed from the star sign description, and the descriptions should be randomly reordered on the page. The following questions may be asked:

- 'Do you know your star sign?' If the client does not know, assist the client to determine their star sign and introduce horoscopes.
- 'Here is a sample of horoscopes from last week's newspaper. The order in which they are displayed on the sheet has been changed. Please read through each one and place a number from 1 to 10 reflecting how accurate the description would be for you over the last week.'
- 'Choose one which seems to be closest to the way that your last week has turned out.' Pause for client to make a choice.
- 'On the next handout you will find the star signs you just read. Is the star sign you chose your correct star sign?'

Horoscope Handout

1. As horoscopes are written in such an open way is it likely that you will relate to most of the horoscope predictions for the coming month (irrespective of which star sign you are)?

2. What does this activity tell you about the relevance and accuracy of horoscopes?

Activity 4: Superstition Questionnaire

This handout is a cognitive restructuring exercise in which a number of superstitions are presented to the client. The logical basis of each superstition is then questioned.

(1a) Many people avoid flying on Friday 13th. Is it possible that plane parts, or bolts, could be impacted by a number on a calendar? How could this occur?

(1b) Is this behaviour foolish? Would you fly on Friday, 13th?

(2a) How could the number of leaves on a 'four-leaf' clover change events in the world?

(2b) How could finding a 'four-leaf' clover make fortuitous events occur?

(3a) Have you ever found a five-cent piece and thought of the saying 'Find a penny pick it up, all day long you will have good luck?'

(3b) How could a five-cent piece be connected to other events that happen in your day? Would good events not occur if you had not found the five-cent piece?

(4a) Some people think that putting up an umbrella inside is bad luck. Would you put an umbrella up inside a bathroom or laundry to dry it?

(4b) How could drying an umbrella in this way bring about something bad within the house?

(5a) Some people believe that owning a green car is unlucky. Do you know anyone with a green car? Do they seem to have worse luck than other people?

(5b) Would you stop yourself buying a green car because of this superstition? How could the colour of a car bring about bad events in the owner's life?

(6a) Some people believe that certain numbers are unlucky and would not rent or buy a house with that particular street number. How could a street number influence how happy a person will be within their residence?

(6b) Is it as important as having sufficient space, a decent kitchen or a sunny room?

(6c) How could a number directly influence a person's career/family/ relationships in a negative way?

(7a) Some people believe that if a mirror is broken, there will be seven years of bad luck to follow. What percentage of people would possess a broken mirror (e.g., a mirror that is cracked or damaged)?

(7b) What would the percentage be if you consider small as well as large mirrors (e.g., mirrors in shaving or cosmetic packs)?

(7c) How do you think that having owned a broken mirror in a blusher/shaving set could physically effect events that would occur to the person in the next seven years?

Activity 5: The Carlos Hoax

A facts sheet describes the fraudulent claims of a channeller invited to Sydney by the current affairs program *60 Minutes*. The facts sheet outlines how the media and public were persuaded to provide both air time and support for the channeller.

FACTS SHEET: THE CARLOS HOAX TARGET ARTICLE

During February 1988, Sydney was visited by a fraudulent channeller. But far from being like all the other fraudulent channellers who have visited Australia, this one was different — he was a fraudulent fraudulent channeller, a hoax organised by Richard Carleton of the Channel 9 '*60 Minutes*' program and US arch-sceptic James Randi.

Preceded by a promotional campaign including a press-kit with fake newspaper clippings, reviews and tapes of radio interviews and theatre performances, and a little book called '*The Thoughts of Carlos*', 'channeller' Jose Alvarez was interviewed on three Sydney TV programs — *Terry Willesee Tonight* (channel 7), the *Today Show* (channel 9) and *A Current Affair* (channel 9).

The culmination of the visit was an appearance at the Drama Theatre of the Sydney Opera House on the afternoon of Sunday, February 21 — a free seminar at which the spirit channelled by Alvarez, a 170-times incarnated spirit from Atlantis, named Carlos, shared his wisdom. When Alvarez's body was taken over by Carlos his pulse slowed down as measured by a nurse sitting next to him. Carlos made predictions about the future, typically New Age pronouncements to 'be nice' to other people. Carlos said that there were UFOs on earth and that they were here to protect earth from danger. On one television interview, Carlos predicted that two world leaders would die in the next year. When asked to be more specific he stated that he could not, as being specific would 'cause panic'. At the Opera House, after his performance, there was a selection of crystals for sale. Crystals were described as fossils of ancient spirits. These ranged from $5 for a simple crystal to $20,000 for the rare Atlantean crystal, and $850 for a bottle of Carlos' tears. Carlos had promotional material available which stated 'For the sake of truth, ignore the disbelievers'.

The seminar was further covered on Channel 9 news that night and the *Today Show* the next morning.

The whole point of the exercise was revealed on the *60 Minutes* program of the following Sunday, February 28, when Richard Carleton exposed the hoax, which he said was designed to show how the Australian media were inadequate in their background research. The programs could have exposed Carlos/Alvarez very simply, he said, by phoning the US to check on his credentials, all of which were total fakes. They failed to do this, and thus allowed Alvarez a free run with the full benefits of promotion in Sydney's media.

On the *60 Minutes* program, it was claimed that Alvarez would not have had the audience he did at the Opera House (and the potential sales therefrom) had the media coverage been more aggressive (and factual). 'The hall was packed' the program said, screening interviews with the credulous and deluded who had come because 'they saw it on TV'. Between 250 and 300 people came to the Opera House to see Carlos.■

Carlos Hoax Handout

1. What did Carlos claim to be?
2. How many people turned up at the Opera House to hear him perform?
3. What did he do in his performance?
4. What was he trying to sell?
5. What did the Carlos Hoax demonstrate about people's willingness to believe in an ability to connect with the past and future?
6. Could other reported channellers also be simple hoaxes?
7. What does the Carlos Hoax do to your belief in channelling?
8. Could anyone have disproved Carlos?

Activity 6: Report of UFO Sighting

This article, by Steve Roberts, originally appeared in the 1996 edition of *The Skeptic* magazine (see following page). Roberts describes a person, Kelly Cahill, who reported having seen a UFO. According to the author, Kelly Cahill was on a 'search for meaning' in her life. The article presents the information described by Kelly after the sighting. Evidence taken from the scene and Kelly's reports is described and critically reviewed. Further information gathered from pranksters casts a further disparaging light onto the topic of UFO's. The aim of the activity is to emphasise the importance of scientific validation and gathering proof before subjective experiences are taken to represent reality. This is helpful in challenging clients' beliefs in thought action fusion.

Case Studies Supporting the Magical Ideation Treatment

Einstein, Menzies, St Clare and Drobny (2007) examined whether magical ideation could be shifted in two adults suffering from OCD with the magical ideation treatment package described in the present chapter. C.P. had a 6-year history of OCD and was suffering from major depression at the time of treatment. R.F. had a 14-year history of OCD and had no concomitant diagnoses at the time of treatment. Throughout treatment R.F. was taking Fluroxamine (Luvox) 100 mg. Dosage was not altered during the study and had commenced 6 months prior to treatment. Magical ideation and superstitious beliefs and behaviours were successfully altered by the intervention. This was demonstrated by the results at 3-month follow-up. According to the two-fold criterion of Jacobson, Follette and Revenstorf (1984) scores indicated that both clients had recovered on the MI, the PI, the Lucky Beliefs scale and the Lucky Behaviours scale. On the OCI-Distress scale (Foa et al., 1998), C.P. was improved but not recovered and on the OCI-SV, R.F. had recovered. Scores on the Thought

REPORT OF UFO SIGHTING

Reprinted from Roberts, S. (1996) I would love to see a UFO, Target Article, *The Skeptic*, *16*(4), 29–30. Copyright 1996 by the Australian Skeptics. Reprinted with permission.

Kelly Cahill was looking for something. Not something you or I could provide, not even something she could achieve for herself, but something spiritual, something not of this world. Something Out There.

Her life in Melbourne and then in a small country town had failed to deliver anything really meaningful, despite a marriage with cute young children. Perhaps the answer to life's mysteries lay in the bible. And if one religion could not provide the answers then perhaps another one could.

Now some people don't even possess a bible; some have one on a shelf; some Christians consult their copy occasionally and a minority read it a lot. A few read it incessantly and that is just what Kelly did, for 6 weeks. There are groups that offer comradeship and guidance in reading and interpreting the scriptures — some nice, some not so nice — but Kelly did not avail herself to any of these; without calling on the centuries of existing analysis or picking up any of the intense modern scholarship, she read the bible all by herself, underlining so many passages that the book eventually required replacement. Closeted in a bedroom, with occasional frantic prayer for six weeks.

Imagine her possible mindsets and attitudes on emerging from this monastic experience to go to a party on the evening of August, 7, 1993. Would there be a sign? Perhaps a stroke of lightning, a heavenly voice; perhaps a distant light; a light in a field; even a UFO sighting would be better than nothing, although short of what a religious experience ought to deliver. The forces of nature obligingly delivered up not one, but three UFO sightings in the one night. Since these are rather hard to establish let's list them:

1. A row of 6 to 8 close bright lights in a field on the edge of suburbia, seen from 150 metres away, at dusk, as the car drove past.

2. A similar set of lights, airborne, a few hours later and 15 kilometres away.

3. Immediately after number 2 — no details except for an intense sheet of light which momentarily blinded Kelly and her husband, who was driving the car, so that neither of them recovered their vision for some seconds, although the car stayed on the road.

The last two events occurred during a 90 minute drive in the early hours of the morning, after a party, in countryside. Her husband easily dismissed all three incidents as unworthy of attention, but Kelly got a lot more mileage out of it over the years following.

The UFO community contains very few people with the persistence and rigour of Kelly Cahill and of John Auchettl, the investigator that she was fortunate enough to stumble across some time later. Kelly's first sally forth into UFOdom was with a certain female who wanted to immediately publish her story without further investigation, causing Kelly to take fright and wisely back off at a hundred miles an hour. Later she went to some trouble to track down as many UFO groups as possible and her book Encounter (Harper Collins, $12.95) contains a very useful appendix of known UFO organisations around the world, despite a few mistakes. The UFO community riven by internal squabbles, has generally failed to compile such lists.

Now although I admire Kelly Cahill's courage and determination and wish that others would similarly step forward to report their experiences, public attention to such claims demands a proper analysis which in turn requires the freedom to ask questions, raise doubts, and apply scientific method to the claims made. John Auchettl did indeed conduct a thorough investigation- by UFO standards, at least — but has met with unspecified problems in issuing a report. This is all the more lamentable since other witnesses are claiming to have been present at one of the sightings. But 3 years with no report, and no good reason for no report, damages the credibility of the claims.

Looking back, what happened at the time was rather ordinary, explicable UFO experiences, although 3 in one night is a bit many. But after obsessive reflection on the incident for 6 weeks, Kelly had a dream. (Hands up, all of you who have woken in the night with a feeling that there was another presence — something or somebody else — in the bedroom.) She also found Auchettl, who later found some other witnesses to those lights in the field on that night. They saw something Kelly missed — a tripod under the row of lights in the field. (A tripod? — this provides a path of thought whereby an inquiring mind could establish exactly what the object was and thus explain the entire set of sightings. But that would spoil the story, wouldn't it?) Which other people? — John is not at liberty to say, for reasons not well defined, even three years later. What did they see? — well Kelly later thought she had seen tall dark figures with huge luminous red eyes; the others it is reported, did not see the red eyes. The other witnesses underwent the traditional regressive hypnosis which gave them the traditional belief that they had been taken into a UFO and strapped to a table; but Kelly shunned hypnosis and had no such memories. Both groups of female observers were accompanied by a male who saw nothing.

What of physical evidence? Kelly later reported marks on her body — a small red triangle and some curious hollow bits — but a doctor who happened to need to examine the relevant parts of her did not notice them. There is no picture of the small triangle and now it has gone away. The hollow bits are beneath the surface and would seem to be common to the species *homosapiens*.

Auchettl closely examined the field of the first sighting and found a slight, U shaped, magnetic anomaly. The 3D graph of this makes a good picture and is much admired by people who have no idea what it really depicts, but the accompanying scale in nanoTesla clearly shows that the variations in magnetic field are about 1/1000 of the usual Earth's magnetic field at that point. The edge of the surveyed area and other parts of the field have comparable anomalies, which therefore appear to be insignificant. In this and in the chemical analysis below, no calibration study or second opinion is reported.

There was some abrasion of the grass, but no pattern is reported. A detailed chemical analysis of the UFO site showed deposits of exotic chemicals. Which exotic chemicals? Answer: pyrene, tannic acid, and sulphur; wax on some leaves of grass; and earthworms. (Putting on my white coat for a moment: Pyrene — formed when gasoline, garbage, or any animal or plant material is burnt, therefore usually found in smoke and soot where it combines with dust particles in the air and is carried into water and soil and onto crops; also found in creosote. Tannic acid — found in bark and hence in river water and plants so watered; also found in peat. Sulphur — used in fungicides and in fertilizers. Wax — present in cell walls of plants in order to reduce water loss. Earthworms — oh, for heaven's sake).

When confronted by two explanations for what she recalled, Kelly immediately rejects the one that, although more plausible, would not make her special (page 166). Consider this — when aliens typically show up, such as when James Cook's expedition first reached our shores, do they generally arrive in full view or do they stealthily approach a single native, providing and leaving no evidence? If the former, then who is different from anyone else?

Although Kelly has built up the details of this whole incident over several dreams, she has had other experiences including poltergeists. Her VCR decided to censor the scary scenes from films it was playing back and was considered for exorcism. And once she had the privilege of being spied on by the traditional black helicopter. This would be unremarkable if the helicopter had not been hovering below roof level in a housing estate. For 15 minutes.

In all these dreams, did the aliens leave a message? Yes, they did — they said 'Look under the car'. On doing so — not immediately but some drives later — a loose flywheel cover was noted. Good thing the aliens warned us, otherwise we would have flywheel covers clattering all over the road. Better still, there is presumably nothing more important upon which advice might have been provided.

Ho hum. Where do we go from here? Well the sleepy town of Narre Warren, where the UFO sighting occurred (in a field at Melway reference 108E5) has ever since been notorious for its rashes of hoax UFO sightings. Young persons who light empty paper garbage bags or fly and illuminate kites are suspected of having a role in this, and some have even fessed up on talkback radio. As for Kelly — gone is the husband and rocky marriage, such a brake on her new role in life; her Christianity is now a wider belief (if it's wider, belief in what?) that, once this UFO story has gone away, will qualify her to lecture on the wacko circuit all over again. Arrived is the super hairdo and makeover — stardom and guest-of-honour spots in the UFO community are hers now. After all, there has never been any good evidence for the existence of UFOs before; now there is someone who dreamed of one.■

Action Fusion-Moral scales (Shafran et al., 1996) had altered positively for both clients. R.F. was recovered on the Beck Depression Inventory-II (BDI-II; Beck, Steer, & Brown, 1996) at follow-up, whereas C.P.'s depression had further deteriorated.

Anecdotally, the magical ideation treatment has been implemented successfully with many treatment-resistant clients with OCD. It is suitable for presentations in which clients are too scared to engage in standard exposure and response prevention; and in cases when the feared outcome cannot be tested (e.g., the belief that one's children will die in 15 years' time if a specific ritual is not carried out today). Magical ideation treatment is not advocated as a stand-alone treatment, it is suggested as an adjunct to engage and assist clients with high magical ideation by lowering their magical ideation prior to conducting other recognised cognitive–behavioural treatments (e.g., DIRT, or exposure and response prevention).

The magical ideation treatment package has not yet been trialled in individuals with high magical ideation occurring within other types of disorders (e.g., anorexia nervosa, schizophrenia, body dysmorphic disorder). Future research should investigate whether the magical ideation package will assist treatment within these disorders.

References

Basoglu, M., Lax, T., Kasvikis, Y., & Marks, I. (1988). Predictors of improvement in obsessive compulsive disorder. *Journal of Anxiety Disorders, 2*, 299–317.

Beck, A.T., Steer, R.A., & Brown, G.K. (1996). *Manual for the Beck Depression Inventory-II*. San Antonio, TX: Psychological Corporation.

Chapman, L., Chapman, J., & Raulin, M. (1978). Body image aberration in schizophrenia. *Journal of Abnormal Psychology, 87*, 399–407.

Eckblad, M., & Chapman, L. (1983). Magical ideation as an indicator of schizotypy. *Journal of Consulting and Clinical Psychology, 51*, 215–225.

Edwards, H. (1992). Astrology today (or perhaps Manana). *The Skeptic, 12*(4), 23–25.

Einstein, D.A., & Menzies, R.G. (2004a). The role of magical thinking in obsessive compulsive symptoms in an undergraduate sample. *Depression and Anxiety, 19*, 174–179.

Einstein, D.A., & Menzies, R.G. (2004b). The presence of magical thinking in obsessive compulsive disorder. *Behaviour Research and Therapy, 42*, 539–549.

Einstein, D.A., & Menzies, R.G. (2006). Magical thinking in obsessive-compulsive disorder, panic disorder and the general community. *Behavioural and Cognitive Psychotherapy, 34*, 351–357.

Einstein, D.A., & Menzies, R.G. (2007). *Does magical thinking improve across treatment for obsessive-compulsive disorder?* Manuscript submitted for publication.

Einstein, D.A., Menzies, R.G., St Clare, T., & Drobny, J. (2007). *The treatment of magical ideation in two individuals with obsessive-compulsive disorder.* Manuscript submitted for publication.

Foa, E.B., Huppert, J.D., Leiberg, S., Langner, R., Kitchik, R., Hajcak, G., et al. (2002). The Obsessive-Compulsive Inventory: Development and validation of a short version. *Psychological Assessment, 14,* 485–496.

Foa, E.B., Kozak, M.J., Salkovskis, P.M., Coles, M.E., & Amir, N. (1998). The validation of a new obsessive compulsive disorder scale: The Obsessive-Compulsive Inventory. *Psychological Assessment, 10,* 206–214.

Forty, J. (1996). *Ancient Egyptian mythology.* New Jersey: Chartwell Books.

Frost, R., Krause, M., McMahon, M., Peppe, J., Evans, M., McPhee, A.E., et al. (1993). Compulsivity and superstitiousness. *Behaviour Research and Therapy, 31,* 423–425.

Hodgson, R., & Rachman, S. (1977). Obsessional compulsive complaints. *Behaviour Research and Therapy, 15,* 389–395.

Jacobson, N.S., Follette, W.C., and Revenstorf, D. (1984). Psychotherapy outcome research. Methods for reporting variability and evaluating clinical significance. *Behaviour Therapy, 15,* 336–352.

Jenike, M., Baer, L., Minichiello, W., Schwartz, C., & Carey, R. (1986). Concomitant obsessive compulsive disorder and schizotypal personality disorder. *American Journal of Psychiatry, 143,* 530–532.

Johnson, C.N., & Harris, P.L. (1994). Magic: Special but not excluded. *British Journal of Developmental Psychology, 12,* 35–51.

Leokum, A. (1972) *Tell me why.* London: Odham Books.

Norman, R., Davies, F., Malla, K., Cortese, L., & Nicholson, I. (1996). Relationship of obsessive compulsive symptomatology to anxiety, depression and schizotypy in a clinical population. *British Journal of Clinical Psychology, 35,* 553–566.

Quirke, S. (1992) *Ancient Egyptian religion.* London: British Museum Press.

Reed, A.W. (1982) *Aboriginal myths, legends and fables.* Sydney: Reed Publishing.

Roberts, S. (1996) I would love to see a UFO. *The Skeptic, 16*(4), 29–30.

Roth, S.L. (1988) *Fire came to the Earth People.* New York: St Martin's Press.

Sanavio, E. (1988). The Padua Inventory. *Behaviour Research and Therapy, 26,* 167–177.

Shafran, R., Thordarson, D., & Rachman, S. (1996). Thought action fusion in obsessive compulsive disorder. *Journal of Anxiety Disorders, 10,* 379–391.

St Clare, T., Menzies, R.G., & Jones, M.W. (2006). *Danger Ideation Reduction Therapy (DIRT) for obsessive-compulsive washers: A comprehensive guide to treatment.* Manuscript submitted for publication.

Woolley, J.D. (1997). Thinking about fantasy: Are children fundamentally different thinkers and believers than adults? *Child Development, 68,* 991–1011.

CHAPTER 3

Mindfulness Meditation and Bipolar Disorder

Jillian Ball, Justine Corry and Philip Mitchell

Originating as a traditional Buddhist practice to enhance spiritual awakening, mindfulness has now become accepted as an effective coping skill in mainstream psychology. Intrinsic to the practice of mindfulness are attitudes of acceptance, nonjudgment, patience, nonstriving and letting go. Mindfulness is regarded by some as closely related to other psychological interventions including acceptance, cognitive defusion and exposure (Hayes, Strosahl, & Wilson, 1999). In the practice of mindfulness, patients are taught through a series of meditation techniques to heighten present-centred awareness; including getting in touch with moment-to-moment changes in the body and to see more clearly the patterns of the mind.

Why Use Mindfulness Meditation in Treating Bipolar Disorder?

Mindfulness is particularly relevant in the treatment of bipolar patients for a number of reasons:

- the relapse rate amongst this group is particularly high
- anxiety and stress play a major role in precipitating and maintaining the disorder
- lowered self-esteem is a significant issue for many patients and
- difficulties in regulating thoughts and feelings are intrinsic to the condition.

Relapse and Recurrence

Repeated relapses for people with bipolar disorder are common and carry with them serious potential consequences. Despite medication, bipolar disorder is recurrent in about 90% of sufferers (Keck et al., 1996). Relapse rates on mood stabilisers are as high as 40% in the first year, 60% in the second year and 73% over 5 years or more (Gitlin, Swendsen, Heller, &

Hammen, 1995). The robustly supported finding that the higher the number of previous episodes in bipolar disorder, the higher the possibility of relapse (Maj, Akiskal, Lopez-Ibor, & Sartorius, 2002), emphasises the need for psychological treatments that interrupt this cycle.

Based on Kabat-Zinn's stress reduction program, Teasdale, Segal, Williams, Ridgeway, Soulsby and Lau (2000) have developed a mindfulness-based cognitive therapy program (MBCT) where patients learn the practice of mindfulness meditation, are educated about their illness, and are taught several exercises from cognitive therapy (CT). MBCT has been found to be particularly effective for patients who have experienced a greater number of depressive episodes (more than three) compared to patients in the earlier stages of their illness (Teasdale et al., 2000). It is encouraging that research shows mindfulness helps patients stay well after recovery from unipolar depression (Ma & Teasdale, 2004). The ease with which mindfulness can be practised in all aspects of daily life should enhance its role in relapse prevention.

Stress and Anxiety

Increasingly, the stress–vulnerability model has been accepted as a useful model in understanding the frequency of bipolar episodes (Scott, 2004), highlighting that factors such as stress influence relapse even when medication is optimal. Psychosocial stressors generally trigger symptoms in bipolar patients who do not have sufficient resources to cope. Furthermore, it has been found that anxiety predicts worse outcomes in patients suffering from bipolar disorder (Boylan et al., 2004; Guardino & Miller, 2005).

Mindfulness has been found to be effective in the management of anxiety and stress (Kabat-Zinn et al., 1992; Miller, Fletcher, & Kabat-Zinn, 1995; Shapiro, Schwartz, & Bonner, 1998). During the practice of mindfulness, anxiety, worry or ruminating thoughts are acknowledged and reactivity to these feelings is discouraged. Old patterns of avoiding distressing feelings or being overly attached to positive feelings may eventually fade when not reinforced.

Self-esteem

Some researchers suggest that hypomania/mania may at times occur as a response to feelings of low self-esteem (Lyon, Startup, & Bentall, 1999). A case study has been reported by Mansell and Lam (2003) of a client who held the belief that he could rise above his depression and feelings of low self-esteem through the pursuit of highly demanding goals and rewarding activity. While still depressed, small increases in positive mood and energy triggered hyperpositive thoughts about himself (e.g., 'I am back to my intelligent and outgoing self again'). Consequently, he engaged in a series of ascent behaviours that were consistent with the pursuit of this view of the world. Extreme drivenness or overly zealous goal attainment has also been described by Lam, Wright and Smith (2004) as a predominant characteristic of hypomania as individuals attempt to ward off feelings of inadequacy.

Traditionally, one of the key aspects of mindfulness is learning not to engage with thoughts of self, particularly those associated with roles, responsibilities and expectations and images of self and others. The drive to alter or control situations in order to enhance a sense of self-esteem is common to mood states of elevation and fear. Segal, Williams and Teasdale (2002) differentiate two basic modes of mind — the doing or driven mode and the being mode. The former is based on making things different from the way they are in the present moment. The latter, which forms the basis of mindfulness practice, is based upon acceptance and contentment with the present moment and the way things are and is useful for enhancing a sense of wellbeing and self-acceptance.

Regulating Thoughts and Feelings

Mindfulness involves consciously paying attention to one's thoughts, feelings and moment-to-moment changes in the body. Individuals learn to see more clearly the patterns of the mind and to learn how to recognise shifts in mood. Segal et al. (2002) highlight the significant effect of mindfulness in halting the escalation of mood and reactions to thoughts that might lead to a depressive or manic relapse. With practice, individuals can develop the capacity to let thoughts, feelings and sensations come and go without having to struggle with them. From a conditioning perspective, this may be viewed as a form of covert exposure thereby desensitising the patient to certain mental processes.

Mindfulness Exercises

To begin mindfulness training with bipolar disorder patients, our preferred exercises are breathing meditation, body scan meditation and mindfulness of walking. These exercises provide good opportunities to practise present moment awareness and the fundamentals of good mindfulness practice. Individuals are encouraged to practise each exercise initially for 20 minutes and then to eventually build up to 40 minutes. Segal et al. (2002) have outlined a number of useful tips and instructions for teaching mindfulness exercises.

Prior to commencing mindfulness, it is useful to highlight several points. Firstly, patients might find it comforting to know that it is common for the mind to wander away from the focus of the breath to distracting thoughts and images. The individual can be encouraged to recognise these thoughts or images as passing events and to gently bring the focus of attention back to the meditation practice. The idea of developing awareness without judgment is also imperative to the practice of mindfulness. Individuals may need to be encouraged to let go of the need to do the exercise well or to strive for a sense of mastery or achievement. The only requirement is for regular and frequent practice, preferably conducted with an open and curious mind. Throughout the practice, emphasis is placed on the individual surrendering expectations and goals of what the mindfulness exercise should achieve (including the need to feel more relaxed). The more individuals try to influence or control their experiences, the less they will benefit.

Breathing meditation, body scan meditation and mindfulness of walking highlight the importance of bringing awareness to the way things are in the present moment without having to change anything. Elaborated instructions for each of these practices may be found in articles by Kabat-Zinn (1990) and Segal et al. (2002).

Necessary Precautions

Bipolar-disorder patients are a diverse group and their individual needs and emotional states need to be considered carefully each session before mindfulness is introduced as a therapeutic tool. Patients who experience highly fragile ego boundaries or are poorly integrated (e.g., patients with comorbid borderline personality disorder or psychosis) may misunderstand or misuse the practice. Furthermore, severely depressed, manic or suicidal patients may lack the mental stability to benefit from mindfulness while distressed.

When introducing mindfulness, the practice needs to be clearly differentiated from self-analysis or rumination. Thinking excessively or heightening awareness of unwanted thoughts may increase anxiety, rather than create a still and calm mind. Furthermore, some patients may find the experience of relaxation unfamiliar, distressing or experience a fear of losing control. Discussion of these possible experiences prior to commencement of mindfulness practice may help to alleviate distress should it occur.

Conclusions

Bipolar-disorder patients have the potential to benefit significantly from the therapeutic functions of mindfulness — including emotional regulation, distress tolerance, disengagement and the deconditioning of unhealthy thought patterns. Feasibility studies are needed to evaluate the clinical suitability and effectiveness of applying mindfulness to this population. Studies are also required to examine precautions which should be taken, prior to commencing mindfulness within this clinical group.

References

Boylan, K.R., Beiling, P.J., Marriott, M., Begin, H., Young, L.T., & McQueen, G.M. (2004). Impact of comorbid anxiety disorders outcome in a cohort of patients with bipolar disorder. *Journal of Clinical Psychiatry, 65,* 1106–1313.

Gitlin, M.J., Swendsen, J., Heller, T.L., & Hammen, C. (1995). Relapse and impairment in bipolar disorder. *American Journal of Psychiatry, 152,* 1635–1640.

Guardino, B.A., & Miller, I.W. (2005). Anxiety disorder comorbidity in bipolar disorder: Relationship to depression severity and treatment outcome. *Depression and Anxiety, 21,* 71–77.

Hayes, S.C., Strosahl, K.D., & Wilson, K.G. (1999). *Acceptance and commitment therapy.* New York: The Guilford Press.

Kabat-Zinn, J. (1990). *Full catastrophe living. Using the wisdom of your body and mind to face stress, pain and illness.* New York: Dell Publishing.

Kabat-Zinn, J., Massion, A., Kristeller, J., Peterson, L.C., Fletcher, K.E., Pbert, L., et al. (1992). Effectiveness of a meditation-based stress reduction program in the treatment of anxiety disorders. *American Journal of Psychiatry, 149,* 7, 936–983.

Keck, P., McElroy, S., Strakowski, S., Kizer, D., Balistreri, T., Bennet, J., et al. (1996). Factors associated with pharmacological non-compliance in patients with mania. *Journal of Clinical Psychiatry, 57,* 292–297.

Lam, D.H., Wright, K., & Smith, N. (2004). Dysfunctional attitudes in bipolar disorder, *Journal of Affective Disorders, 79,* 193–199.

Lyon, H.M., Startup, M., & Bentall, R.P. (1999). Social cognition and the manic defence: Attributions, selective attention and self-schema in bipolar disorder. *Journal of Abnormal Psychology, 108,* 273–282.

Ma, S.H., & Teasdale, J.D. (2004). Mindfulness-based cognitive therapy for depression: Replication and exploration of differential relapse prevention effects. *Journal of Consulting and Clinical Psychology, 72,* 31–40.

Maj, M., Akiskal, H.S., Lopez-Ibor, J.J., & Sartorius, N. (2002). *Bipolar disorder.* New York: John Wiley & Sons.

Mansell, W., & Lam, D. (2003). Conceptualising a cycle of ascent into mania: A case report. *Behavioural and Cognitive Psychotherapy, 31,* 363–367.

Miller, J.J., Fletcher, K., & Kabat-Zinn, J. (1995). Three-year follow-up and clinical implications of a mindfulness meditation based stress reduction intervention in the treatment of anxiety disorders. *General Hospital Psychiatry, 17,* 192–200.

Scott, J. (2004). Treatment outcome studies. In S.L. Johnson & R.L. Leahy (Eds.), *Psychological treatment of bipolar disorder* (pp. 226–244). New York: The Guildford Press.

Segal, Z.V., Williams, J.M.G., & Teasdale, J.D. (2002). *Mindfulness based cognitive therapy for depression: A new approach to preventing relapse.* New York: The Guilford Press.

Shapiro, S.L., Schwartz, G.E., & Bonner, G. (1998). Effects of mindfulness-based stress reduction on medical students and premedical students. *Journal of Behavioral Medicine, 21,* 581–599.

Teasdale, J.D., Segal, Z.V., Williams, J.M.G., Ridgeway, V.A., Soulsby J.M., & Lau M.A. (2000). Prevention of relapse/recurrence in major depression by mindfulness-based cognitive therapy. *Journal of Consulting and Clinical Psychology, 68,* 615–623.

CHAPTER 4

Mindfulness as Therapy From a Buddhist Perspective

Malcolm John Huxter

Mindfulness refers to remembering to bring attention to present moment experience in an open and nonjudgmental manner. Mindfulness is the heart of Buddhist meditation and these practices have been utilised in western cultures for generations (Kabat-Zinn, 2003). In the last 20 years mindfulness has become popular with psychotherapists using cognitive and behavioural therapies. Approaches where mindfulness is a key component include mindfulness-based stress reduction (MBSR; Kabat-Zinn, 1990), dialectical behaviour therapy (DBT; Linehan, 1993a), acceptance and commitment therapy (ACT; Hayes, Strosahl, & Wilson, 1999), and mindfulness-based cognitive therapy (MBCT; Segal, Williams, & Teasdale, 2002). With the exception of ACT, the source of the mindfulness practices used and taught in these approaches has been credited to Buddhist roots.

As a focused psychological strategy or skill, mindfulness is gaining clinical credence for many psychological disorders (Baer, 2003). There has been much discussion and debate about how mindfulness can be incorporated into psychology as a scientifically validated construct and there has been a tendency to separate mindfulness from Buddhism (e.g., Bishop et al., 2004; Brown & Ryan, 2004; Hayes & Shenk, in press). The separation has been helpful to enhance acceptance of this powerful therapeutic tool (Dimidjian & Linehan, 2003). However, as our contemporary psychotherapeutic community becomes more willing to accept ancient psychotherapeutic approaches, they may also be more willing to consider the theoretical systems from where they originated.

This chapter will describe the basics of Buddhist psychology and place mindfulness within the context of a therapeutic pathway. Firstly, it will provide some reasons why the Buddhist perspective of mindfulness may be helpful for psychologists. Then, for the most part, it will highlight some of the psychotherapeutic systems found in Buddhism. Reference to clinical practice and some similarities to contemporary mindfulness-based approaches and Buddhism will also be mentioned. The comments about using mindfulness in clinical practice are based on the author's professional experience. The information on Buddhism is based on the author's personal experience with several teachers over three decades. Respectful acknowledgment and complete references are given in Huxter (2006a).

Rationale for Keeping Mindfulness and Buddhism Connected

Two ways mindfulness has been defined for psychotherapy include:

- awareness of present experience with acceptance (Germer, Siegel, & Fulton, 2005)
- 'Open or receptive attention to, and awareness of ongoing events and experience' (Brown & Ryan, 2004, p. 245).

In psychotherapy mindfulness is regarded as:

- a personal practice and therapeutic stance used by therapists
- a theoretical framework to support therapy
- a skill that can be taught to patients or clients (Germer, 2005).

For the most part, psychotherapists who use mindfulness have personal experience with this practice. Of these therapists, many base their theoretical orientation of mindfulness on Buddhist processes and principles (e.g., Germer et al., 2005; Kabat-Zinn, 2003; Marlatt, 2002. See also *Cognitive and Behavioral Practice,* Vol 9 No. 1, 2002, pp. 38–79). Buddhist psychology offers a comprehensive and in-depth conceptual framework from which to understand both the theoretical and practical aspects of mindfulness. Yet, when Baer (2003) wrote a comprehensive conceptual and empirical review of mindfulness training as a clinical intervention, Buddhist ideas were only given a token, yet respectful, mention.

It is understandable that many psychologists wish to distance themselves from Buddhism in order to make mindfulness scientifically acceptable, culturally relevant, and not confused with religion. However, separating mindfulness from its spiritual connection could be diluting its psychological effectiveness (Dimidjian & Linehan, 2003). In the 21st century, as mindfulness-based practices become more mainstream, our society and psychotherapeutic community may be more willing to accept that Buddhism could be a valid psychological approach to reducing human suffering. For those psychologists who already have a Buddhist orientation, the tendencies by other therapists and researchers to discard, not acknowledge, and simply ignore the relevance of mindfulness from a Buddhist perspective is like throwing the baby out with the bath water.

According to Buddhist traditions, respectfully acknowledging the origins of practices helps to provide confidence and credibility in teaching these practices. Patients need not have heard about Buddhism to benefit from mindfulness. If, however, psychologists wish to teach Buddhist practices it is helpful to have an understanding of Buddhist principles. Such an understanding helps to clarify the similarities and differences between various approaches, manage problems when they arise, extend the teaching of skills beyond that which is in the teacher's personal experience as well as competently answer questions when they arise.

Buddhism

In my understanding, the word 'Buddha' comes from an ancient Indian language called Pali and the verb root *budh,* which means 'to awaken' or 'to understand'. The Buddha (or an awakened one) taught ways to understand or awaken to the truth and these teachings were called the Dharma. The truth, from a Buddhist perspective, refers to the way things are and conveys a sense of lawfulness about causes and effects, actions and consequences. Interdependence is, according to Buddhism, a key feature of reality.

Unlike linear ideas of causality where 'A' leads to 'B' leads to 'C', the Buddhist understanding of causality is interdependent. If there is no 'B' then 'C' does not arise. Alternatively, as 'C' is part of a system that cannot be separated from the whole, the arising or nature of 'A' is dependent upon the nature of 'C' or 'B'. In other words, as symbolised in Figure 1, the interdependent co-arising of phenomena are reciprocally modified by their interaction.

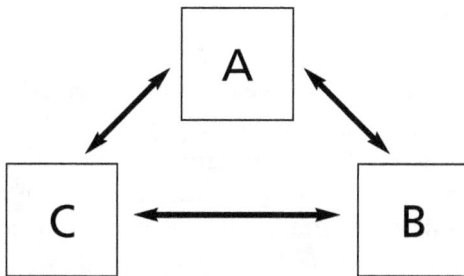

Figure 1
Interdependent co-arising.

The Dharma is not confined to Buddhism and is universal as the truth of the way things are. The Buddha had the foresight to organise the teachings so that they could be adapted to different cultures, regardless of time or place. He also taught in such a way that the beneficial results of Dharma practices, such as mindfulness, could be realised by individuals for themselves, by themselves and not depend upon an external authority.

Generally, Buddhism is seen as a religion. Often, however, those who call themselves 'Buddhist' prefer not to subscribe to beliefs, are not religious, and consider themselves more aligned with being agnostic (e.g., Batchelor, 1997).

The Four Truths

There are many different schools or traditions of Buddhism. Regardless of traditions, however, the primary aim of Buddhism is the realisation of the four noble truths. The four truths are, in essence, two cause and effect relationships. That is, anguish and its causes, freedom from anguish, and the causes of this freedom. Using medical model analogies the truths could be explained as (a) disorder, (b) aetiology, (c) health, and (d) treatment.

The four truths are:

- There is unsatisfactoriness, discontent, anguish or suffering.
- Discontent has origins or root causes.
- There is freedom from anguish.
- There are pathways to freedom.

The term *dukkha* (Pali) is used in reference to the first truth of suffering. The dimensions of *dukkha* are infinite and can be gross and/or subtle. *Dukkha* includes all the varied forms of mental/emotional distress found in psychological disorders.

According to Buddhism, the root causes of *dukkha* (the 2nd truth) are contextually dependent on mental, emotional and behavioural tendencies that incline towards:

- addiction to pleasant feelings, or craving and clinging
- rejection, avoidance, or struggle with unpleasant feelings, or aversion
- not knowing or ignoring and being psychologically unconscious (This can range from a lack of clarity to total confusion and gross delusions. From a Buddhist perspective, ignorance refers to being blind to the four noble truths, and the way things are.).

According to Buddhism, *dukkha* arises and continues because of an interdependent cyclic relationship between environmental conditions and tendencies based on greed, ignorance and aversion. Depending on one condition, the next condition in the cycle will arise. Interestingly, cognitive–behavioural therapists will often describe mental disorders as having reactive and cyclic patterns. Panic cycles, for example, involve triggers, predisposing vulnerabilities, fight or flight responses, mental and physical symptoms, catastrophic interpretations and safety avoidant behaviours (Wells, 1997).

Nirvana (a Sanskrit term) is used in reference to the third truth. A metaphor used for *Nirvana* was the extinguishing of a fire. According to one translation, the word literally means Un (*nir*) + binding (*vana*) (Thanissaro, 1996). Thus, freedom is defined not in terms of what it is but in terms of what it is not. Here, freedom means that one is unbound by patterns and habits that lead to *dukkha*. *Nirvana* is the result of exiting unhelpful cycles of interdependent arising. At a very relative level, freedom with panic, for example, may occur when the panic cycle is short-circuited. Short-circuiting the panic cycle can occur at any point in the cycle. No longer believing catastrophic misinterpretations about physical experience, for example, is one way to exit panic cycles.

Being free from *dukkha* (the third truth) arises from practising the fourth truth. If ignorance and clinging are amongst the root causes for anguish then developing insight and simply letting go of reactive patterns are ways to be free from *dukkha*. The noble eight-fold path generally represents the fourth noble truth and the path of Dharma practice. The eight factors on this path are divided into three basic categories, which have an interdependent relationship (see Figure 2).

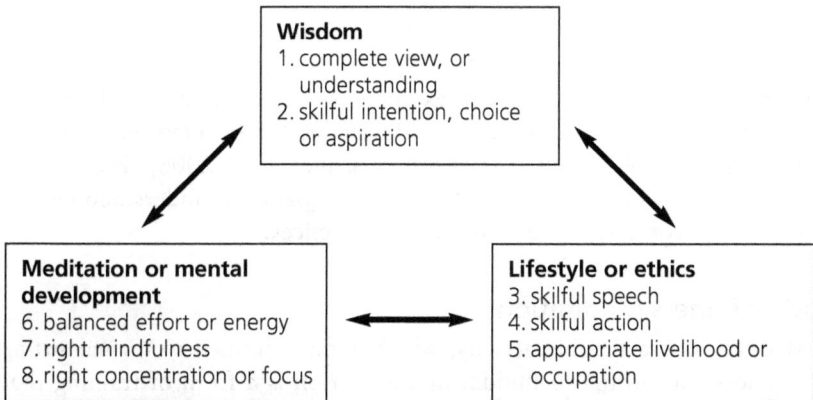

Figure 2
The eight-fold path.

According to some practitioners, the path has two levels — basic and refined or noble (Thanissaro, 1996). The refined level includes the realisation of Nirvana. The basic level involves the amelioration of *dukkha*. At the basic level, wise understanding leads to making decisions and commitments (skilful intentions). The choices we make are crucial in how things will unfold. With firm resolve it is possible to act in ways that reduce anguish and that are conducive to mental development. Mental development is not always easy and often involves courageous effort. However, when we bring focused non-judgmental attention to our self or our situation, wisdom may arise.

For a Buddhist, the path of Dharma is process and product, or the means of transport and place of deliverance. The path of Buddha Dharma could be compared to a high performance motor vehicle built to cope with all terrains. The basic vehicle design based on the movement of a wheel, is simple. However, driving the wheels are many refined mechanical and electronic components and systems working together as a whole. In Buddhism, mindfulness is one factor contextually embedded in several awakening systems.

There are numerous differences and similarities between contemporary mindfulness approaches and Buddhism. However, only a few similarities will be mentioned. ACT developed independently of Buddhism, yet despite the distance there are many theoretical similarities. The key features of the ACT hexagram, for example, bear close resemblance to the Buddhist basic eight-fold path. The hexagram involves acceptance, contact with the present moment, values, committed action, self as context and defusion (Hayes, 2004).

The basic conceptual and practical framework of MBSR is from Theravada Buddhism. Kabat-Zinn's (1990) seven attitudinal foundations of mindfulness practice are, for example, skilful adaptations of some of the Buddhist awakening systems. Additionally, MBSR often refers directly to the four noble truths (e.g., Roth & Calle-Mesa, 2006). Providing a context such as the four truths can enhance patients' understanding and motivation for mindfulness and related practices.

Mindfulness Meditation

Meditation is a flexible activity, which is not confined to formal sitting practices. According to Buddhism, meditation is a form of training that involves energy, mindfulness and concentration. The two categories of meditation in Theravada Buddhism are tranquillity meditation, and insight (*vipassana*) meditation. Important components in the awakening systems, such as loving kindness and compassion are calm meditation practices, and ways of relating to self and others. Mindfulness meditation is considered as an insight practice and a way of being.

In the Theravada Buddhist traditions, mindfulness meditation is called *satipatthana vipassana*. According to Pali scholars *Sati* means awareness, keeping in mind, attention or memory. *Patthana* means keeping present and foundation or source (Kearney, 2002). Thus, *satipatthana* means the foundations of mindfulness and refers to remembering to deliberately place close attention to what is happening right now. Another way of describing mindfulness meditation is 'presence'.

Vipassana translates as insight, where *vi* denotes separate, intense or distinct and passana means seeing. Therefore *vipassana* means seeing separately and seeing distinctly (Kearney, 2002). *Vipassana* results from practicing *satipatthana*. Insight can refer to 'the clear perception of the object as it really is' (Goleman, 1988, p. 123).

Insight

In Buddhism, insight directly counters ignorance and is a key factor to exit cycles of *dukkha*. Insight includes realising the four noble truths and knowing, at an experiential level, three characteristics of existence. The three marks or characteristics of life according to Buddhism are:

- impermanence or change
- unreliability, ambiguity or uncertainty
- interdependence, no-thing-ness, no self-ness, insubstantiality, contingency or emptiness.

As all things change they are also uncertain, unreliable and ambiguous. That is, we can never be certain about the future. In line with laws of interdependence, all situations, events, people and things are contingent on other things for their existence. In Buddhist terminology 'emptiness' and 'not self' mean that all things, including that which we call 'self' are empty of separate existence. Emptiness can also mean that things are empty of unrealistic assumptions and unhelpful opinions. Being empty of assumptions means that nothing is added or taken away. In Buddhism, the positive correlate of emptiness is 'such-ness' where things are just as they are (Batchelor, 1997).

Insight about the three characteristics of existence has a generalising effect with clinical implications. Seeing the impermanence of a falling autumn leaf can, for example, be generalised to knowing the fleeting change and emptiness of a distorted thinking pattern or knowing how a painful emotion need not be taken personally. It is often a liberating relief to individuals suffering with tormenting emotions (such as those with borderline personality disorder) to realise that they need not identify with their emotions.

There are many connections, both theoretically and otherwise, between DBT and Buddhism (Linehan, 1993a). One connection to Buddhism is how DBT uses a dialectical view of reality and human behaviour to direct therapy. The three features of this view are (a) interdependence, (b) balance and transformation (yin yang), and (c) change — which bear similarities to the Buddhist characteristics of existence.

It seems that insight into the marks of existence is a therapeutic feature of ACT. One cause of suffering, according to ACT, is 'cognitive fusion' where we take what we think about ourselves literally (Hayes et al., 1999). ACT describes many innovative and creative defusion techniques. From a Buddhist perspective, these techniques can lead to having insight about the nature of thoughts and emotions and seeing clearly that they are not who or what we are.

MBCT is basically a reformulation of MBSR with the addition of contemporary cognitive–behavioural practices and empirically based theories. One strong similarity to Buddhism is the MBCT description of meta-cognitive insight. Meta-cognitive insight refers to 'experiencing thoughts as thoughts (that is as events in the mind rather than direct readouts on reality)' (Teasdale et al., 2002, p. 286). Meta-cognitive insight involves shifting the focus to the relationship with thoughts rather than their content. Seeing the such-ness of thoughts means that they are just thoughts and not necessarily facts to be believed. In situations where patients are prone to depression, realising the such-ness and ambiguity of thought is liberating.

The Satipatthana Sutta

The Buddha taught for 45 years and gave hundreds of discourses that were recorded as Suttas (Pali). In the Satipatthana Sutta he described, in detail, the four foundations of mindfulness, each with numerous subdomains. The four foundations seem to encompass the full spectrum of body–mind experience, as well as processes that are appropriate for awakening and the reduction of *dukkha*. They can also be adapted to temperament and situation, thus they are relevant for psychotherapeutic situations. Some of the foundations and their sub-domains seem well established in contemporary mindfulness-based therapies, whilst others are not. The following is a very brief overview. For more details about the four foundations as therapy see Huxter (2006a and 2006b). For a translation and comprehensive commentaries please refer to Analayo (2003).

The discourse says, practicing Satipatthana requires the establishment of four mental qualities:

- being ardent or applying diligence
- being alert or clearly knowing and comprehending
- mindfulness
- being able to put aside greed and distress with reference to the world or, detachment.

According to one translator, the Buddha also spoke about three stages in the development of mindfulness (Thanissaro, 1996). Roughly these stages are:

- focusing in the present moment
- noticing how the object changes and the factors related to the change
- bare attention to the object, without clinging or grasping and with equanimity.

Mindfulness of Body

Mindfulness of body involves contemplating the body in all possible ways and circumstances. The several sub-domains within this foundation include mindfulness of breath, postures, clear comprehension of actions, and physical sensations. Therapeutically, being grounded in the body can provide respite from battles with difficult thoughts and emotions. Mindfulness of body can provide a way to cultivate insight without depending on rational analysis. Mindfulness of breath and body scan (awareness of sensations) are two common mindfulness of body practices in modern psychology. However, they are not always suitable. With those prone to panic, both of these practices can, initially, easily shift to self-focused attention and precipitate an anxious reaction. Similarly, with those who have a history of sexual abuse, body scan can trigger abreactions. Shifting attention to external phenomena (such as sound), or mindfulness of postures (walking), or being mindful with action can be helpful in these circumstances. Sometimes patients are too restless to sit still, and being mindful in movement or with actions may be a suitable alternative. Being mindful of daily activities with clear comprehension of purpose and suitability can, for example, be helpful with disorders related to impulse control, such as bulimia or deliberate self-harm. By purposely bringing non-judgmental attention to activities, insight about cause–

effect relationships is developed and the likelihood of choices in line with insight is increased.

Mindfulness of Feelings

In Buddhism, feelings refer to the affective tone of an experience and not emotions as they are considered in our everyday language. The affective tones of experiences are pleasant, unpleasant or neutral. Feelings can arise in relation to physical experience or mental experience. Other dimensions of feelings include whether they give rise to unhelpful reactive patterns or not. In interdependent reactive cycles, feelings usually come before craving to either push away or pull in. We cannot control our feelings about experiences as they arise because of conditions. We can choose, however, how we respond. Being aware of feelings, as feelings, can short-circuit unnecessary overreactions to experiences that come our way. Despite having painful feelings arising from the body (as an example) our mind can be peaceful and mindfulness can be helpful for pain management. The term 'urge surfing' (Marlatt, 2002) aptly describes how mindfulness of feelings and cravings can help substance abusers interrupt cycles of their substance addictions.

Mindfulness of Mind

This domain of mindfulness includes helpful and unhelpful emotions and thought patterns, as well as subtle states of mind.

For the most part we identify with our mind. Practising this domain helps to provide some space from this identification as well as rein in the tendency for destructive emotions to run rampant. Mindfully tracking the changing nature of painful emotions helps to break reactive patterns often associated with these states. Being aware of worry as worry and not getting entangled with the thoughts related to the worry can short-circuit this tendency. Being able to mindfully label aggressive emotions, as another example, can help to provide choice with these states rather than feeling at their mercy. Linehan (1993b) accesses this domain of mindfulness when she teaches those with borderline personality disorder how to tolerate and regulate distressing emotions.

Mindfulness of Phenomena

This domain is also referred to as mindfulness of mind objects and includes a range of qualities and patterns. This frame of reference includes, for example, awareness of the ways tendencies interact. The five sub-domains in this foundation include mindfulness of five hindrances to practice and mindfulness of the seven factors of awakening. The five hindrances are sense desire, aversion, restlessness/worry, lethargy and sceptical doubt. The seven factors of awakening is one of the many awakening systems within the eight-fold path. It includes mindfulness, investigation or enquiry, energy, joy, tranquillity, concentration and equanimity.

This foundation requires more active engagement and intelligent discrimination than the other three foundations. In particular, it emphasises maximising the skilful and minimising the unskilful. The fourth foundation is very relevant for therapy because it encompasses the essence of the Buddha's teaching. Working with the hindrances and cultivating the factors of awakening are, for example, much of the business of psychotherapy.

Final Comment

Mindfulness cannot be confined to any one psychological approach such as Buddhism. Nonetheless, many of the mindfulness practices used in contemporary psychology originate from this tradition. For psychologists grounded in Buddhist understanding, contemporary mindfulness-based approaches have added empirical evidence and innovative ways to apply Dharma with clinical populations. The basic Dharma wheel design, however, has not been superseded.

Just as stripping a multi-purpose vehicle of its functioning systems will eventually render it useless, attempts to distil and separate mindfulness from Buddhism run the risk of losing the skill, knowledge and conceptual framework that this tradition offers. Buddhist psychology is a sophisticated and comprehensive approach to realising freedom from a diverse range of mental and emotional disorders. Attempts to reinvent the wheel, without reference to earlier models are, perhaps, a retrograde step. With respect to interdependence, an approach that is inclusive of Buddhism rather than exclusive may be more progressive for integrating mindfulness in contemporary psychology.

References

Analayo, Ven. (2003). *Satipatthana: The direct path to realization*. Birmingham, UK: Windhorse.

Baer, R.B. (2003). Mindfulness training as a clinical intervention: A conceptual and empirical review. *Clinical Psychology: Science and Practice, 10*, 125–143.

Batchelor, S. (1997). *Buddhism without beliefs. A contemporary guide to awakening*. London: Bloomsbury.

Bishop, S.R., Lau, M., Shapiro, S. Carlson, L. Anderson, N.D., Carmody, L., et al. (2004). Mindfulness: A proposed operational definition. *Clinical Psychology: Science and Practice, 11*, 230–241.

Brown, K.W., & Ryan, R.M. (2004). Perils and promise in defining and measuring mindfulness: Observations from experience. *Clinical Psychology: Science and Practice, 11*, 242–248.

Dimidjian, S., & Linehan, M. (2003). Defining the agenda for future research on the clinical application of mindfulness practice. *Clinical Psychology: Science and Practice, 10*, 166–171.

Germer, C.K. (2005). Mindfulness: What is it? What does it matter? In C.K. Germer, R.D. Siegel, & P.R. Fulton (Eds.), *Mindfulness and psychotherapy* (pp. 3-27). New York: The Guilford Press.

Germer, C.K., Siegel, R.D., & Fulton, P.R. (2005). *Mindfulness and psychotherapy*. New York: The Guilford Press.

Goleman, D. (1988). *The meditative mind: The varieties of meditative experience.* London: Thorsons.

Hayes, S.C., & Shenk, C. (in press). Operationalizing mindfulness without unnecessary attachments. Reply to Bishop et al. (2004). *Clinical Psychology: Science and Practice.*

Hayes, S.C., Strosahl, K.D., & Wilson, K.G. (1999). *Acceptance and commitment therapy*. New York: Guilford Press.

Hayes, S.C. (2004). Acceptance and commitment therapy and the new behavior therapies. In S. Hayes, V.M. Follette, & M.M. Linehan (Eds.), *Mindfulness and acceptance: Expanding the cognitive-behavioural tradition* (pp. 1-29). New York: Guildford Press.

Huxter, M. (2006a). *Mindfulness and a path of understanding. A workbook for the release from stress, anxiety and depression.* Manuscript submitted for publication.

Huxter, M. (2006b). The Buddha's discourse on the foundations of mindfulness. *Contemplative Views.* 7(1), 2–9. (Available from www.malhuxter.com)

Kabat-Zinn, J. (1990). *Full catastrophe living. Using the wisdom of your body and mind to face stress, pain, and illness.* New York: Guilford Press.

Kabat-Zinn, J. (2003). Mindfulness based interventions in context: Past present and future. *Clinical Psychology: Science and Practice, 10*, 144–156.

Kearney, P. (2002). Personal communications.

Linehan, M.M. (1993a). *Cognitive-behavioral treatment of borderline personality disorder.* New York: Guilford Press.

Linehan, M.M. (1993b). *Skills training manual for treating borderline personality disorder.* New York: Guilford Press.

Marlatt, G.A. (2002). Buddhist philosophy in the treatment of addictive behavior. *Cognitive and Behavioural Practice,* 9(1), 44–50.

Roth, B., & Calle-Mesa, L. (2006). Mindfulness-based stress reduction (MBSR) with Spanish- and English-speaking inner-city medical patients. In R. Baer (Ed.), *Mindfulness-based treatment approaches: Clinicians guide to evidence base and applications* (pp. 263-284). Burlington, MA: Academic Press.

Segal, Z.V., Williams, J.M.G., & Teasdale, J.D. (2002). *Mindfulness-based cognitive therapy for depression.* New York: Guilford Press.

Teasdale, J.D., Moore, R.G., Hayhurst, H., Pope, M., Williams, S., & Segal, Z. (2002). Metacognitive awareness and prevention of relapse in depression: Empirical evidence. *Journal of Consulting and Clinical Psychology,* 70(2), 275–287.

Thanissaro B. (1996). *The wings to awakening*. Barre, MA: The Dhamma Dana Publication Fund.

Wells, A. (1997). *Cognitive therapy of anxiety disorders: A practical manual and conceptual guide*. Chichester, UK: John Wiley & Sons.

CHAPTER 5

Cognitive–Behavioural Treatment of Trauma-Related Nightmares in Children: A Developmental Adaptation of Imagery Rehearsal Therapy

Jason S. Encel and Hayley K. Dohnt

Chronic nightmares occur frequently in children with posttraumatic stress disorder (PTSD) and other traumatic stress reactions. However, PTSD-related nightmares are rarely the primary target of cognitive–behavioural treatment (Davis, de Arellano, Falsetti, & Resnick, 2003; Krakow, Sandoval, et al., 2001). Practitioners of cognitive–behavioural therapy (CBT) tend to favour treatments directed towards more general or waking symptoms of PTSD. The assumption is made, often incorrectly, that when trauma-focused and other interventions are implemented, the client's distressing dreams will resolve (Davis et al., 2003; Krakow, 2004). Moreover, CBT practitioners are frequently not trained to work with dreams (Freeman & White, 2002). Given that trauma-related nightmares may be persistent, cause high levels of emotional distress in children and their caregivers, and interfere with day-to-day functioning, consideration should be given to direct treatment of trauma-related nightmares.

Nightmares are one of the most commonly reported 're-experiencing' symptoms of PTSD in children. A nightmare is generally defined operationally as a disturbing or frightening dream leading to awakening from sleep (American Psychiatric Association [APA], 2000; Krakow, 2004). Traumatic nightmares may cause considerable sleep disruption leading to excessive daytime sleepiness, poor concentration, depression, and increased anxiety (APA, 2000). Krakow (2004) argues nightmare sufferers develop psychophysiological insomnia as a by-product of bad dreams.

Trauma-related nightmares differ from 'typical' or 'nontrauma-related' nightmares (Davis et al., 2003). Trauma-related nightmares are characterised by content associated with the original trauma and may replay the trauma, whereas 'typical' or 'nontrauma-related' nightmares may include more unrealistic content (Davis et al., 2003). Individuals may experience the same nightmare repeatedly or nightmares with thematic similarities. Initially, trauma-related nightmares may replicate the traumatic event(s) and change over time to include themes involving danger and threat. In children, traumatic nightmares may take a more generic form such as monsters or frightening animals (Cohen & Mannarino, 2004). It has been postulated that dreaming facilitates cognitive–emotional processing of traumatic events (Punamäki, Ali, Ismahil, & Nuutinen, 2005).

Importantly, in adults, it has been demonstrated that interventions targeting posttraumatic nightmares lead to clinically significant improvement in subjective sleep quality and psychological distress, including PTSD symptoms (Krakow, 2004). However, little is known about the efficacy of targeting traumatic nightmares in children with PTSD.

Mounting evidence demonstrates the efficacy of trauma-focused CBT in treating PTSD in children (Cohen & Mannarino, 2004; Dalgleish, Meiser-Stedman, & Smith, 2005). However, these studies typically do not examine whether more generic PTSD treatments reduce nightmare frequency, distress or adverse effects. Prolonged exposure to the traumatic memory itself may reduce or eliminate nightmares (Giarratano, 2004). However, there is a dearth of evidence-based information available on treating trauma-related nightmares, especially in children and adolescents (Davis et al., 2003; Krakow, Sandoval, et al., 2001).

Aims

In recent years, a specific form of nightmare therapy, imagery rehearsal therapy (IRT), has been shown to be efficacious in reducing nightmare frequency and distress and associated sleep disturbances in adults with PTSD. The present chapter examines the rationale for exploratory modifications to IRT so that it is more developmentally sensitive and 'child friendly'. The aims are to (1) provide an overview of the 'nuts and bolts' of IRT, (2) provide an overview of the evidence-base for IRT, (3) report on suggested procedural issues and guidelines for adapting IRT for use with traumatised children based on our own clinical experience, and (4) provide suggestions for future research. The emphasis is on practical implementation of the treatment approach.

Imagery Rehearsal Therapy

Numerous variations of techniques now described as IRT were practised before the advent of the scientific literature (e.g., Krakow, 2004; Kroese & Thomas, 2006). IRT has much in common with a range of story-line alteration, and possibly 'face and conquer' techniques. However, IRT may be distinguished from the 'pack' of story-line alteration interventions on four fronts: (1) IRT *explicitly* builds in a *systematic* rehearsal component, (2) The efficacy of IRT in adults is supported by a significant evidence base, which includes randomised controlled trials (RCTs), (3) IRT has explicit procedural guidelines, which means that the technique is amenable to replication and consistent clinical implementation — this facilitates treatment fidelity and research, and (4) IRT, at least insofar as adults are concerned, has available a range of educational and therapeutic support materials, including web-based options.

The 'How to' of IRT

What follows is a selective overview of IRT as reported in the adult literature. IRT has been characterised as a 'cognitive-imagery restructuring paradigm' (Krakow, Hollifield, et al., 2001). IRT treatment *packages* have the following components, which are presented sequentially: psychoeducation about nightmares, sleep and PTSD and principles of sleep hygiene; practise in evocation of pleasant, nonthreatening imagery prior to traumatic dream work; coping skills training to manage distressing images or intense affect which may be activated (i.e., anxiety management); and IRT. In IRT, the client is taught a three-step process:

- selecting a target nightmare
- changing the nightmare with the instruction 'change it in any way you wish'
- rehearsing the images of the 'new dream' scenario in the waking state.

In the adult literature, IRT has typically been conducted in a small group format. As part of an IRT package, education is provided about the role of nightmares in the acute posttrauma phase. However, when nightmares persist months posttrauma they may not be helpful in the recovery process. Within the IRT framework, chronic nightmares are conceptualised as being *trauma-induced* and *habit-sustained* (Krakow, 2004). Clients are given the rationale that nightmares can be regarded as *learned* behaviour and the notion of 'unfinished business' is de-emphasised. Krakow (2004) states: 'it helps ... to consider their disturbing dreams as learned behaviour triggered by the trauma but sustained by a malfunctioning imagery system that has lost its natural self-corrective capacity' (p. 102). It follows that if nightmares are treated as 'habits' or learned, they can be controlled when the client learns to replace them with a 'new habit' (new imagery). Clients are instructed, 'we will now rehearse the new dream only, *not* the nightmare'. Since the focus is on a *new* dream, clients are discouraged from describing traumatic experiences or traumatic nightmare content throughout the IRT program in order to minimise the role of exposure as a therapeutic component. When a client wants to talk about trauma material, it may be preferable to suspend IRT in favour of trauma-focused work.

Within the IRT framework, it is argued that irrespective of what causes or maintains them, chronic nightmares disturb sleep. Therefore, successful treatment of nightmares may lead to better sleep and daytime functioning. The client is *not* asked to discount their trauma or PTSD. Rather, they are invited to work on their sleep problems (nightmares or insomnia or both; Krakow, 2004). The client is also provided with the rationale that techniques implemented in the *waking* state can reduce nightmares because what an individual dreams about often reflects what they think about when they are awake (Krakow, 2004). This is broadly consistent with the cognitive model of dreaming (Freeman & White, 2002).

It is beyond the scope of the present chapter to provide comprehensive details of the specifics of implementing IRT. More detailed theoretical and procedural information can be obtained from research and review articles, the book '*Turning Nightmares into Dreams*' (Krakow, 2002) and the official website for 'new dream therapy', http://www.nightmaretreatment.com.

Evidence Base for IRT

Case reports, uncontrolled trials and RCTs have established IRT as an effective treatment for chronic nightmares in adult trauma survivors suffering PTSD (e.g., Krakow, Hollifield, et al., 2001; Krakow, Johnston, et al., 2001). While the evidence base for the efficacy of IRT in treating chronic nightmares in traumatised adults is building, the IRT literature pertaining to children and adolescents is in a nascent form. Generally, child trauma treatment research lags behind its adult counterpart (Dalgleish et al., 2005). It is not surprising, therefore, that the same is true for a specific nightmare treatment such as IRT.

To the best of our knowledge, there is no published RCT pertaining to use of IRT with traumatised children. Only a handful of studies have reported use of IRT with children (St-Onge et al., 2000) and adolescents

(Davis et al., 2003; Krakow, Sandoval, et al., 2001). Firstly, the efficacy of IRT has been documented in treating chronic nightmares in adolescent girls who have suffered sexual trauma (Krakow, Sandoval, et al., 2001). However, unlike many of the adult studies, there was not a significant amelioration in associated sleep complaints or PTSD symptoms. Secondly, a recent case study used IRT with an adolescent rape victim with PTSD (Davis et al., 2003) and reported that nightmare-focused treatment was effective in reducing nightmare frequency and arousal to PTSD-specific nightmares. Finally, only one small-scale study has been conducted examining the efficacy of IRT in treating moderate to severe nightmares in children *without* PTSD (St-Onge et al., 2000). This small study offered preliminary support for the applicability of IRT in children. Further research is needed vis-à-vis the benefits and effectiveness of using IRT in treating trauma-related and nontraumatic nightmares in children.

Adapting IRT for Use With Children

The finding that IRT is effectively used with adults and adolescents, and can be successfully used for those with a developmental disability, raises the possibility that IRT can be used with children. However, it cannot be assumed that procedures developed for adults can be 'transplanted' holus bolus to traumatised children. There is increasing recognition of the need to design developmentally sensitive approaches to therapeutic intervention when working with children (Barrett, 2000). The authors of the present chapter have trialled procedural modifications to adapt IRT for use with traumatised preadolescent children, to make it more 'child-friendly'. These adaptations have been conducted in an individual therapy context. Modifications are suggested at all three stages of IRT.

Selecting a Nightmare

IRT is conducted initially using a self-selected distressing dream of low-moderate level of emotional intensity. Forbes et al. (2003) suggest that clients select a recurrent nightmare. As with adults, it is important that children do not select the 'most difficult' nightmare first up. Clients work up to more distressing or threatening nightmares after they have practised the imagery rehearsal technique successfully and built up confidence in using it. When a nightmare is being selected, we recommend use of a subjective units of distress scale. Use of a 'fear thermometer' will allow the therapist to monitor the intensity of subjective distress activated by recalling the nightmare.

Changing the Nightmare

Given the importance of implementing clinical interventions from a child-based perspective, we have trialled the use of therapeutic drawings within an IRT framework. Art, drama and play may assist traumatised children to express their experiences, thoughts and feelings (e.g., Johnson, 2000). The fact that children may display trauma re-experiencing symptoms through posttraumatic drawing and play suggests that they gravitate naturally to these as a means of personal expression. Methods such as therapeutic drawing may therefore capitalise on children's developmental capabilities. Nonverbal methods may facilitate access to, and processing of, traumatic memories. In trauma-focused therapy with children, therapeutic drawing is well accepted (e.g., Smith, Perrin, & Yule, 1999). Within the IRT literature, there is a precedent for modification of 'standard' adult-oriented IRT techniques in a developmentally sensitive way, albeit with intellectually disabled adult survivors of sexual abuse (Kroese & Thomas, 2006). Drawings were used to provide a concrete illustration of the images represented in a new dream.

We have adopted a flexible position in relation to the key task of changing the nightmare. Some children are quite capable of writing out a new dream and prefer to do so. We invite a child to write or draw a new dream scenario, whichever they prefer, for example: 'change the nightmare in any way you wish and then write it down or draw it'. This offers an alternative to the standard adult-oriented modality which involves writing out the new dream scenario. We have also added the instruction: 'tell me about your new dream while you are drawing it'. We ensure the child has access to lined and blank paper, pencils, felt markers and ink pens. At times, we have found it necessary to stress that the important part is the new dream story, not the quality of the drawing.

In our experience, children respond favourably to drawing a changed dream prior to imagery rehearsal. Children who find it too difficult to talk about their trauma may be willing to draw it. Further, children with developmental difficulties, including handwriting or written or oral expressive language problems, may find drawing to be a more 'friendly' way to communicate. The authors conducted a case study (Dohnt & Encel, 2006), reporting a favourable treatment response, using IRT, with developmental adaptations. The client was a traumatised girl with expressive language problems. As she was a child who liked to draw, she enjoyed drawing her new dream prior to imagery rehearsal. This made it easier for her to deal with a highly distressing traumatic memory of the nightmare. By reducing demands on her expressive language skills, the child found it easier to consider alternative (new) endings to the nightmare.

When a child chooses to write a new dream, additional prompting may be required to produce a coherent narrative. Instructions may include (1) speak/write in the present/past tense, (2) break description into beginning, middle and end, (3) ask questions such as, 'what are you thinking and feeling?', 'who is in your new dream?', 'what happens next', 'what is different/what has changed in your new dream?', 'what are the characters doing?' (such assistance may also be appropriate when a child draws a new dream). Another option includes writing the new dream on a word processor. Alternatively, to allow the child to focus on generating a new dream, the therapist can 'scribe' for the child by writing or typing *their* new dream. If a child decides to write their new dream, it is helpful to have them read it aloud, as suggested by Davis et al. (2003). As with adults, after the initial imagery rehearsal exercise, children briefly describe how they have changed the nightmare. Some children may benefit from recording their new dream onto an audiotape or CD/digital format. Children may also have the option of 'showing your new dream' by acting it out using puppets, dolls or other relevant toy props. This can apply to the rehearsal phase as well.

In children, an additional neutral instruction to formulate a vivid image has been suggested: 'make sure you *see* the images in your head' (St-Onge et al., 2000). Drawing makes this visualisation explicit. If the child becomes 'stuck' on the nightmare, instead of generating a new dream, it is reasonable to add the statement, suggested by St-Onge et al. (2000): 'so that it is not a nightmare anymore'. This statement could be positively valenced: 'so that it is a good dream' or 'so that it ends more happily/safely/better'. Typically, in IRT, the instruction to change the nightmare, including the process of *how* to rescript the dream, is nondirective. Krakow (2004) points out that some individuals change the minutiae of the dream while others create an entirely new story-line. Anecdotally, in our experience, the same can be said of children.

Davis et al. (2003) suggest that when changing the traumatic nightmare into a new dream, it may be helpful to incorporate challenges or alternatives to cognitive errors represented in the target nightmare. They propose that alternatives might include themes of regaining power and control, support and validation. For example, around themes of power and control, in a domestic violence scenario, where a child's mother is the victim of an assault by a male partner witnessed by the child, the alternative dream ending might include 'she calls the police', 'she asks him to leave', 'the police arrive and take him away', or 'I call the police' (instead of 'I'm helpless, I stand there watching paralysed with fear'). Equally, cognitive challenges around themes of vulnerability (e.g., 'I'm gonna die'), responsibility and guilt (e.g., 'I *should* have done more'), or self-worth (e.g., 'I'm a wuss') could be incorporated into the new dream. Anecdotally, we have observed that some children make imaginative changes in generating a new dream. For example, transforming a 'Rambo' knife into a soft rubber knife, overpowering an attacker, making monsters hoarse with laryngitis or make it squeak as if it had been breathing helium, shrinking a monster in size, or making a monster lose its teeth.

As with adults, we have not found it necessary to work on or change every nightmare with children. There is a generalisation effect. Krakow (2004) states that 'working on just a few bad dreams and turning them into new dreams will have a ripple effect on other nightmares' (p. 97).

Rehearsing the Nightmare

In children, minor changes enhance the prospects of effective rehearsal. We have developed the phrase: 'practise when you are awake so you have better dreams when you are asleep'. The prospect of avoiding or better controlling nightmares may be an incentive for homework practice. Children are invited to place a picture of their new dream on their bedroom wall (when they have been made during treatment). As with adults, coping skills should be practised in treatment. The therapist can encourage their implementation in the event that children become particularly distressed by IRT homework.

Various minor differences in the duration of daily IRT practice have been recommended from a few minutes to 20 minutes. In children, we have found that rehearsal time may be reduced to as little as 2–5 minutes. It is important not to overpractice because the novelty may wear off and boredom may quickly become a salient factor with children. The optimal timing and frequency of rehearsal has not been examined in children. As with adults, we have generally asked children to conduct rehearsal practice at night. When we have thought that a child would benefit from additional rehearsal time, we have asked them to practise earlier in the day as well.

In our experience, children typically require more support and direction than adults around when to move onto a new dream. We have often found a telephone call between therapy sessions to be helpful. This may provide an opportunity to collaboratively set goals regarding selection of new dreams, generating new dreams or to review imagery rehearsal homework.

Additional Treatment Guidelines

Measurement instruments for nightmares in children are an area requiring development. We suggest clients record the following information: (1) frequency of the target nightmare, (2) frequency of other nightmares, (3) nightmare-related distress, (4) nightmare interference/effects and (5) general sleep quality. Data should be recorded at baseline, during treatment and at follow-up. Daily recording of traumatic nightmare *content* is generally contraindicated within the IRT paradigm regarding the development and maintenance of nightmares (Krakow, 2004). However, in one IRT pilot study, children were asked to tape record their nightmares and dreams each morning and record them in a journal (St-Onge et al., 2000).

Traumatic nightmares may be beneficial immediately posttrauma by providing warnings necessary to safety, security and emotional processing. IRT should be considered for implementation beyond the acute trauma phase so as not to interfere with natural recovery processes. As with trauma-focused therapy in general, therapeutic dream work should commence when the client is in a safe environment posttrauma, in the context of a client–therapist relationship. IRT may be considered when nightmare-related distress and interference are prominent and nightmare-focused treatment is desired. IRT may be helpful if clients do not favour more exposure-based therapy or if trauma-related nightmares do not respond to more standard trauma-focused interventions. IRT is applicable to single or multiple traumas.

Parent involvement is frequently advocated when treating anxious children (e.g., Dalgleish et al., 2005). We have found it useful to socialise parents into the IRT approach. Parents can support their child by encouraging use of coping skills and helping with recording sleep data. A structured system for rewarding homework based on contingency management principles may facilitate IRT homework practice, for example, a 'better dreams' chart.

How Do Children Respond to IRT?

Our experience suggests that IRT and the child-friendly adaptations, are well received by children. This is important, since effective engagement of children in the therapeutic process will increase the likelihood of favourable outcome. IRT has the advantage that it focuses on using the client's own resources and healing capacities. Informally, we have observed that through IRT, children reappraise their initial unhelpful beliefs about the uncontrollability of nightmares. For example, (1) 'I feel safe to go to bed because I will have good dreams', (2) 'I've made the monsters go away', (3) 'I may have some good dreams tonight'. Beliefs about being able to have better dreams may challenge trauma-related cognitions pertaining to powerlessness and hopelessness and facilitate cognitions pertaining to control.

As with adults, we have found that changing nightmares bestows upon children a sense of mastery, or self-efficacy, which may be transferred into their waking lives. For example, children may become more confident to face difficult situations. After IRT, one child told his therapist that he no longer performed night-time rituals (counting special numbers) to prevent bad dreams. Anecdotal reports from children indicate a number of positive changes associated with IRT, including (a) reductions in other PTSD-related symptoms, (b) more rapid sleep onset and fewer presleep fears and worries (e.g., 'criminals' entering the house at night), (c) fewer nocturnal awakenings and greater total sleep time, (d) reduced avoidance of going to bed and sleeping, (e) sleeping independently, (f) reduced checking that doors and windows are locked, (g) feeling more confident and capable of managing bad dreams when they do occur, (h) a reduced sense of reliving traumatic events (i.e., 'it's a dream, it's not real' or 'it's over'), (i) reduced nocturnal panic attacks on awakening from a nightmare, (j) greater ease of resettling to sleep, (k) improved mood and energy level, and (l) better concentration at school. Recent research may be a pointer to the therapeutic value of changing dream endings. 'Happy' dream endings have been found to moderate the negative impact of traumatic events on children's mental health (Punamäki et al., 2005).

Using IRT in Multicomponent Treatment Programs for Traumatic Stress Reactions in Preadolescent Children

IRT is generally not a 'stand alone' treatment since it has specific applicability for posttraumatic nightmares. However, traumatised children often present with multiple concerns and so direct nightmare therapy may be a *component* of a multicomponent treatment plan. IRT is compatible with more common components of CBT for PTSD. A recent case study reports successfully integrating IRT into a broader trauma-focused treatment program (Davis et al., 2003). IRT may be regarded as an adjunctive therapeutic approach within staged trauma-focused treatment programs. However, IRT may be a specific intervention where posttraumatic nightmares are a circumscribed problem.

Future Directions

There is a need for a RCT regarding the efficacy of IRT in treating trauma-related nightmares in children. An RCT could examine using

IRT with nightmares related to a variety of trauma types; the impact of IRT on sleep quality and diurnal PTSD symptomatology in children; and compare the efficacy of IRT to other treatments such as exposure therapy, cognitive restructuring and eye movement desensitisation and reprocessing. Research on the utility of developmental adaptations when working with traumatised children is warranted. The relative merits of individual versus group-based IRT, in children, could be examined. There is scope for psychometric work validating various nightmare measures and for research examining the most useful instructions to give to clients (neutral or positively valenced). It has been argued that in some individuals who suffer trauma-related nightmares, it may be necessary to identify and target cognitive distortions represented in nightmares and incorporate the corrective information into the changed dream (Davis, et al., 2003). This question warrants further research.

Summary

While chronic nightmares are a common after-effect of traumatic stress, they are rarely the primary target of treatment. IRT is a technique to directly target chronic posttraumatic nightmares. It involves imaginal rehearsal of a nonthreatening 'new dream' that the patient elaborates by altering elements of the original nightmare scenario. There is mounting evidence for the efficacy of IRT with adults and to a lesser extent, adolescents. To the best of our knowledge, studies on trauma-related nightmares in children are yet to be reported in the clinical literature. This chapter has outlined exploratory procedural modifications to make IRT more developmentally sensitive when working with traumatised children.

References

American Psychiatric Association. (2000). *Diagnostic and statistical manual of mental disorders* (4th ed., text Rev.). Washington, DC: Author.

Barrett, P.M. (2000). Treatment of childhood anxiety: Developmental aspects. *Clinical Psychology Review, 20*(4), 479–494.

Cohen, J.A., & Mannarino, A.P. (2004). Posttraumatic stress disorder. In T.H. Ollendick & J.S. March (Eds.), *Phobic and anxiety disorders in children and adolescents: A clinician's guide to effective psychosocial and pharmacological interventions* (pp. 405–432). Oxford: Oxford University Press.

Dalgleish, T., Meiser-Stedman, R., & Smith, P. (2005). Cognitive aspects of posttraumatic stress reactions and their treatment in children and adolescents: An empirical review and some recommendations. *Behavioural and Cognitive Psychotherapy, 33*, 459–486.

Davis, J.L., de Arellano, M., Falsetti, S.A., & Resnick, H. (2003). Treatment of nightmares related to post-traumatic stress disorder in an adolescent rape victim. *Clinical Case Studies, 2*(4), 283–294.

Dohnt, H.K., & Encel, J.S. (2006). *A cognitive–behavioural intervention for traumatic nightmares in children: A case study.* Manuscript in preparation.

Forbes, D., Phelps, A.J., McHugh, A.F., Debenham, P., Hopwood, M., & Creamer, M. (2003). Imagery rehearsal in the treatment of posttraumatic nightmares in Australian veterans with chronic combat-related PTSD: 12-month follow-up data. *Journal of Traumatic Stress, 16*(5), 509–513.

Freeman, A., & White, B. (2002). Dreams and the dream image: Using dreams in cognitive therapy. *Journal of Cognitive Psychotherapy, 16*(1), 39–53.

Giarratano, L. (2004). *Clinical skills for treating traumatised adolescents: Evidence based treatment for PTSD.* Mascot, NSW: Talomin Books.

Johnson, D.J. (2000). Creative therapies. In E.B. Foa, T.M. Keane, & M.J. Friedman (Eds.), *Effective treatments for PTSD: Practice guidelines from the International Society for Traumatic Stress Studies* (pp. 586–588). New York: The Guilford Press.

Krakow, B. (2002). *Turning nightmares into dreams.* Albuquerque, NM: The New Sleepy Times.

Krakow, B. (2004). Imagery rehearsal therapy for chronic posttraumatic nightmares: A mind's eye view. In R.I. Rosner, W.J. Lyddon, & A. Freeman (Eds.), *Cognitive therapy and dreams* (pp. 89–109). New York: Springer Publishing Company.

Krakow, B., Hollifield, M., Johnston, L., Koss, M., Schrader, R., Warner, T.D., et al. (2001). Imagery rehearsal therapy for chronic nightmares in sexual assault survivors with posttraumatic stress disorder: A randomized controlled trial. *Journal of the American Medical Association, 286*(5), 537–545.

Krakow, B., Johnston, L., Melendrez, D., Hollifield, M., Warner, T.D., Chavez-Kennedy, D., et al. (2001). An open-label trial of evidence-based cognitive behavior therapy for nightmares and insomnia in crime victims with PTSD. *American Journal of Psychiatry, 158*, 2043–2047.

Krakow, B., Sandoval, D., Schrader, R., Kuehne, B., McBride, L., Yau, C., et al. (2001). Treatment of chronic nightmares in adjudicated adolescent girls in a residential facility. *Journal of Adolescent Health, 29*(2), 94–100.

Kroese, B.S., & Thomas, G. (2006). Treating chronic nightmares of sexual assault survivors with an intellectual disability—two descriptive case studies. *Journal of Applied Research in Intellectual Disabilities, 19*(1), 75–80.

Punamäki, R-L., Ali, K.J., Ismahil, K.H., & Nuutinen (2005). Trauma, dreaming, and psychological distress among Kurdish children. *Dreaming, 15*(3), 178–194.

Smith, P., Perrin, S., & Yule, W. (1999). Cognitive behaviour therapy for post traumatic stress disorder. *Child Psychology and Psychiatry Review, 4*(4), 177–182.

St-Onge, M., Bisson, V., Legault, M., Kahalé, N. Belzil, M., & De Koninck, J. (2000). Imagery rehearsal for nightmares in children: A pilot study. *Journal of Sleep Research, 9*(suppl. 1), 180.

CHAPTER 6

Treatment Programs for Children With Selective Mutism

Elizabeth Ann Woodcock, Maria Ivanka Milic
and Susan G. Johnson

Selective mutism (SM) is defined in the *Diagnostic and Statistical Manual of Mental Disorders* (fourth edition, text revision; DSM-IV-TR) as a persistent failure to speak in social situations in which there is an expectation for speaking (e.g., at school) despite speaking in other situations and being able to comprehend language (American Psychiatric Association [APA], 2000). Children with SM generally speak freely and comfortably with immediate family members within the family home. How much they continue to speak with family members and others outside of the home appears to vary according to the presence of other factors that increase or lower the child's anxiety (e.g., nonfamily members, unfamiliar environments). These children often fail to speak with their teachers and classmates at school, and in recreational and community settings.

Whilst earlier studies suggest the disorder is relatively rare, affecting approximately 0.01% of the population (Cline & Baldwin, 2004), recent methodologically improved school-based prevalence studies reveal substantially higher rates that range between 0.7% and 1.9% of children in the first 3 years of school (Bergman, Piacentini, & McCracken, 2002; Elizur & Perednik, 2003). SM typically presents around 3 years of age (Black & Uhde, 1995; Dummit et al., 1997). A proportion of children have a transient form of mutism that tends to remit without treatment (Bergman et al., 2002); however, for other children the failure to speak can persist into adolescence or early adulthood. Treatment is often sought once the child has failed to speak for 4 to 5 years, at which time the child may experience secondary social and emotional problems and treatment is much more difficult (Pionek Stone, Kratochwill, Sladezcek, & Serlin, 2002). Of those children who do begin to speak without treatment, a proportion continue to experience clinically significant levels of anxiety as well as social, academic, and communication deficits (Bergman et al., 2002).

Although SM is categorised in DSM-IV-TR under 'Other Disorders of Infancy, Childhood and Adolescence', there is strong empirical evidence that it is an anxiety disorder (Anstendig, 1999; Vecchio & Kearney, 2005). For example, almost all children with SM meet diagnostic criteria for social phobia and about half meet criteria for an additional anxiety disorder (Black & Uhde, 1995; Dummit et al., 1997; Vecchio & Kearney, 2005). Further support for SM being an anxiety disorder is the higher incidence of social phobia and avoidant personality traits in first-degree relatives (Black & Uhde, 1995) and the positive response of SM to SSRIs that are known to have anxiolytic properties (Black & Uhde, 1994; Dummit, Klein, Tancer, Asche, & Martin, 1996).

Until the late 1990s, there was a paucity of research on treatments for SM, with the majority being single-case research designs and case studies. There were only a handful of studies with more than 20 cases, very few between-groups designs, and no independent replication studies (Cline & Baldwin, 2004). In the only meta-analysis to date (Pionek Stone et al., 2002) the existing treatments for SM, which were predominantly behavioural, were shown to be more effective than no treatment. Applying these interventions in clinical practice was difficult as the existing treatment studies provided brief descriptions of interventions and the process of treatment was not clearly delineated. No manualised treatment programs were available to guide treatment. As a result of these limitations, a structured program (described below) was developed by the second author to provide clear guidelines for the management and treatment of children with SM (Milic, 1999, 2005).

'I can talk. I do talk!': A School-Based Cognitive–Behavioural Treatment Program

The program developed by Maria Milic is a cognitive–behavioural (CB) treatment that views SM as an anxiety-based disorder in which anxiety limits the child's ability to communicate. It was developed for children from 4 years of age. Within the program, 'talking' is defined as exchanging ideas by any appropriate means, including speech, whispering, sounds, gestures and writing. This broader definition places talking on a continuum such that most children with SM can be perceived to 'talk' in settings where others describe them as mute. The central goal of treatment is to help the child feel relaxed and confident in using more ways of talking/communicating, with the final stage being use of speech in all situations where the child needs or wants to speak.

The program is conducted over a 12-month period at the child's school (or preschool) and consists of four primary components:

- training sessions, in which the parent(s) and teacher are trained by the clinician in CB strategies for anxiety and SM
- behavioural strategies for the school staff
- thrice-weekly play sessions (for approximately 6 months)
- generalisation and maintenance of talking.

If other difficulties are identified that are not part of SM or social anxiety (e.g., school refusal, parental anxiety disorder, family disharmony), a referral is made for concurrent outpatient treatment.

Training Sessions

Ten to 12 training sessions are attended by the parent(s), classroom teacher and other relevant school personnel. One session is held approximately every 4 weeks of the school term. The content of the sessions (described below) is modelled on well-researched family-orientated treatment programs for children with anxiety disorders (Barrett, Lowry-Webster, & Holmes, 1999; Rapee, 2003).

Session 1:   Provide rationale. Describe CB model for anxiety. Introduce graded exposure. Establish play sessions. Implement basic behavioural strategies.

Session 2:   Psychoeducation about, and management of, physiological symptoms of anxiety (slow breathing, exercise, distraction techniques such as play). Review graded exposure. Establish reward program.

Session 3:   Psychoeducation about relationship between thoughts and feelings, and common patterns of unhelpful thinking. Review graded exposure and reward program.

Session 4:   Train adults to help the child identify and challenge unhelpful self-talk. Review graded exposure and reward program.

Sessions 5 to 12: Review graded exposure, focusing increasingly on generalising gains from play sessions to classroom, playground, community and social events. Continue practising cognitive challenging. Discussions around pacing exposure, normal patterns of recovery, setbacks, expectations, and helping the child manage new situations and change. Monitor social functioning and implement skills training (if relevant).

A significant part of each training session is helping the adults to break down the exposure tasks for 'talking' into achievable steps and plan the sequence of steps to be practised over the following 4 weeks. The continuum of communication is divided into five stages:

- Stage 1: Nonverbal communication.
- Stage 2: Indirect verbal communication which involves video/audio tapes or computer recordings of the child speaking.
- Stage 3: Whispering through a 'safe' person (e.g., to a parent in the teacher's presence)
- Stage 4: Speaking freely with the teacher.
- Stage 5: Speaking freely with children and adults at school and in the community.

Within each stage there is an extensive hierarchy of steps. It is expected that the child will take small steps and practise each step over a number of occasions.

Basic Behavioural Strategies

Guidelines were developed to help the adults to encourage the child's communication in the least threatening manner. They include:

- Expect the child to communicate for themselves in whatever way they find least anxiety-provoking.
- Give the child opportunities to communicate by adopting a style of questioning (e.g., closed questions or choices) that allows the child to respond.
- Give the child adequate time to communicate as their anxiety frequently results in hesitancy.
- Show interest in and praise the content of the child's responses, rather than the fact that they have communicated.
- When the child's voice is heard for the first time, act in a 'matter of fact way' without surprise or celebration.

Strategies are also implemented to increase the child's interaction with peers at, and outside of, school, and to include the child in all aspects of school life.

Play Sessions

The child begins to face their fear of using their voice in play sessions with their parent and classroom teacher. Prior to the session, the parents negotiate with the child what steps will be practised, and the teacher and parent together implement an individualised reward program. Ideally, the play sessions are held three times a week for 20 minutes in a closed room. One parent attends the play sessions to support the child to practise using modes of 'talking' that are progressively more anxiety-provoking. Although children with SM are more likely to start speaking with a child than an adult (Black & Uhde, 1995), the classroom teacher is used because they are present in the majority of school situations with the child and in a position to be able to meet the child's needs. The play sessions provide the child with a space to learn to feel secure in their teacher's presence and to learn that their teacher can be a reliable support. Once the child can speak confidently with the teacher, the teacher can help them generalise their speaking to the school environment.

For stage 1 (nonverbal communication), the play sessions are structured as 20 minutes of free play. The child chooses a game or activity and decides how the game will be played. For the first 2 weeks the only expectation on the child is to enjoy playing. This allows the child time to become familiar and comfortable with the room and their teacher. From the third week the child begins to work on the steps in stage 1 of the hierarchy. During the child-led free play, the adults chat, make statements, and ask questions about the activity. Initially, the parent asks more questions than the teacher and both adults ask the child one question for every five statements to prevent the child from becoming overwhelmed. Strategies to manage the child's hesitancy and failure to respond to questions are discussed to ensure that the child is not pressured to respond in any way. Strategies include acknowledging the anxiety, simplifying questions, and returning to the question later.

From stage 2 (Indirect Verbal Communication) the child practises the exposure task for the first 10 minutes with the final 10 minutes devoted to child-directed free play. Ending the session with play provides the child with a strategy to calm their anxiety and to end their interaction with their teacher in a positive way, thus challenging any unhelpful thoughts they may have about the exposure task.

Generalisation and Maintenance of 'Talking'

Once the child is able to speak to their teacher during the play sessions, the teacher supports the child to practise talking with them in the classroom, and gradually use their voice with classmates and other adults. The parent helps the child to generalise speaking to the playground and to various community settings, such as shopping centres, extracurricular activities, friends' houses, and in the home with visitors.

Comparisons Between Resources and Treatment Programs for Selective Mutism

A number of resource manuals and structured treatment programs emerged whilst the 'I can talk. I do talk!' program was being developed. These programs, and their main differences, are outlined in Table 1.

There are a number of similarities between these programs. All view SM as being an anxiety-based disorder and underscore a collaborative approach between parents, schools and professionals. The main goal of the interventions is for the child to gradually face their fear of speaking without being pressured to speak. They consider lack of speech to be the first stage of a continuum of communication, with speaking being a later, more anxiety-provoking, stage. Common components of the programs include psychoeducation about anxiety, changes to the school environment to make it less anxiety-provoking, and other behavioural techniques such as systematic desensitisation, stimulus fading, shaping, and contingency management. Adults are encouraged to assess which situations the child finds anxiety-provoking and develop an individualised graded hierarchy. Generalisation of speaking to all children and adults is considered unlikely to occur without specific intervention.

Preliminary Results From the 'I can talk. I do talk!' Program

The program was offered by the second author as a solely school-based intervention from 2002. The progress of children who participated in this treatment between January 2002 and June 2005 will be qualitatively reviewed here. Fifteen children diagnosed with SM were offered treatment within that period. Four of those 15 are not included; two did not complete the program and two were engaged in concurrent individual and family outpatient treatment in their local area. Thus, the progress of eleven children (five females, six males) is reviewed.

Age (mean + SD) at referral was 5.8 + 1.28 years (range = 4.2 to 8.3 years) with the children having failed to speak for 3.3 + 0.8 years (range = 2.2 to 4 years). The children commenced treatment at a younger age than the literature suggests with four children commencing treatment in preschool. English was not the first language of seven of the children. This is consistent with the higher prevalence of SM in children of parents of non-English speaking background (Elizur & Perednik, 2003). A family clinical interview revealed a high prevalence of comorbid anxiety disorders (seven children had social phobia, three had separation anxiety disorder, and two had generalised anxiety disorder). Furthermore, 10 (91%)

Table 1
Differences Between Resources and Programs for Selective Mutism

Program/resource	Cognitive component	Adult responsible for school exposure program	Number of stages of communication
Boggs (2005)	Yes	Not specified, possibly clinician	Not specified
Fung et al. (2000) Kenny et al. (2000)	Yes	Parent	13
Goetze Kervatt (1999, 2004)	No	School personnel	Not specified, 5 stages described
Johnson & Wintgens (2001)	No	Clinician	10
McHolm et al. (2005)	No	Parent	11
Milic (1999, 2005)	Yes	Clinician	5
Shipon-Blum (2003a, 2003b)	Yes	Not specified, possibly clinician	5

of the 11 mothers and four (36%) fathers identified experiencing their own clinically significant anxiety.

The average number (mean + SD) of training sessions was 8.9 + 4.5 (range = 2 to 18 sessions), with a treatment duration of 16.5 + 8.47 months (range = 4 to 32 months), which was increased by school holidays and the change of the school year. There were two children who took considerable time to complete the program and required additional training sessions. One of these children commenced the treatment in preschool and was making good progress, but experienced a setback with the transition to school. The second child's parents had clinical levels of anxiety but did not wish to commence outpatient therapy until the end of the school program.

At the beginning of treatment, some of the children could speak to their parents on the school grounds. No children spoke comfortably to their teacher, although two children could whisper to their teacher. The program successfully helped all children begin to speak freely with their parents, adults, and classmates at school (see Table 2). Three of the children continued to find speaking in front of an audience difficult. In contrast, two of the children talked on the microphone at the school assembly. Ten children were also speaking freely in all community and social settings.

Table 2
Number of Children Speaking Freely in Various School Situations Pre-
and Post-Treatment

	Pre-treatment ($n = 11$)	Post-treatment ($n = 11$)
Speaks freely, with classroom teacher	0	11
Speaks freely, with other adults at school	0	11
Speaks freely, with friends at school	1	11
Speaks freely, with classmates	0	11
Speaks freely, in front of the class	0	8

Case Example of a Clinic- and School-Based Adaptation of the 'I can talk. I do talk!' Program

The 'I can talk, I do talk!' program was adapted by the first author to use in her privately-based selective mutism clinic, as illustrated in the following case example.

Background Information

Sally, a 6-year-old girl, was referred by her school counsellor due to concerns that she had entered her second year of school without yet speaking at school and was becoming increasingly isolated in the playground. Sally could talk to her parents in any setting, except school or situations in which adults or children outside of her extended family could see or hear her speaking. She could talk freely with her extended family, but only responded nonverbally to family friends, neighbours, and strangers. Whenever her parents had raised the issue of her difficulty talking, Sally usually replied with 'I like to talk, but can't'. Parents and school staff identified no other academic, social, or psychological concerns.

Sally was born in Sri Lanka and moved to Australia when she was 4 years old. English was the primary language spoken in the home, with Tamil being a secondary language. Sally's early development was unremarkable. When Sally was 3 years old her parents noticed that she only spoke with familiar members of the extended family. Sally attended preschool in Sri Lanka for 1 year and day care in Australia for 3 months, and did not speak at either.

Overview of Intervention

The intervention consisted of three primary components:

(1) Clinic sessions with Sally and her mother to provide psychoeducation about anxiety and SM, demonstrate the play sessions, and work on an

exposure hierarchy for community situations. Greater emphasis was given to teaching Sally about anxiety compared to the school-based version, using a variety of resources (e.g., Barrett, 2004; Rapee, 2003). Eighteen sessions were held over a 9-month period. The family's finances limited the frequency, length (reduced from 60 to 30 minutes after the third session), and termination of these sessions.

(2) School training sessions as per the 'I can talk. I do talk!' program, except that they were less frequent (four sessions over 7 months) and with less attention to the community-based component as this was addressed in the clinic.

(3) School play sessions, with Sally, her mother, and the classroom teacher.

The various components of the program and Sally's progress are presented in Table 3.

Sally's progress was followed up 6 months after the clinic sessions had stopped. The teacher's aide was continuing to conduct play sessions with Sally and help generalise Sally's speaking to all school situations. Sally was speaking to almost every child or teacher that came into her class. She was regularly raising her hand to answer questions, participating in class discussions (using one sentence), presenting news to the class (using multiple sentences), and verbally participating in peer support with older children. Sally was depending less on Amy, her best friend, and was playing with other children in the playground. In the community, Sally was talking freely to her mother. When there were visitors to the house she answered questions from adults and talked spontaneously to children, but not adults. In church she answered questions from adults, but was not talking spontaneously to anyone in this environment.

Outstanding Issues

Treatment programs for children with SM appear to be heading in the right direction with progressively more focus on the anxiety underlying the mutism and greater involvement of the school. However, there is a paucity of research on this topic and many questions that are as yet unanswered. For example, the relative importance of specific treatment components is still unclear, such as the optimal combination of school-, clinic-, and community-based components, the importance of adding a cognitive component to behavioural treatments, the role of medications, and the optimal frequency and number of sessions. Now that manualised programs are available that differ with respect to the above factors, randomised controlled treatment studies need to be conducted. Such studies

Table 3
Sally's Progress and Key Gains With the Treatment Program

Month	Program components	Sally's progress and key gains
Assessment	Used 'talking map' (Johnson & Wintgens, 2001) to communicate places at school/community where Sally could talk. Conducted play session to build rapport.	Prior to the session Sally instructed her parents to 'tell her (the clinician) that I'm shy'. Visibly anxious throughout interview. Responded to most questions with slight head movements. Could not whisper to parents with clinician's back turned, but spoke when clinician left the room.
1	Commenced clinic nonverbal games (e.g., modified versions of 'I spy', 'Simon Says') and recordings of Sally's voice.	Keen to engage in activities. Played recording stating, 'To Dr Elizabeth, I'm looking forward to seeing you and playing games with you'. Noticeably anxious during playback (wringing hands, looking down-wards).
2	Established communication hierarchy and reward system. Taught progressive muscle relaxation and deep breathing. Conducted first school training session.	Keen to practise steps on hierarchy and earn points on chart. Disliked experience of relaxing and did not practise. Recorded a reading on tape for classroom teacher and thereafter brought similar recordings to clinic sessions.
3	Psychoeducation about anxiety. Continued clinic play sessions with nonverbal games and tape-recordings. Started to elicit speech in clinic play sessions. Started school play sessions.	Demonstrated good understanding of anxiety. Made loud sounds and large movements with hands/arms, took more lead in games. Smiling whilst playing recordings. Answered clinician's questions by whispering to mother whilst clinician turned around with fingers in her ears, making noises. Laughed out loud. Whispered 'How many stickers will I get?' to her mother.

Table 3 (CONTINUED)
Sally's Progress and Key Gains With the Treatment Program

Month	Program components	Sally's progress and key gains
4		More confident nonverbal behaviour in classroom (smiling, eye contact, requesting help by putting up hand). Playing with children in play-ground when initiated by others. Speaking to best friend, 'Amy', at home using structured tasks (e.g., singing songs, reading). Speaking to mother in playground. Talking to mother when passing people on way to school.
5	Continued play sessions, recordings, psychoeducation.	Whispering answers to mother in clinic/school play sessions before clinician/teacher turned around or put fingers in ears.
6		Unstructured, spontaneous speaking (few words) to Amy at home. Spontaneous, unstructured voice recordings (e.g., describing swimming lessons). Louder whispering in play sessions such that clinician/teacher could respond directly to Sally (Sally looked surprised/anxious but continued at same volume).
7	Amy (friend) joined school play sessions. Cognitive strategies taught in clinic.	Talking spontaneously (short sentences) at Amy's house in front of Amy's family. Whispering directly to teacher in play sessions. Whispered to Amy in class. Initiating play in playground.
8	Replaced Sally's mother/teacher in school play sessions with boy in Sally's class, 'Mark', and teacher's aide.	Spoke to clinician/teacher in low voice using structured tasks (e.g., reading). Said 'goodbye' to clinician. Whispering to Mark and teacher's aide in play sessions.
9+	Clinic sessions ended. Teacher's aide continued play sessions. Teacher helped generalise talking at school.	Spoke out loud in class during structured task (i.e., spelling game).

are understandably challenging, however, given the difficulty recruiting subjects (due to the low incidence and poor recognition of the disorder) and the slow response to treatment. However, short research trials may be possible if they adopt outcome measures such as the number of 'stages of communication' through which the child has progressed, rather than whether the child is speaking. Another important issue is to determine the best time to intervene. Because interventions at a younger age have more positive outcomes (Pionek Stone et al., 2002) it may be more efficacious to implement treatments in the preschool. Thus, treatments may need to be modified to suit the preschool and the cognitive capabilities of this age group. The play sessions in the 'I can talk. I do talk!' program appear particularly suitable for this purpose. If early intervention is indeed important, then another issue to address is how to facilitate early detection of SM and referral to appropriate services.

References

American Psychiatric Association. (2000). *Diagnostic and statistical manual of mental disorders* (4th ed., text Rev.). Washington, DC: Author.

Anstendig, K.D. (1999). Is selective mutism an anxiety disorder? Rethinking its DSM-IV classification. *Journal of Anxiety Disorders, 13*(4), 417–434.

Barrett, P. (2004). *FRIENDS for life: Workbook for children.* Brisbane, Australia: Australian Academic Press.

Barrett, P., Lowry-Webster, H., & Holmes, J. (1999). *The FRIENDS anxiety prevention program. Group leader's manual for children.* Brisbane, Australia: Australian Academic Press.

Bergman, R.L., Piacentini, J., & McCracken, J.T. (2002). Prevalence and description of selective mutism in a school-based sample. *Journal of the American Academy of Child & Adolescent Psychiatry, 41*(8), 938–946.

Black, B., & Uhde, T.W. (1994). Treatment of elective mutism with fluoxetine: A double-blind, placebo-controlled study. *Journal of the American Academy of Child & Adolescent Psychiatry, 33*(7), 1000–1006.

Black, B., & Uhde, T.W. (1995). Psychiatric characteristics of children with selective mutism: A pilot study. *Journal of the American Academy of Child & Adolescent Psychiatry, 34*(7), 847–856.

Boggs, A.E. (2005). *Selective mutism anxiety reduction therapy: A multiple case study.* Proquest/UMI.

Cline, T., & Baldwin, S. (2004). *Selective mutism in children* (2nd ed.) London: Whurr.

Dummit, E.S., Klein, R.G., Tancer, N.K., Asche, B., & Martin, J. (1996). Fluoxetine treatment of children with selective mutism: An open trial. *Journal of the American Academy of Child & Adolescent Psychiatry, 35*(5), 615–621.

Dummit, E.S., Klein, R.G., Tancer, N.K., Asche, B., Martin, J., & Fairbanks, J.A. (1997). Systematic assessment of 50 children with selective mutism. *Journal of the American Academy of Child & Adolescent Psychiatry, 36*(5), 653–660.

Elizur, Y., & Perednik, R. (2003). Prevalence and description of selective mutism in immigrant and native families: Controlled study. *Journal of the American Academy of Child & Adolescent Psychiatry, 42*(12), 1451–1459.

Fung, D., Kenny, A., & Mendlowitz, S. (2000). *Meeky Mouse Notebook: A cognitive behavioral treatment program for children with selective mutism.* Unpublished manuscript.

Goetze Kervatt, G. (1999). *The silence within: A teacher/parent guide to helping selectively mute and shy children.* Oak Ridge, NJ: Author.

Goetze Kervatt, G. (2004). *Supplement to 'The silence within': A teacher/parent guide to helping selectively mute and shy children.* Oak Ridge, NJ: Author.

Johnson, M., & Wintgens, A. (2001). *The selective mutism resource manual.* Oxon, UK: Speechmark.

Kenny, A., Fung, D.S.S., & Mendlowitz, S.L. (2000). *Parent and school manual: Developing an intervention plan for selective mutism.* Unpublished manuscript.

McHolm, A.E., Cunningham, C.E., & Vanier, M.K. (2005). *Helping your child with selective mutism: Practical steps to overcome a fear of speaking.* Oakland, CA: New Harbinger.

Milic, M.I. (1999, November). *A pilot school-based program for treatment of selective mutism.* Paper presented at Pitfalls in Practice: A Clinician's Conference, the first AACBT conference, NSW Branch, University of Sydney, Australia.

Milic, M.I. (2005, March). *Helping children with selective mutism in the school environment.* Training Workshop for School Personnel, Redbank House, Westmead Hospital, Sydney, Australia.

Pionek Stone, B., Kratochwill, T.R., Sladezcek, I., & Serlin, R.C. (2002). Treatment of selective mutism: A best-evidence synthesis. *School Psychology Quarterly, 17*(2), 168–190.

Rapee, R. (2003). *Cool Kids program: Family version.* Sydney, Australia: Macquarie University Anxiety Research Unit.

Shipon-Blum, E. (2003a). *Easing school jitters for the selectively mute child* (2nd ed.). Pennsylvania, PA: Smart-Center Inc.

Shipon-Blum, E. (2003b). *The ideal classroom setting for the selectively mute child: A guide for parents, teachers, and treating professionals* (2nd ed.). Pennsylvania, PA: Smart-Center Inc.

Vecchio, J.L., & Kearney, C.A. (2005). Selective mutism in children: Comparison to youths with and without anxiety disorders *Journal of Psychopathology & Behavioural Assessment, 27*(1), 31–37.

CHAPTER 7

Developing and Delivering Computer-Based CBT for Anxiety Disorders in Young People

Mike J. Cunningham, Caroline L. Donovan and Sonja March

Anxiety disorders afflict between 5% to 10% of children and adolescents (Costello, Mustillo, Erkanli, Keeler, & Angold, 2003) and are associated with a range of adverse academic, vocational and social consequences if left untreated (Costello, Angold, & Keeler, 1999; Ginsburg, LaGreca, & Silverman, 1998; Last, Hansen, & Franco, 1997). Face-to-face cognitive–behavioural therapy (CBT) programs for child and adolescent anxiety disorders have been shown empirically to be highly effective (see James, Soler, & Weatherall, 2005 for a review), yet only one in four young people suffering with an anxiety disorder receives professional help. Barriers that prevent young people from accessing mental health professionals for assistance with their anxiety include privacy and anonymity, stigma, cost, geographic isolation, access to therapists, and discomfort with traditional therapy procedures (Booth et al., 2004). Thus, the need for alternative treatment approaches that potentially circumvent these barriers appears highly necessary.

Computer-based CBT (CCBT) represents one such approach. Indeed, a number of authors have suggested that CCBT may lead to an improvement in mental health services, a cost reduction in therapy, more innovative service and democratisation of health care, facilitation of consumer empowerment, lower perceived stigmatisation, and generally a more convenient form of mental health practice (e.g., Christensen, Griffiths, & Evans, 2002; Kaltenthaler et al., 2002; Senate Select Committee on Mental Health, 2006). Since it is highly structured and has well-delineated procedures, CBT lends itself well to computerisation (Proudfoot, 2004). Indeed, CCBT has been shown to be effective in a number of randomised control trials for the treatment and prevention of a variety of adult psychological disorders (see Griffiths & Christensen, 2006 for a review). To date, however, there has been a paucity of research in the use of computer programs in the psychological treatment of youth.

Despite the absence of youth as a target population in CCBT psychological treatment research, there are several reasons why such an approach may be particularly suited to this demographic. First, youth view the Internet as one of the most important sources of information, with one study finding that 90% view the Internet as a tool for acquiring information, communication and trade (Tsai, 2004). Second, youth in general, and anxious youth in particular, are somewhat inhibited when confiding in, and communicating with, adults. Internet communication has a 'disinhibition effect' where higher self-disclosure levels are evident in computer-mediated compared to face-to-face interaction, due in part to the anonymity and invisibility of Internet communication (Joinson, 2001; Suler, 2004). Thus, anxious youth may be more likely to self-disclose and subsequently benefit from CCBT treatment. Third, 85% of Australian households with a child aged 15 years or younger have a computer at home and 68% have home Internet access (Australian Bureau of Statistics, 2004). Thus, CCBT programs may be particularly accessible for young people.

Two innovative Australian projects targeting youth anxiety disorders are currently underway. 'The Cool Teens' program, developed at Macquarie University, is an interactive, multimedia CD-ROM targeting adolescents aged 14–18 years with anxiety disorders (Cunningham, Rapee, & Lyneham, 2006a; Cunningham, Rapee, Lyneham, Schniering, & Wuthrich, 2006). The program consists of eight CCBT modules, each taking between 15–30 minutes to complete. Developed as a home-based program for independent use, Cool Teens uses a combination of media (text, audio, illustrations, cartoons, and live video) to deliver information, examples, interactive exercises, hypothetical scenarios, and case studies.

The BRAVE program, developed at The University of Queensland, began as an anxiety program for children aged 7–12 years in which half the sessions were delivered in a traditional face-to-face group therapy format, and half were delivered as an Internet program (Spence, Holmes, March, & Lipp, in press; Holmes, Spence, & March, in press). Subsequently, this program has been extended into a full Internet-based intervention called BRAVE for Children—ONLINE, that targets anxious children aged 8–12 years (Spence, March, & Holmes, 2005). BRAVE for Teenagers—ONLINE has also been developed at The University of Queensland as a full Internet-based intervention whose target audience are anxious adolescents aged 13–17 years (Spence, Holmes, Donovan, & Kenardy, 2006). Both BRAVE for Children—ONLINE and BRAVE for Teenagers—ONLINE involve ten, 1-hour youth sessions, 5–6 parent sessions, and two booster sessions conducted 1 month and 3 months after completion of the initial program.

The majority of existing CCBT programs fall into 2 formats: Online Internet experiences (websites) and offline products (CD-ROMs or computer DVDs). Cool Teens is an example of a CD-ROM-based CCBT program, while BRAVE is an illustration of an Internet-based format. Discussion will now centre on the practical issues involved in designing and developing CCBT programs, using the Cool Teens and BRAVE programs as examples. Information is presented as a series of questions and answers, supported by examples, highlighting specific experiences from the development of these two projects.

How Will the Program Be Used?

The first challenge in developing a CCBT program is to decide exactly how the final product will be used. Each of the following questions must be considered thoroughly in order to provide an overall guiding framework for design, development, and delivery:

- What disorder(s) are to be targeted?
- Which population will be targeted?
- Where will the program be used (e.g., at a clinic, at home, at school)?
- What level of professional psychological assistance will be involved and, if there is any, will communication with a professional be integrated within the program?
- Will others (e.g., parent, teacher, mentor) be involved in therapy, or is the program purely for independent use?

In terms of how the programs are used, Cool Teens and BRAVE demonstrate both similarities and differences. Both programs are home-based and target anxiety disorders in youth. The level of professional assistance and the involvement of others in therapy however, differs between the two programs. Integrated and nonintegrated interaction between therapist and young person is evident in the BRAVE program. Throughout the course, the young person completes a variety of exercises and home tasks online that are accessible to the therapist, who in turn provides help or reinforcement as appropriate. E-mails are sent to participants upon completion of each session, congratulating the young person on their involvement and providing clarification of activities or skills as necessary. In addition, a phone call is made by the therapist to the young person upon the construction of their exposure hierarchy, to ensure that it is appropriate and practical. Finally, families are encouraged to telephone the therapist if difficulty is experienced with any component of the program. Thus, the BRAVE program allows the therapist to track the progress of the young person, and to redirect and reinforce their efforts where necessary. With respect to the involvement of others in the program, BRAVE includes concurrent parent programs designed to teach parents about the concepts involved in the youth program and to provide specific strategies for managing their child's anxiety.

In contrast, Cool Teens involves no direct therapist or parental involvement. The decision to make Cool Teens a self-help CBT program for independent home use by teenagers presented several major overall challenges. In order to provide sufficient instruction and support for the young person within the program, a considerable amount of high quality video is used on the CD-ROM. Six young actors role play specific anxiety problems throughout the program, and two psychologists provide answers to common questions in an 'Ask the Experts' section. In addition, two young presenters introduce and summarise each module with a 30–60 second video, a feature that has proven to be one of the most popular in the program. Although Cool Teens is designed for pure self-help delivery without professional assistance, the addition of a weekly e-mail or telephone support from a professional is being evaluated for increased efficacy of the program.

An important difficulty faced by both BRAVE and Cool Teens researchers was the plan to target a broad range of ages and anxiety types with programs that provide all users with the same content. The danger in this approach is that the product may be too general and will demonstrate varying levels of efficacy depending on the particular age and anxiety disorder of the young person. Both programs have attempted to overcome this difficulty by providing numerous examples incorporating a balanced variety of ages and anxiety types, to illustrate the different strategies and information presented. A future option may be to offer alternative content pathways, or perhaps different versions of the programs, based on the particular anxiety disorder in question.

What Project Approaches Will Help to Bring Success?

The overall success of a CCBT program depends on the appropriate involvement and combination of efforts from many people, and the facilitation of all project steps. Four strategies may be particularly useful:

- break the project into phases
- involve young people
- develop an overall long-term plan
- involve a multidisciplinary team

In the world of IT, projects are often divided into three phases of a software cycle: design, development and testing. Combining psychological research components with this cycle produces a generic set of phases to direct program production: (a) prototype design and development, (b) prototype evaluation, (c) full program development (including any redesign), (d) pilot evaluation, and (e) clinical trial. It is critical to involve young people by seeking their opinions and input regarding program design, content creation, and delivery formats and features. Feedback and suggestions should be elicited early and regularly. Both the BRAVE and Cool Teens programs were pilot tested with teenage audiences to ensure that the content, graphics, and examples provided were appealing and age appropriate.

Due to the uncertain nature of personnel and funding continuity involved in many university-based projects, it is important to develop a long-term plan that helps to maximise commitment and investment in the program. A full research, funding and publication plan, including future program distribution and enhancement preferences, will help guide decisions and provide long-term incentive to succeed. Proudfoot et al. (2003) also stresses the importance of a multidisciplinary team approach. Psychotherapy seems to lag behind other fields in the use of computer-based tools. However, it is important that clinical psychology researchers involve professionals with nonclinical expertise (e.g., information technologists, graphic artists, instructional designers) from the outset of their research.

What CBT Components Will Be Included?

Most CBT programs involve some combination of psycho-education, somatic symptom management, cognitive restructuring, problem-solving, exposure, and relapse prevention (Velting, Setzer, & Albano, 2004). Since the selection of multimedia formats will depend on the type of content to be delivered, the choice of components has a major influence on design and technical decisions. The challenge is to decide which components to include and which to omit.

The Cool Teens project set out to adapt a group therapy manual (Lyneham, Schniering, Hudson, & Rapee, 2005) already in use with an anxious teenage population. Component CBT strategies of the Cool Teens program include cognitive restructuring and exposure, complemented by psycho-education, goal setting, coping skills, and a section on maintenance and relapse. These components were thought to be the most necessary and adaptable for a self-help version of the existing clinic-based program, whilst providing an appropriate overall number and combination of techniques for independent use.

The BRAVE project designed Internet sessions for young people and parents to be identical in content to individual clinic-based therapy versions of the BRAVE program (Donovan, Holmes, Spence, & Kenardy, 2006a, 2006b; Holmes, March, & Spence, 2005; March, Holmes, & Spence, 2005). BRAVE is an acronym for each of the CBT strategies presented during the program. 'B' stands for 'body signs' and refers to training in the detection of the physiological responses to anxiety. 'R' is for relaxation, introduced as a method for calming down one's anxious body signs, and comprising the strategies of deep breathing, progressive muscle relaxation, and imagery. 'A' refers to 'activating helpful thoughts' and involves the cognitive restructuring component of the program. 'V' stands for 'victory over your fears' and incorporates the strategies of both graded exposure and problem solving. Finally, 'E' stands for 'Enjoy! Reward yourself' and refers to teaching both the young person and parent about the virtues and practicalities of positive reinforcement. The program also incorporates psychoeducation, strategies for parenting an anxious young person, and relapse prevention.

For all CCBT programs, a major challenge is to balance consistency in both the presentation and length of CBT components, with a reasonable amount of variety in the presentation of content. Developers of Cool Teens designed a model for presenting each module, based on Learning Objects from the world of e-Learning (Cisco Systems Inc., 2000). These 'Therapy Objects' (Figure 1) provided a framework for consistent delivery and helped guide the selection of appropriate multimedia.

Even using an overall model, each module must be analysed on an individual basis and decisions must be made as to what information, demonstrations, and examples to include. For components such as psychoeducation, transformation from clinic-based delivery to computer-based delivery may not be particularly difficult. In fact, computer-based delivery of this information may be more interesting and therefore more likely to be remembered, compared to standard clinic procedures. However, the presentation of other CBT strategies, such as graded exposure, may be more difficult and challenging to deliver via computer.

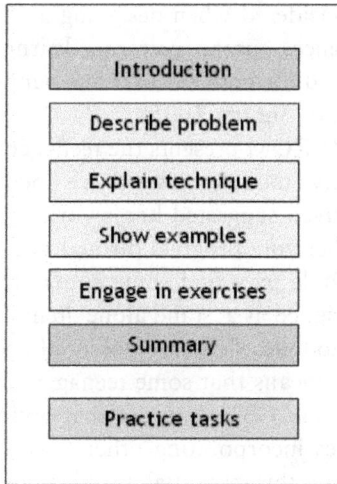

Figure 1
Cool Teens 'Therapy Object'.

In an attempt to ensure the success of graded exposure over the Internet, the BRAVE program includes telephone contact with a therapist for hierarchy development. In addition, tip sheets on hierarchy construction and potential problems that young people may encounter when doing exposure are provided, and the exposure component of the teenage program is completed over two sessions to prevent information overload. The Cool Teens program includes an animated series of steps with voiceover explanations of the process of creating an exposure 'stepladder' that are easily re-accessed at any time. Many examples are included as well as a specific 'Tips and Traps' section in a follow-up module to help the teenager to reinforce their knowledge of this important technique. Thus, although the effectiveness of transforming clinic-based graded exposure into computer-based versions is yet to be determined, both Cool Teens and BRAVE programs have acknowledged and attempted to guard against, the potential problems that may occur.

What Overall Experience Do You Want to Provide for the User?

A complete understanding of the final expected user experience is essential to developing a CCBT program that is easy to use and that contains the correct sequence and combination of information. Individual differences that must be considered when designing a CCBT program include learning style preferences, usage patterns, learning abilities, and the amount of time involved for both the user and supporting parent or therapist (Coyle, Doherty, & Sharry, 2005).

The Cool Teens CD-ROM presents the teenager with a series of eight, 15–30 minute interactive modules. Users have open access to all modules at all times and are given suggested homework upon the completion of each. Teenagers can therefore progress through the program at their own pace. Since young people may find some components more useful than others, each one is designed as a 'stand alone' item. Despite the many benefits of open access modules, there are potential problems as well. Open access to the modules means that some teenagers may access later modules comprising particular CBT strategies that optimally require completion of earlier modules incorporating other CBT strategies. Cool Teens attempts to circumvent this potential problem by providing a recommended order of module completion and by crossreferencing various modules at critical points. Furthermore, the navigation system allows extremely easy initial- and return-access to all program sections.

The overall experience for BRAVE program users is substantially different to that of Cool Teens. The BRAVE program comprises 10 sessions of approximately 1-hour duration that are accessed in a prescribed order and rate. That is, teenagers can only progress through the 10 sessions in a particular order, and are only able to access the next session 7 days following their completion of the previous session. Although this bypasses the problem of completion order experienced by Cool Teens, it does not allow the teenager to progress at a rate that may be more suitable or convenient to them. However, a 7-day interval was chosen to maximise program effectiveness by allowing participants sufficient time to implement and practise skills before progressing to the next sessions that build upon previous skills. It would appear that there are positives and negatives associated with both open- and closed-access options. Until evidence from trials involving the usability and efficacy of these types of programs is available, each research team can only choose the mode they believe is most appropriate for their particular client base and format of CCBT delivery.

What Technical Implementation is Most Appropriate?

As noted above, the most commonly used methods of delivering interactive computer programs are online websites and offline CD-ROMs, or some combination of both. Many pros and cons have been suggested for these options including initial and maintenance costs, integration of support tools, quality of multimedia components, current and future access to IT equipment and expertise, the need for future updates or program versions, and data collection or monitoring. Cool Teens was programmed using Macromedia Flash MX and the resulting application is an autorun CD-ROM for both Windows and Mac. The major reasons for the program being developed as a CD were requirement for high-quality live video files (too large to download via a website other than with fast broadband access), a 10% greater home access to computers than to the Internet (National Office for the Information Economy, 2003), the ongoing funding that may be required for a website, and familiarity of the CD format to teens who are very familiar with buying music and game products. The major disadvantages of this method are a potentially higher unit cost for future delivery and the lack of central storage for user data which limits potential therapist involvement.

The choice of Internet rather than CD-ROM delivery of the BRAVE program was made for a number of reasons. First, program designers hoped that common problems associated with CCBT programs such as noncompliance and dropout, would be somewhat alleviated using a web-based program where the therapist is in at least weekly contact with participants via the Internet. Second, data from the exercises and homework, as well as information on when sessions are completed and how long the child/teenager takes to complete the sessions, are automatically stored in a format compatible with SPSS. Third, the therapist is able to monitor the participants' responses and guide and assist them when necessary. The biggest disadvantage of the choice of Internet over CD-ROM was the exclusion of high-level audio and video files that are particularly appealing to teenagers.

It should be noted that successful projects have been (and continue to be) completed using both websites and CDs and that overall, the choice is probably not a critical barrier to the user experience. Since today's leading software development tools are often used for creating interactive programs for both of these delivery formats, experience delivered to the user can, in many respects, be the same no matter which option is used.

What Graphic and Design Style Will be Used?

In a study of teenagers from the United States of America and Australia, leading Internet design analyst Jakob Nielsen (2005) found that teens paid more attention to visual appearance and gave the highest ratings to websites with a modest, clean design. Furthermore, this study highlights the dangers of making assumptions during the design process. Although

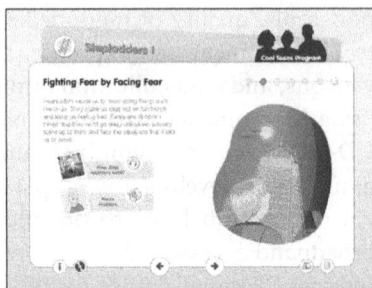

Figure 2
Example screens from the BRAVE and Cool Teens programs.

one may assume that teenagers would find websites easier to use than adults, Nielsen (2005) found that adults were more successful on a set of web tasks compared to teenagers. The author suggested that teens may have 'a lower patience level' that should be taken into consideration when designing computer-based programs. Both the BRAVE and Cool Teens programs have attempted to provide the teenager with a maximum amount of information using a minimum amount of text and interesting, clear graphics (see Figure 2).

With several overall design values in mind, Cool Teens aimed to create a user experience that was informative, engaging, user-friendly, visually appealing, and age appropriate. To achieve this goal, a balanced combination of mixed media components (text, audio, illustrations, cartoons, and live video) was used to present the individual content pages of the modules. The language used in the scripts for all audio and video components was written to be appropriate for the entire age spectrum targeted. Given feedback from several sources that younger teens are likely to be more willing to listen to older teens than vice versa, video characters from the older end of the age range were chosen.

Without the audio and video available in the Cool Teens program, the BRAVE programs rely on animations, the inclusion of quizzes, games and interactive exercises, colourful pages and small amounts of text to enhance the likelihood that the information is attended to and processed by the young person and parent. Since the target population of the BRAVE program ranges from 8–17 years, it was essential that two versions were constructed: one for 8- to 12-year-olds and one for 13- to 17-year-olds. While the content of the two versions is identical, the presentation is

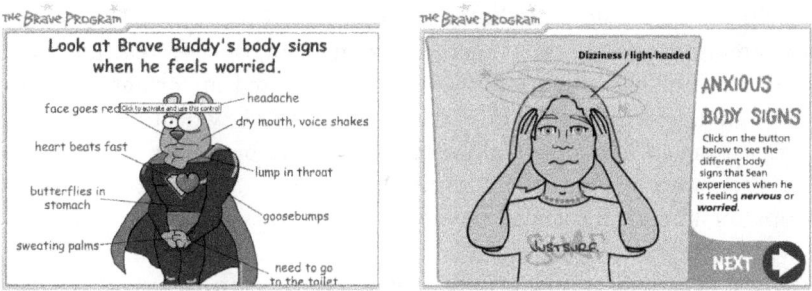

Figure 3
Age appropriate screens from both versions of the BRAVE program.

vastly different (see Figure 3 for an example). The teenage program involves more complex text, examples and stories, has more advanced graphics, and is interspersed with many interactive exercises to maintain interest and increase compliance to the program. Cool Teens and BRAVE have addressed the issue of age appropriate graphics and design well, with both programs being rated positively on these aspects by pilot audiences.

What Can Be Added to Enhance the Therapeutic Alliance?

Higher levels of therapeutic alliance have consistently been found to predict more effective psychological treatment outcome (see Howgego, Yellowlees, Owen, Meldrum, & Dark, 2003 and Martin, Garske, & Davis, 2000 for reviews). This poses an obvious problem for CCBT: How do you establish therapeutic alliance within CCBT programs?

The BRAVE program involves a small amount of contact with an online therapist and attempts to bolster the therapeutic alliance in a number of ways. Telephone contact between therapist and young person is made prior to program commencement in order to discuss goals and requirements. Each participant is assigned their own 'BRAVE trainer' who is introduced via a photograph and short biography. In Session 1, teenagers and therapists complete a 'getting to know you' exercise in which they provide each other with information about themselves through a series of guided questions. BRAVE participants also receive weekly, standardised e-mails both before and after each session, and receive personalised therapist feedback on their performance of various tasks and homework exercises. Finally, telephone contact is made in order to discuss and help construct the young person's exposure hierarchy.

Specific features have been added to the Cool Teens program in an attempt to compensate for the lack of therapist involvement. Video and audio of two experts answering common and important questions throughout the program, in addition to video of two program guides introducing each module and practice task, have been particularly popular program components. Nonspecific components of therapy such as hope for improvement and empathy for the types of problems encountered, have also been included within the character examples. Finally, users are encouraged to engage a program mentor (friend or parent) who can assist them as they progress through the program. Both BRAVE and Cool Teens have therefore acknowledged the importance of the therapeutic alliance, and have attempted to address the issue within their computer-based programs in a variety of ways.

What Incentive and Monitoring Systems Can Be Added?

Face-to-face therapy sessions allow regular opportunities for a therapist to motivate clients and to monitor their progress throughout the course of therapy. It is essential that CCBT designers make some attempt to incorporate incentive and monitoring systems within their programs.

In order to maximise treatment completion and compliance, BRAVE participants are sent reminders about available sessions if they have not logged on within 2 days of the session becoming accessible. In addition, at the beginning of each session, participants complete a number of exercises to provide their online therapist with information about their homework tasks. The online therapist then provides feedback to the participant about their attempts. Methods to ensure understanding of BRAVE program material are attempted within the format of each session. After information is provided to the young person or parent, the participant then applies it first to hypothetical examples and then to their own examples of anxiety. At the end of each session, participants complete a quiz on session material in an attempt to review the session and ensure their understanding. Similarly, participants are given a quiz at the beginning of each session to remind them of the previous session's content.

The Cool Teens program provides users with a weekly set of questions that allows them to monitor their progress based on an overall anxiety score. This progress is analysed by the computer, and a subsequent motivational audio file is played based on their positive or delayed progress. The Practice Task section of each module is an important monitoring system designed by Cool Teens researchers. Users have a shortcut icon to quickly access a menu page that allows them to add, update and track implementation of the techniques they are putting into practice in real life situations. While specific feedback is not provided, summary charts of overall progress provide the teenager with a sense of task completion and progression. Finally, the user's mentor may provide both motivation and monitoring of progress through the program. Using different strategies and features, both BRAVE and Cool Teens have integrated a number of incentive and monitoring systems into their programs.

Effectiveness and User Satisfaction

After taking all the abovementioned points into consideration, and subsequently designing and developing a CCBT program, it is essential that the program is then tested in a randomised clinical controlled trial to determine its effectiveness. At present, evaluation of both the Cool Teens and BRAVE programs remain in the preliminary stages. In a user satisfaction evaluation of a shortened prototype version of the Cool Teens program involving 22 adolescents (Cunningham, Rapee, & Lyneham, 2006b), all multimedia components and general aspects of the program, such as navigation and appearance, were rated positively. Feedback suggests that this therapy option would be acceptable to a considerable proportion of young people. Results of a pilot clinical study of the CD-ROM involving a small number of participants with a primary diagnosis of anxiety will soon be available. A full randomised clinical control trial involving 150 young people is ongoing.

At present, three separate randomised controlled trials are being conducted on the BRAVE program. The first (Spence, Holmes, March, & Lipp, in press) investigated the efficacy of the BRAVE for Children's program partially delivered via the Internet (CLINIC-NET), compared to a group-based, clinic version of the BRAVE program (CLINIC) and a waitlist control group. At posttreatment, 65% of the CLINIC group no longer met diagnosis for an anxiety disorder, compared to 56% of the CLINIC-NET group and 17% of the waitlist control group. These effects were maintained over time, with 89.5% of the CLINIC group and 73.9% of the CLINIC-NET group remaining diagnosis free at the 12-month follow-up. Although there was a trend for the CLINIC program to be more effective than the CLINIC-NET program, the difference was not statistically significant.

The second study investigating the BRAVE Program for Children, is a randomised controlled trial involving two subsidiary studies. The first compares a full Internet version of the BRAVE program to a waitlist control group. The second investigates whether a variety of factors including treatment compliance, therapeutic alliance, self-efficacy, and client expectancy relate to successful treatment outcome. An underlying aim of these studies is to determine which factors are necessary to facilitate positive change in Internet-based interventions. These studies are presently ongoing, with no data available as yet.

The third study is a randomised controlled trial of the BRAVE for Teenagers program and involves three subsidiary studies. The first investigates the effectiveness of a full Internet version of the BRAVE for Teenagers program compared to an individual clinic-based version of the BRAVE program and a waitlist control group. The second study will compare the full Internet version of the BRAVE for Teenagers program to a waitlist condition, with participants from rural areas of Australia. The third study will investigate the predictors of treatment outcome in order to determine characteristics of teenagers most likely to benefit from Internet-based therapy for anxiety. These studies are also ongoing, with data as yet unavailable.

Cool Teens and BRAVE are therefore both testing the efficacy of their programs through treatment outcome studies. Preliminary results are positive, and researchers from both projects look forward to being able to make important contributions to the future of CCBT.

Conclusions and Future Developments

As clinical trial data for BRAVE, Cool Teens and other similar programs become available we will be better positioned to examine the necessary ingredients for the efficacy and effectiveness of CCBT. Some major questions include: What level and type of support is best for young users? Can we identify people who are more likely to have success or failure with this type of delivery? Can we explore other models and components to enhance delivery (e.g., virtual reality or gaming environments such as Thinking Worlds or Personal Investigator; Coyle et al., 2005). Could customised program development for specific types of anxiety increase user satisfaction and efficacy? As Richardson and Richards (2006) suggest, development of the next generation of self-help materials will benefit from the evaluation of the clinical outcomes with programs that combine common and specific CCBT components in different formats and combinations.

Clinical anxiety in young people is a widespread problem and is associated with high levels of suffering and interference in daily activities. Although effective CBT treatments exist, they are frequently not accessed by this age group. We believe that CCBT programs such as BRAVE and Cool Teens can lead the way in addressing this problem by providing accessible, low-cost treatment options for the many young people who would otherwise not receive help.

Acknowledgments

Mike Cunningham is a PhD student under the academic supervision of Professor Ron Rapee, and holds an international Macquarie University Research Scholarship. We acknowledge and thank the Cool Teens team and the Macquarie University Vice Chancellor's Development and Australian Rotary Health Research Funds.

Caroline Donovan is a Postdoctoral Fellow at The University of Queensland and Sonja March is a PhD student under the academic supervision of Caroline Donovan and Professor Sue Spence. We would like to acknowledge the NH&MRC for their funding of the BRAVE project and thank profusely the BRAVE teams at both The University of Queensland and Macquarie University.

References

Australian Bureau of Statistics. (2004). *Household use of information technology, Australia, 2002 and 2003* (No. 8146.0). Canberra, Australia: Author.

Booth, M.L., Bernard, D., Quine, S., Kang, M.S., Usherwood, T., Alperstein, G., et al. (2004). Access to health care among Australian adolescents—young people's perspectives and their sociodemographic distribution. *Journal of Adolescent Health, 34*, 97–103.

Christensen, H., Griffiths, K.M., & Evans, K. (2002). *e-Mental health in Australia: Implications of the Internet and related technologies for policy* (ISC Discussion Paper No 3). Canberra, Australia: Commonwealth Department of Health and Ageing.

Cisco Systems, Inc. (2000). *Reusable Learning Object Strategy—Definition, creation process, and guidelines for building (Version 3.1)*. Retrieved March 14, 2007, from http://www.reusable learning.org/Docs/Cisco_rlo_roi_v3-1.pdf

Costello, E.J., Angold, A., & Keeler, G.P. (1999). Adolescent outcomes of childhood disorders: The consequences of severity and impairment. *Journal of the American Academy of Child and Adolescent Psychiatry, 38*(2), 121–128.

Costello, E.J., Mustillo, S., Erkanli, A., Keeler, G., & Angold, A. (2003). Prevalence and development of psychiatric disorders in childhood and adolescence. *Archives of General Psychiatry, 60*, 837–844.

Coyle, D., Doherty, G., & Sharry, J. (2005). *The design of computer systems for talk-based mental health care interventions* (Trinity College Dublin Technical Report). Retrieved July 14, 2006, from https://www.cs.tcd.ie/publications/tech-reports/reports.05/TCD-CS-2005-50.pdf

Cunningham, M.J., Rapee, R.M., & Lyneham, H.J. (2006a). The Cool Teens CD-ROM: A multimedia self-help program for adolescents with anxiety. *Youth Studies Australia, 25, 50–56.*

Cunningham, M.J., Rapee, R.M., & Lyneham, H.J. (2006b). *Feedback to a prototype self-help computer program for anxiety disorders in adolescents.* Australian e-Journal for the Advancement of Mental Health, 5(3). Retrieved Jan 15, 2007 from http://www.auseinet.com/journal/vol5iss3/cunningham.pdf

Cunningham, M.J., Rapee, R.M., Lyneham, H.J., Schniering, C.A., Hudson, J.L., & Wuthrich, V. (2006). *The Cool Teens CD-ROM—An anxiety management program for young people.* Sydney, Australia: Macquarie University Anxiety Research Unit (MUARU).

Donovan, C.L., Holmes, J.M., Spence, S.H., & Kenardy, J. (2006a). *BRAVE for Teenagers: A program for adolescents with anxiety.* Brisbane, Australia: School of Psychology, The University of Queensland.

Donovan, C.L., Holmes, J.M., Spence, S.H., & Kenardy, J. (2006b). *BRAVE for Teenagers: A program for parents of adolescents with anxiety.* Brisbane, Australia: School of Psychology, The University of Queensland.

Ginsburg, G.S., LaGreca, A.M., & Silverman, W.K. (1998). Social anxiety in children with anxiety disorders: Relation with social and emotional functioning. *Journal of Abnormal child Psychology, 26*(3), 175–185.

Griffiths, K.M., & Christensen, H. (2006). Review of randomised controlled trials of Internet interventions for mental disorders and related conditions. *Clinical Psychologist, 10,* 16–29.

Holmes, J.M., March, S., & Spence, S.H. (2005). *BRAVE for Children: A program for children with anxiety.* Brisbane, Australia: School of Psychology, The University of Queensland.

Holmes, J.M., Spence, S.H., March, S. (in press). Use of the Internet in the treatment of anxiety disorders with children and adolescents. In G. Martin (Ed.), *Using the Internet for mental health.*

Howgego, I.M., Yellowlees, P., Owen, C., Meldrum, L., & Dark, F. (2003). The therapeutic alliance: The key to effective patient outcome? A descriptive review of the evidence in community mental health case management. *Australian and New Zealand Journal of Psychiatry, 37*(2), 169–183.

James, A., Soler, A., & Weatherall, R. (2005). Cognitive behavioural therapy for anxiety disorders in children and adolescents. *The Cochrane Database of Systematic Reviews* (4) CD004690.

Joinson, A.N. (2001). Self-disclosure in computer-mediated communication: The role of self-awareness and visual anonymity. *European Journal of Social Psychology, 31,* 177–192.

Kaltenthaler, E., Shackley, P., Stevens, K., Beverley, C., Parry, G., & Chilcott, J. (2002). A systematic review and economic evaluation of computerized cognitive behavioural therapy for depression and anxiety. *Health Technology Report, 6,* 22.

Last, C.G., Hansen, C., & Franco, N. (1997). Anxious children in adulthood: A prospective study of adjustment. *Journal of the American Academy of Child and Adolescent Psychiatry, 36*(5), 645–652.

Lyneham, H.J., Schniering, C.A., Hudson, J.L., & Rapee, R.M. (2005). *The Cool Kids Program—Adolescent Version*. Sydney, Australia: Macquarie University Anxiety Research Unit.

March, S., Holmes, J.M., & Spence, S.H. (2005). *BRAVE for Children: A program for parents of children with anxiety*. Brisbane, Australia: School of Psychology, The University of Queensland.

Martin, D.J., Garske, J.P., & Davis, M.K. (2000). Relations of the therapeutic alliance with outcome and other variables: A meta-analytic review. *Journal of Consulting and Clinical Psychology, 68*(3), 438–450.

National Office for the Information Economy. (2003). *The current state of play. Online participation and activities*. Retrieved March 14, 2007, from http://unpan1un.org/intradoc/groups/public/documents/APCITY/UNPAN020593.pdf

Nielsen, J. (2005). *Usability of websites for teenagers*. Retrieved July 14, 2006, from http://www.useit.com/alertbox/20050131.html

Proudfoot, J. (2004). Computer-based treatment for anxiety and depression: Is it feasible? Is it effective? *Neuroscience and Biobehavioural Reviews, 28*, 353–363.

Proudfoot, J., Swain, S., Widmer, S., Watkins, E., Goldberg, D., Marks, I., et al. (2003). The development and beta-test of a computer-therapy program for anxiety and depression: Hurdles and lessons. *Computers in Human Behavior, 19*, 277–289.

Richardson, R., & Richards, D.A. (2006). Self-help: Towards the next generation. *Behavioural and Cognitive Psychotherapy, 34*, 13–23.

Senate Select Committee on Mental Health. (2006). *A national approach to mental health—from crisis to community—A first report*. Commonwealth of Australia. Retrieved March 15, 2007, from http://www.aph.gov.au/senate/committee/mentalhealth_ctte/report/report.pdf

Spence, S.H., Holmes, J., Donovan, C.L., & Kenardy, J. (2006). *BRAVE for Teenagers—ONLINE: An internet based program for adolescents with anxiety*. Brisbane, Australia: School of Psychology, The University of Queensland.

Spence, S.H., Holmes, J., March, S., & Lipp, O. (in press). The feasibility and outcome of clinic plus internet delivery of cognitive-behavioural therapy for childhood anxiety. *Journal of Consulting and Clinical Psychology*.

Spence, S.H., March, S., & Holmes, J. (2005). *BRAVE for Children—ONLINE: An internet based program for children with anxiety*. Brisbane, Australia: School of Psychology, The University of Queensland.

Suler, J. (2004). The online disinhibition effect. *CyberPsychology, 7*(3), 321–326.

Tsai, C. (2004). Adolescents' perceptions toward the internet: A 4-T framework. *CyberPsychology, 7*(4), 458–463.

Velting, O., Setzer, N., & Albano, A.M. (2004). Update on advances in assessment and cognitive-behavioral treatment of anxiety disorders in children and adolescents. *Professional Psychology: Research and Practice, 35*, 42–54.

CHAPTER 8

Cognitive Therapy With Older Adults: Are Adaptations Necessary?

Deborah-Anne Koder

At first, a chapter dedicated to what is one of the most heterogeneous client groups seems incongruous, as an arbitrary age cut-off should not define treatment access or delivery. Indeed, there is now strong evidence for the efficacy of cognitive–behaviour therapy for adults aged 65 years and over and the general flavour of such treatment outcome studies is that cognitive–behaviour therapy — with its central tenets of client–therapist collaboration, flexibility and empiricism — is highly suitable for older clients (Laidlaw, Thompson, Dick-Siskin, & Gallagher-Thompson, 2003).

However, despite recent positive directions in the evidence base for the efficacy of nonpharmacologic interventions in treating depression (Mackin & Arean, 2005) and anxiety (Wetherell, Sorrell, Thorp, & Patterson, 2005), older adults are less likely to receive psychological therapy from specialist mental health providers and psychologists compared to their younger counterparts (Crabb & Hunsley, 2006; Jorm, 1994). This is despite projective increases within Australia's demographic composition with the largest subgroup of elderly adults comprising of those aged 85 years and over. This group is expecting to be around 1.2 million or a proportion of nearly 5% of the Australian population by 2051 (Bishop, 1999).

Therefore, it is timely to discuss possible issues that may arise when working with older adults: such issues are not prescriptive and not necessarily content driven but may be encountered more frequently with this population. Process variables in terms of how therapy is to be introduced and structured are worth examination within the context of the therapeutic alliance with older clients. In terms of content, much discussion has ensued since Church's initial premise that cognitive therapy had to be adapted to suit the deficits in abstract thinking as a consequence of the 'ageing brain' (Church, 1983; Koder, Brodaty, & Anstey, 1996). The flexibility and collaborative nature of cognitive therapy should allow for any individual differences, regardless of age. The aim of this chapter is to outline the use of cognitive therapy in potentially challenging contexts more commonly found in older populations (for example, in dementia care settings or with the frail aged). Such discussion serves not only to dispel ageism regarding the applicability of cognitive therapy with this population, but also gives therapists valuable insights and confidence in working in aged care settings.

Process Variables in the Practice of Cognitive–Behaviour Therapy With Older Adults

The Influence of Nonspecific Variables

Before discussing the practice of cognitive–behaviour therapy per se, age-related issues pertaining to the client–therapist relationship and other influences on the therapeutic alliance need to be considered.

In examining the role of the therapeutic alliance in reducing hopelessness in depressed older clients, the central theme of losses emerges (Floyd & Scogin, 1998). Changes such as a loss of one's role in society, loss of health, loss of residence, independence and so on tend to be more common as we grow older (although not necessarily a definite part of old age), leading to feelings of disempowerment and loss of control. The efficacy of cognitive therapy may be in part due to a reduction of hopelessness evidenced by lowered scores on the Beck Hopelessness Scale compared to the Dysfunctional Attitudes Scale in Floyd and Scogin's research with older adults (Floyd & Scogin, 1998). Similarly, the social aspect of a therapeutic relationship has been discussed in promoting positive outcomes with ruptures in the therapeutic alliance possibly accounting for the higher drop out rates in older age groups (Hyer, Kramer, & Sohnle, 2004).

Another aspect of early therapy sessions within the cognitive–behaviour therapy framework that is of particular importance is induction to therapy, where rationale for treatment is explained in order to challenge various beliefs the client may hold regarding their condition (Thompson, Davies, Gallagher, & Krantz, 1986, Table 1). These may include beliefs relating to the person's perceived ability to benefit from therapy ('I'm too old to change'), beliefs related to the origin of their depression ('Isn't it just part of old age?') or pain — particularly in the context of concomitant medical treatment ('Why am I seeing a psychologist? It's a physical

Table 1
Common Assumptions Regarding Psychological Therapy
and Rational Responses

Examples	Responses
'I'm too old to change', 'You can't teach an old dog new tricks'	'Age is a number', 'I can always learn new skills and new ways of looking at things', 'I don't know 'till I try'
(Therapist can present information regarding the brain's ability to acquire new information, even at an advanced age, as evidenced by programs such as 'University of the 3rd Age'. Therapist can focus on concrete goals.)	
'People will think I'm mad', 'I'm not crazy'	'I am learning about my depression and that it is acceptable', 'Just because I feel down doesn't mean I've failed', 'Talking about how I feel does not equal being crazy'
(Therapist can emphasise the role of stereotypes in developing such belief systems and challenge these with education on the nature of depression. Therapist needs to explain the goals of cognitive therapy in a straightforward manner.)	
'Why am I seeing a psychologist? It's my body, not my head'	'I feel down a lot of the time, so it's important to talk about my feelings and understand them', 'It is not an either/or question — that's my black and white thinking talking!'
(Therapist focuses on collaborative, active role of client and provides education on how symptoms of depression can overlap with medical symptoms such as poor appetite, low energy. Education on the effects of cognition on emotions, and of the physical consequences of stress.)	
'Isn't this just a natural part of growing old?', 'It's to be expected because old age is depressing'	'No, there are many positive aspects of ageing', 'It is not due to old age but a separate problem that I'm learning to manage', 'This is another part of my life and not the worst thing that can happen'
(Therapist discusses expectations of therapy with client in challenging hopelessness and provides education to challenge stereotypes regarding normal ageing. Focus is on active role in therapy and challenging dichotomous thinking and generalising.)	

problem'), or holding long-term views regarding mental health and therapy, in general ('I'm not crazy').

Clear explanation of the link between the therapy session content and the client's 'story' is vital (Table 2). The process in cognitive therapy is not one of the 'all-knowing' therapist applying a technique to help the passive client, which in itself may require some induction — particularly in clients

Table 2
Key Skills in Conducting Psychological Therapy With Older Adults

- Focus on the therapeutic alliance as well as 'techniques'.
- Clear rationale for therapy. Challenge erroneous beliefs regarding depression.
- Develop and explain working formulation, or provide an explanation regarding biopsychosocial factors involved in each client's current presentation.
- Set clear, concrete goals and break these down into manageable steps that are scheduled.
- Focus on behavioural experiments to test assumptions (e.g., 'I can't do it', 'I'm such a failure'), providing specific opportunities and information regarding activities (e.g., volunteer work, community transport).
- Identify the need for and utilise reinforcement strategies such as printed hand-outs, cue cards, repetitions, rehearsals and additional sessions.
- Provide clear rationale for homework, tailoring to client's sensory and cognitive needs.
- Involve relevant family members/care staff in management as required, especially in frail aged, being mindful of confidentiality.
- Adapt rate of therapy, with sensitivity to therapy termination.

with a long history of medical involvement. Rather, collaborative analysis of evidence through therapy session content and homework are used to increasingly expose and challenge long-held belief systems detrimental to mood and self-esteem. Developing and explaining a working formulation to clients as to the role of various factors leading to their current presentation is essential, not only in fostering and maintaining a good therapeutic relationship but in anticipating difficulties during therapy (Laidlaw et al., 2003).

The Structure of Therapy With Older Adults (Table 2)

The concrete methods used in cognitive–behaviour therapy assume particular importance in a client group that can present with more complex issues (for example, medical, family-related). Clear establishment of homework guidelines, setting therapy and sessional goals and agendas and differences in the rate and duration of therapy are practical aspects of therapy with older adults (Kazantzis, Pachana, & Secker, 2003).

Homework assignments can appear daunting at first in a population that may not have received as much formal education or where there have been many years since they encountered homework! Sensory difficulties in vision and hearing also need to be accounted for, together with problems writing caused by praxis deficits secondary to organic involvement (for example, hemiparesis following a stroke). These must be carefully assessed or the client will be experiencing failure, rather than success, with accentuation of helplessness and loss of control. The rationale for homework needs to be clearly explained, together with discussion of where and when homework could be done in order to anticipate difficulties and enhance compliance. Writing down homework tasks in a regular, structured predictable fashion (for example, by using a designated notebook where session content can also be summarised) may further boost compliance. Personalising homework and session content, rather than sole reliance on pre-determined handouts, is recommended. Such sessional summaries, using the client's own language and idioms for common terms (for example, 'black and white' thinking as opposed to 'dichotomous' thinking or 'I'm jumping to conclusions, again' replacing 'selective abstraction' or 'arbitrary inference') is more likely to enhance consolidation and generalising of new material (Tanner & Ball, 1991, Table 3).

Reinforcement strategies may also include reworking of issues, linking content from one session to another and slowing the pace of therapy dependent on the client's abilities and needs. Sessions can be anchored by agenda setting at the beginning of each session combined with finishing each session with both client and therapist providing feedback as to the client's understanding in terms of content and their experiences (Secker, Kazantzis, & Pachana, 2004).

Given the aforementioned predominance of loss themes often seen in older clients with depression, sensitivity regarding termination of therapy is important. It is recommended that sessions be gradually terminated with deceleration of session frequency as opposed to a sudden cut-off from weekly sessions (Koder et al., 1996).

Specific Client Issues Within the Practice of Cognitive–Behaviour Therapy With Older Adults

Adapting Cognitive–Behaviour Therapy for Clients With Cognitive Impairment

Neuropsychological examination of patients with major depression highlights compromised executive functioning with a correlation between severity of depression and deficits in speed of information processing and executive skills (Boone et al., 1995). There has also been recent interest in the role of executive functions in older patients suffering from anxiety and/or mood disorders, with research findings suggesting that patients with compromised executive functioning do not benefit as much from cognitive–behaviour therapy compared to those anxious patients with intact executive functions (Mohlman, 2005). This has led to a range of treatment modifications such as 'enhanced cognitive–behaviour therapy' where midweek homework reminders, trouble-shooting phone calls, rehearsal and expanded reviews aim at improving accessibility to central cognitive therapy skills (Mohlman et al., 2003). Common techniques to help teach management of worry — such as thought-stopping, distraction and setting aside 'worry time' — have also been described (Laidlaw et al., 2003).

There are a variety of practical concerns that need to be considered in conducting therapy with cognitively impaired elderly patients, such as transport and mobility. The use of memory prostheses is another key feature such as cue cards, large print summaries and taped summaries of sessions (Koder, 1998). The two major features, however, of work with this population, are the emphasis on behavioural strategies and the role of carers.

The aforementioned theme of a loss of control and learned helplessness can be magnified further in those with cognitive impairments also suffering from depression (Table 3). Therefore, collaborative setting of concrete goals is a key feature of therapy. Increasing exposure to pleasant activities with the help of the primary caregiver can promote a sense of mastery, as well as directly improving mood through enjoyable pursuits. Teaching caregivers problem-solving strategies, as well as training them in the direct application of common cognitive–behavioural techniques (for example, prompting relaxation practice) is another focus (Teri, McKenzie, & Lafazia, 2005).

Specific adaptations to existing tools are being examined. One major advance has been to adapt pleasant event schedules to elderly populations with dementia (Teri & Logsdon, 1991). Relaxation training with older patients suffering from cognitive decline needs to take into account memory impairments and difficulties sustaining concentration. Longer, taped relaxation sessions can be replaced by highly structured slow breathing relaxation where the client is taught to firstly recognise the earliest symptoms of anxiety (for example, clenched fists, feeling tight in the stomach) and then use imagery whilst breathing slowly (Koder, 1998). It is the author's experience that modelling slow, gentle, diaphragmatic breathing and prompting an anxious person with dementia to slow down their breathing can be effective in regaining a sense of control, particularly when carried out at the first sign of distress when agitated. This is particularly relevant in the residential care setting, where nursing staff can act as prompts and cue relaxation use.

Although discussion has centred on more common behavioural techniques, cognitive therapy via challenging strongly held ideas regarding the dementing illness per se, is highly relevant and has been discussed in the literature (Scholey & Woods, 2003). The belief that depression is a natural consequence of dementia is challenged early on in the therapy induction phase, together with examining anxiety regarding the future. Education regarding the nature of dementia in order to challenge any guilt or blame is recommended with active involvement from carers (Scholey & Woods, 2003). Therapy style is generally more active, flexible and directed (Koder, 1998).

The Practice of Cognitive–Behaviour Therapy in the Context of Chronic Illness and With the Frail Aged

Older adults are more likely to suffer from comorbid physical illnesses and disabilities (Leon et al., 2003) — one of the distinguishing features of work with this population. Primary care physicians need to screen for depression within an assessment of a patient's physical condition as it can be seriously debilitating, as well as impeding recovery from surgery and other physical illness (Arean & Ayalon, 2005). The Geriatric Depression Scale is a brief instrument designed for such screening purposes that has been well-validated (Yesavage, Brink, Rose, et al., 1983).

A potential barrier to psychological work with patients suffering from comorbid medical conditions is the commonly held assumption that depression is either a natural reaction to the illness or that it is part of the illness per se, thus intractable or 'to be expected'. The system involved in caring for the patient, including the patients themselves, needs to be aware of such a bias that promotes passive acceptance of depression.

Therapy focuses on education regarding depression and helping the patient cope with the impact of the disease. A range of physical conditions has been examined in the literature on the efficacy of cognitive–behaviour therapy in older patients, most notably Parkinson's disease (for a review see Cole & Vaughan, 2005), chronic pulmonary disease (Kunik et al., 2001) and post-stroke depression (Laidlaw et al., 2003).

Specific themes in this population who are at the highest risk of depression involve flexibility of treatment (for example, where to see the patient and for how long if they tire easily), challenging of beliefs and generalisations regarding their illness (for example, unrealistic expectations about abilities), the loss of self-esteem consequent to role loss and dealing with fears such as burden (Rybarczyk et al., 1992). Table 3 outlines common examples of such thinking and suggested responses.

Table 3
Common Thinking Errors Associated With Ageing and/or Cognitive
Impairment and Their Rational Alternatives

Type of error (Tanner & Ball, 1991)	Example	Rational response
Dichotomous or 'black and white' thinking	'I must be able to work or I am worthless.'	'There are other things I can do with my time. I have other interests I've now got the time to pursue.'
Over-generalising	'I couldn't remember her name, I can't remember anything. I'm so hopeless.'	'What's the evidence? There's none, I can still remember lots of things.'
Magnifying unpleasantness	'I can't drive, my life is over'	'It's disappointing, but there are other ways of getting around.'
Personalising	'I can't hold my fork properly since the stroke and everyone is staring at me.'	'I'm not the centre of attention here and I really think people are too concerned with themselves. It's okay to feel a little self-conscious. Let me focus on something else and my anxiety should pass.'
Arbitrary inference, Jumping to conclusions	'My heart was racing so much after that walk. It must be another stroke.'	'What's the evidence? I know that exertion naturally causes a rise in heart rate, but I can always check it out.'
Catastrophising, 'Crystal balling', 'Mind reading'	'I have such trouble getting up in the morning. My wife is getting so frustrated, she'll probably put me in a home. I'm such a burden.'	'I do not know what she is thinking. I should let her know how I feel and also give her a chance to say how it affects her. We may be able to develop a plan together to manage this. I understand it is part of my depression and not my fault.'

A subset of clients with similar issues is the 'old-old'. Old age mental health has been defined as delivering services to adults over the age of 65 years. With increasing numbers of adults living past 80 years of age, therapies previously only evaluated with relatively educated subjects with the average age being in the 60s (Engels & Vermey, 1997; Karel &

Hinrichsen, 2000) need to be trialled specifically on older samples who may be more clinically representative. Age has been found to be a predictor of treatment outcome, favouring younger subjects.

Lowered response rates in the oldest age groups may rise if conditions specific to more frail elderly people were identified and incorporated into existing programs (Engels & Vermey, 1997).

Modifications to cognitive–behavioural programs for physically frail older adults who may suffer from a lack of energy or stamina possibly impacting on their ability to carry out behavioural tasks or have any number of difficulties ranging from impaired concentration, slowing of mental abilities or physical illnesses have been anecdotally described. Again, further research is needed before such recommendations can be scientifically established (Grant & Casey, 1995). However, adaptations such as simplifying material and reducing the number of problems dealt with in any one session, structuring daily timetables (for example, when an in-patient) and rehearsal of homework tasks are in a similar vein to those described earlier in reference to older adults with cognitive impairment. Careful, individualised assessment of abilities and tailor making treatment to incorporate assets and deficits are central to therapy, rather than prescriptive 'programs', given the complexity of presentations.

Conclusion

The efficacy of cognitive–behaviour therapy in older adults is well established with positive results from an increasing number of meta-analytic studies (Mackin & Arean, 2005). However, their validity in generalising to specific clinical situations found more commonly in old age samples needs to be further investigated.

This chapter summarised cognitive–behavioural strategies in special populations within the field of aged care, together with a focus on skills involved in the process of delivering effective psychotherapy to older adults. Individual assessment is emphasised rather than holding assumptions about 'the elderly', a heterogeneous group with a wide age span.

The number of older adults is increasing at a more rapid rate than any other age group and current cohort effects are likely to change with the advent of the 'baby boomers' into the old age categories. Their influence on current psychotherapy dynamics, beliefs and practices is likely to be considerable, resulting in exciting developments and more scope for psychological therapy. Encouraging psychologists to consider working in the field of aged care to meet the needs of this increasing and varied client population will be the next challenge facing modern psychology.

References

Arean, P., & Ayalon, L. (2005). Assessment and treatment of depressed older adults in primary care. *Clinical Psychology: Science and Practice, 12,* 321–335.

Bishop, B. (1999). *The National Strategy for an Ageing Australia: Background paper.* Canberra, Australia: Commonwealth of Australia.

Boone, K.B., Lesser, I.M., Miller, B.I., Wohl, M., Berman, N., Lee, A., et al. (1995). Cognitive functioning in older depressed outpatients. Relationship of presence and severity of depression to neuropsychological test scores. *Neuropsychology, 9,* 390–398.

Church, M. (1983). Psychological therapy with elderly people. *Bulletin of the British Psychological Society, 36,* 110–112.

Cole, K., & Vaughan, F.L. (2005). The feasibility of using cognitive behaviour therapy for depression associated with Parkinson's disease: A literature review. *Parkinsonism and Related Disorders, 11,* 269–276.

Crabb, R., & Hunsley, J. (2006). Utilization of mental health care services among older adults with depression. *Journal of Clinical Psychology, 62*(3), 299–312.

Engels, G.I., & Vermey, M. (1997). Efficacy of nonmedical treatment of depression in elders: A quantitative analysis. *Journal of Clinical Geropsychology, 3,* 17–35.

Floyd, M., & Scogin, F. (1998). Cognitive-behavior therapy for older adults: How does it work? *Psychotherapy, 35,* 459–463.

Grant, R.W., & Casey, D.A. (1995). Adapting cognitive behavioural therapy for the frail elderly. *International Psychogeriatrics, 7,* 561–571.

Hyer, L., Kramer, D., & Sohnle, S. (2004). CBT with older people: Alterations and the value of the therapeutic alliance. *Psychotherapy: Theory, Research, Practice, Training, 41,* 276–291.

Jorm, A.F. (1994). Characteristics of Australians who reported consulting a psychologist for a health problem: An analysis of data from the 1989–90 National Health Survey. *Australian Psychologist, 29,* 212–215.

Karel, M.J., & Hinrichsen, G. (2000). Treatment of depression in late life: Psychotherapeutic interventions. *Clinical Psychology Review, 20,* 707–729.

Kazantzis, N., Pachana, N., & Secker, D.L. (2003). Cognitive behavioural therapy for older adults: Practical guidelines for the use of homework assignments. *Cognitive and Behavioural Practice, 10,* 324–332.

Koder, D.A. (1998). Treatment of anxiety in the cognitively-impaired elderly: Can cognitive-behaviour therapy help? *International Psychogeriatrics, 10,* 173–182.

Koder, D.A., Brodaty, H., & Anstey, K.J. (1996). Cognitive therapy for depression in the elderly. *International Journal of Geriatric Psychiatry, 11,* 97–108.

Kunik, M.E., Braun, U., Stanley, M.A., Wristers, K., Molinari, V., Stoebner, D., et al. (2001). One session cognitive behavioural therapy for elderly patients with chronic obstructive pulmonary disease. *Psychological Medicine, 31,* 717–723.

Laidlaw, K., Thompson, L.W., Dick-Siskin, L., & Gallagher-Thompson, D. (2003). *Cognitive-behaviour therapy with older people.* Chichester, UK: Wiley.

Leon, F.G., Ashton, A.K., D'Mello, D.A., Dantz, B., Hefner, J., Matson, G.A, et al. (2003). Depression and comorbid medical illness: Therapeutic and diagnostic challenges. *Journal of Family Practice, 52*(12), S19–33

Mackin, R.S., & Arean, P. (2005). Evidence-based psychotherapeutic interventions for geriatric depression. *Psychiatric Clinics of North America, 28,* 805–820.

Mohlman, J. (2005). Does executive dysfunction affect treatment outcome in late-life mood and anxiety disorders? *Journal of Geriatric Psychiatry and Neurology, 18,* 97–108.

Mohlman, J., Gorenstein, E.E., Kleber, M., de Jesus, M., Gorman, J., & Papp, L. (2003). Standard and enhanced cognitive-behavior therapy for late-life generalized anxiety disorder. *American Journal of Geriatric Psychiatry, 11,* 24–32.

Rybarczyk, B., Gallagher-Thompson, D., Rodman, J., Zeiss, A., Gantz, F.E., & Yesavage, J. (1992). Applying cognitive-behavioural psychotherapy to the chronically ill elderly: Treatment issues and case illustration. *International Psychogeriatrics, 4,* 127–140.

Scholey, K., & Woods, B. (2003). A series of brief cognitive therapy interventions with people experiencing both dementia and depression: A description of techniques and common themes. *Clinical Psychology and Psychotherapy, 10,* 175–185.

Secker, D.L., Kazantzis, N., & Pachana, N. (2004). Cognitive behavior therapy for older adults: Practical guidelines for adapting therapy structure. *Journal of Rational-Emotive and Cognitive Therapy, 22,* 93–109.

Tanner, S., & Ball, J. (1991). *Beating the blues.* Sydney, Australia: Doubleday.

Teri, L., & Logsdon, R.G. (1991). Identifying pleasant activities for Alzheimer's disease patients: The pleasant events schedule-AD. *The Gerontologist, 31,* 124–127.

Teri, L., McKenzie, G., & LaFazia, D. (2005). Psychosocial treatment of depression in older adults with dementia. *Clinical Psychology: Science and Practice, 12,* 303–316.

Thompson, L.W., Davies, R., Gallagher, D., & Krantz, S.E. (1986). Cognitive therapy with older adults. *Clinical Gerontologist, 5,*245–279.

Wetherell, J.L., Sorrell, J.T., Thorp, S.R., & Patterson, T.L. (2005). Psychological interventions for late-life anxiety: A review and early lessons from the CALM study. *Journal of Geriatric Psychiatry and Neurology, 18,* 72–82.

Yesavage, J.A., Brink, T.L., Rose, T.L., Lum, O., Huang, V., Adey, M.B., et al. (1983). Development and validation of a geriatric depression screening scale: A preliminary report. *Journal of Psychiatric Research, 17,* 37–49.

CHAPTER 9

The Application of Acceptance and Commitment Therapy to Chronic Pain

Anthony Merritt, Susan Pervan and Jo Sheedy

Acceptance and commitment therapy (ACT) is an empirically derived and theoretically driven approach that views all human suffering, and therefore psychopathology, as a problem of language and cognition (Hayes, Luoma, Bond, Masuda, & Lillis, 2006). Specifically, it is claimed that mental rules serve to restrict the range of behavioural responses available to an individual, and that this inflexibility prevents the realisation of a meaningful life. In this way ACT is essentially a behavioural therapy.

The ACT model identifies six core processes that maintain behavioural inflexibility — experiential avoidance; cognitive fusion; attachments to the conceptualised self; inaction versus impulsivity; lack of clarity regarding values; and dominance of the narrative past together with fear of the future (Hayes et al., 2006). In concert, there are also six core treatment processes — acceptance, cognitive fusion, being present, self as context, values, and committed action. The most important of these concepts is experiential avoidance and acceptance. These processes involves appraisal of internal events as undesirable, and refers to the subsequent attempts to control, diminish or abolish these experiences. The centrality of experiential avoidance can be found in most psychological therapies, such as that of repression (Freud, 1966), self-denial (Rogers, 1961) and staying present (Perls, 1973).

Several clinical studies have shown the utility of the ACT approach to chronic pain (e.g., McCracken & Eccleston, 2005; McCracken, Vowles, & Eccleston, 2005). These studies have found that acceptance-based approaches result in better emotional, social and physical functioning, less health care utilisation, reduced medication use, and better work status. Acceptance has also been shown to be associated with less pain, depression, pain-related anxiety, and time spent at rest (McCracken & Eccleston, 2006).

The multidisciplinary treatment of chronic pain involves the application of the biopsychosocial model. As such, it is important to stress that psychological treatments should not be delivered in isolation, but instead should be part of a broader treatment plan that involves both medical and physical therapies. Indeed, it is the authors' opinion that the primary goal of psychological approaches to chronic pain is the reduction of psychological barriers that prevent enhanced physical functioning and limit quality of life.

Clinical Application of Acceptance and Commitment Therapy

ACT utilises treatment techniques such as experiential exercises and metaphors. These techniques are applied to the avoidance and control of internal experiences, language and cognitive fusion, mindfulness practice, identification of values and committed action. The following outlines some of the treatment strategies used when ACT is applied to chronic pain. The order in which these ACT concepts are presented in this chapter is not necessarily the prescription for its application in treatment. Progress through the various treatment components will be contingent upon the therapeutic judgment of the clinician, since achieving ACT goals, such as willingness or cognitive defusion, are not binary concepts but instead are viewed as a matter of degree. The ultimate test of success on any stage of ACT, however, is the observation of increases in behavioural activation and the resulting goal and value-directed action. It should also be noted clinicians will find that they return to previously covered concepts throughout the treatment process. This is the nature of ACT.

Values

The identification of values is often a very difficult exercise for individuals. The authors introduce 'values' early in the treatment process and then revisit the area as treatment progresses. Value and goals then become the basis of engaging in the other stages of the ACT treatment process. Other authors, however, have suggested that values work occur towards the end of treatment (e.g., Hayes, Strosahl, & Wilson, 1999).

Initially, we use the following exercise to demonstrate how people lose focus on things that matter.

Exercise 1

Hold your index finger out in front of you and stare at it for a few minutes. What is your experience? What occurs? Do you see that in focusing on your finger, all objects in the distance or past your finger become blurred and out of focus. Now try to relate this to your experience of chronic pain. Can you see that focusing on pain comes at the expense of losing focus and direction in your life? Now hold up your finger again, place the focus into the distance, and look past your finger for a few minutes. What happens to your finger? Can you see that your finger is still present in the line of sight but objects in the distance are clearer? How does this relate to your pain?

We also use other experiential exercises to identify values. One of these involves the person identifying what they would want to be said about them at their funeral or a going away party. This exercise can sometimes take place during mindfulness meditation, since it can be useful to try such exercises while the person is in a more relaxed state.

Following these exercises, individuals then articulate and prioritise values across a range of life domains, using a modified version of the Valued Living Questionnaire (Hayes, Strosahl, & Wilson, 1999). This allows the person to then develop a clearer sense of how to live their life according to their values — such as being a loving parent, being independent, or contributing to the local community.

Goal Setting

Goals are achievable, quantifiable and measurable. Values, on the other hand, provide the direction in which the individual wishes to live their life, but they are neither quantifiable nor achievable. In essence, goals become the means by which an individual can live their life according to their values.

In a chronic pain context, goal setting is an integral part of the treatment process. Chronic pain patients typically lose sight of the important aspects of their lives and goal setting facilitates them moving back towards the activities and directions that they value. Goals are often set across social, leisure, family and vocational domains. Functional goals are also essential to ensure that people upgrade physical and functional tasks. In completing the goal work, actions are identified that need to be undertaken in order to work towards achieving goals. In the case of functional goals, for example, participants are encouraged to list specific aspects of their physical functioning they wish to improve and are asked to record steps that might be taken towards achieving each functional goal.

The concept of barriers is introduced in order to help the person recognise that obstacles, either internal or external, may present themselves in the execution of their goals and stop them living according to values. The individual is encouraged to see that living life according to one's values involves a willingness to make choices, accept obstacles and continue with the valued-direction.

The bubble in the road metaphor is used to illustrate this point:

Metaphor 1

Imagine that you are a bubble travelling on a road and you are met with another bubble that blocks the path. When you try and move around it, the bubble blocks all your attempts to get by. You now have a choice, stop moving in your valued direction, or embrace the bubble, encapsulate it and continue to move forward along the path with the bubble inside.

This metaphor emphasises that willingness is an action rather than a thought or feeling. Relating this to chronic pain, individuals need to choose to live their life according to their values, in the presence of continued pain and other unpleasant internal experiences.

The physical activity component of a chronic pain management programme implements the concepts of willingness to experience unpleasant physical sensations related to chronic pain, whilst engaging in specific activities that lead the individual to live their life in their valued direction. The concept of willingness is frequently revisited during the physical activity component of the programme, as pain is inevitably experienced when physical functioning is upgraded.

Goal setting also has particular importance in the domain of chronic pain, as it allows the clinician to identify whether the individual believes that successful living is contingent upon the eradication of chronic pain. If this is the case then the clinician needs to address the idea that pain can be eradicated. This must occur before other goals can be achieved and before life can be lived according to values.

Creative Hopelessness

This is typically the first time that experiential exercises are used. The focus is on helping the individual to recognise the futility of struggling with internal experiences, such as pain and negative affect. The concept of experiential avoidance is central to this issue. It is also important to note at this point that individuals may be sensitive to feeling blamed during this part of treatment and this should be handled gently. A number of metaphors and experiential exercises can be utilised in order to illustrate the futility of the struggle with internal experiences and to encourage the consideration of alternatives. For example, the individual is asked to list the types of pain management that they have tried. For each of these, they then identify the short-term and long-term effects on pain, as well as the long-term effects on quality of life (Dahl & Lundgren, 2006). Typically some short-term relief in using various interventions thus far is reported. However, individuals largely report limited long-term benefits and often negative consequences of these interventions on their long-term quality of life. This exercise encourages the person to recognise the patterns in their approach to chronic pain. Typically, the list also reflects the elimination or significant reduction of chronic pain as motivating factors that perpetuate their struggle with chronic pain.

A further illustration of creative hopelessness uses the Tug of War exercise:

Exercise 2

The clinician takes a belt or similar item, hands one end to the client and asks them to pull. The clinician then pulls on the other end and explains that if the person loses they will fall into a pit and be destroyed. The clinician encourages the person to pull, and the clinician pulls back. The emphasis is, however, that for every extra effort they put in, the clinician will respond with equal effort.

This exercise demonstrates that the client's situation is like being in a tug-of-war with a monster (whether it is dealing with physical pain, anxiety or depression). The more they pull and dig in their heels the harder it becomes. The person is then encouraged to consider (a) that they do not need to listen to the monster and (b) that maybe it is not their job to win the tug of war, but to drop the rope instead.

Control as the Problem

Human beings have been enormously successful in problem-solving and exercising control over their environment. However, according to the ACT perspective, problem-solving and attempts at control, when applied to the internal world, maintain psychological distress. The thought suppression literature very much supports this point. In the case of chronic pain this is particularly a problem, as pain is an unavoidable and relatively uncontrollable stimulus, and failed attempts at control may result in low self-efficacy and depression.

There are a large number of ACT exercises that demonstrate the futility of control of inner experiences. We use the Perfect Polygraph exercise, which as described here is a variant of the perfect polygraph exercise developed by Hayes et al. (1999) that has been modified by Dahl and Lundgren (2006). It demonstrates the paradox of attempted control.

Metaphor 2

Imagine a perfect polygraph that is able to detect even minute levels of anxiety. Imagine that you have been connected to this machine and you are sitting above a tank of sharks. You are told that if you experience any anxiety you will be dropped into the tank of sharks. All you need to do, however, is stay relaxed and everything will be fine. How do you think you will go?

It is like you are in a tug-of-war with a big, strong, ugly monster. In between you and the monster is a pit, and as far as you can tell it is bottomless. If you lose this tug-of-war, you will fall into the pit and be destroyed. So you pull and pull, but the harder you pull, the harder the monster pulls, and you edge closer and closer to the pit. The hardest thing to see is that our job here is not to win the tug-of-war; our job is to drop the rope. In doing this exercise the person is able to see the paradox of their behaviour: Greater attempts at control increase the risk of the feared outcome.

The Cards exercise is often used next as it is a useful bridge between demonstrating control as a problem and the role of defusing language.

Exercise 3

Write some unpleasant thoughts and feelings related to your chronic pain down on cards. Now hand me the cards. Your task is to not let any of the cards land on or touch your lap. Now I am going to flip the cards towards you and I want you to deflect them away. What was your experience of this exercise? What about it is important? Now, I'm going to do the exercise again and this time just let the cards land wherever they do and just watch them as they do. Now, what was that exercise like for you? Again, how was it relevant to your problems?

The person is encouraged to see that it takes more effort to push the cards away than to just observe them. It is also frequently reported that it is more distressing to push things away than to just let them happen. Finally, at the end of this exercise, the person is asked to carry the cards around with them. Later it is discussed how they were able to have the thoughts with them and still continue with their life.

Defusing Language

Defusing language primarily involves developing distance from one's own thoughts in order to break down the typically unquestioned relationship between thoughts and action. This, in turn, breaks down the mental rules that restrict behavioural responses.

The notion of mental rules is introduced to illustrate how minds are able to view largely arbitrary relationships as absolute truths. This can create problems when applied to how an individual sees themselves and their life. In relation to chronic pain, individuals are asked to identify a range of different rules they have in relation to their chronic pain. The idea of 'rules' can also be applied to experiences during physical activity. For example, it may be helpful to draw awareness to a rule that states 'exercise can only be undertaken when one is pain-free', and to discuss how this rule limits behaviour in the pursuit of achieving goals and value-based living.

Mindfulness meditation is an important tool for defusion. It allows the individual to observe thoughts without giving them valence or an action potential. Mindfulness of breath is typically the first exercise taught. This exercise can be found in many books and websites. A second exercise develops the distancing skill further. Initially it starts with mindfulness of breath then develops as follows:

Exercise 4

Imagine you are sitting by a stream or river. You watch the water flow and leaves floating on top. Now see that the leaves flow with the river but that they are not the same thing. Now take a thought and place it on a leaf. Notice that the leaves and thoughts are not the river and that similarly you are not your thoughts.

This type of exercise is necessary to demonstrate how people fuse to their thoughts and accept them without question. Further, because fusion is a language-based process, demonstrating it is best achieved experientially.

In the setting of the physical activity component of a pain management programme, nonjudgmental labelling is also used to separate the emotional and cognitive aspects of pain from the physical. Training in mindfulness assists in this process and encourages participants to simply notice their thoughts and feelings in relation to their pain. For example, people with pain often catastrophise about their pain, using statements such as 'I can't cope' or 'when will this ever end?' To the person with pain these statements are just accepted as true. Unfortunately, these statements are associated with affect and behaviour inconsistent with living a meaningful life. By developing defusion during physical activity the person recognises when such thinking is impacting on them becoming more active and therefore living life more consistent with their values.

An additional strategy that can be employed to defuse language involves deliteralising the meaning of words:

Exercise 5

This exercise helps to defuse verbal meaning from a word. The person is asked to think about milk, how it tastes, what it looks like etc. They are then asked to repeat the word milk for a period of 1 minute. Following this a discussion is held about what happened to the meaning of the word (i.e., it became just a sound). This exercise is repeated with the word 'pain' and any other salient pain related words or brief statements. Similarly, this exercise can be modified by asking the person to sing the words and thoughts, or to say them in a comical voice.

This exercise is very useful for helping people to see that words, such as pain, are merely sounds that only have meaning in context. This then allows the clinician to suggest alternative ways of employing words in the service of values-based living.

Willingness

Willingness is presented as the alternative to control. It is an 'all or nothing' concept in that it is not possible to be half-willing; a person is either willing or they are not. In order to illustrate this, willingness can be likened to jumping (Hayes et al., 1999). More specifically, the process of jumping is explained as an action that requires launching into the air and allowing gravity to take its course. It is not possible to half jump. What can be modified is the magnitude of the jump. This can be demonstrated by jumping off a roof, as compared to a chair, as compared to a sheet of paper. Similarly, a person may initially choose to be willing with their family, but not at work (although, of course they would be encouraged to build on willingness with the goal of becoming willing, in this example, at work).

A demonstration of the problem of control, as well as willingness, is a metaphor involving two dials:

Metaphor 3

One dial can be pain or any other psychological distress that is relevant for the individual. The dial is introduced at being 10 on a scale of 0 to 10 and that is what brings them into treatment (i.e., wanting to reduce the level of distress). A second dial is then introduced and called willingness. Willingness is described as the willingness to experience a range of thoughts, feelings, or memories as they occur in life without trying to change, avoid or control them. When willingness is 0, the other dial becomes locked at distressing levels.

This notion illustrates that the absence of willingness results in the individual being locked into the realm of distress. That is, being unwilling to have certain experiences results in experiential avoidance that maintains distress. On the other hand, willingness will not necessarily result in less distress, but it creates the conditions by which this might occur. Importantly, willingness cannot be 'faked', the person must be truly willing for this approach to be fully effective.

Importantly, willingness and acceptance does not imply resignation when it comes to chronic pain. In fact, while acceptance and willingness involve disengaging from the struggle with pain *in the present moment*, they also imply ongoing engagement in functional activities in pursuit of one's goals and values (McCracken & Eccleston, 2003).

Committed Action

The final stage of ACT involves committed action towards values-based living, whilst being challenged by various expected and unexpected events in the person's life. The individual must respond to these challenges by maintaining willingness in the cause of continuing with values-based living.

In order to put a perspective on the notion of committed action, and living according to one's values in preparation for engagement in action, the swamp metaphor is used (Hayes et al., 1999):

Metaphor 4

You are on a journey to a beautiful mountain and just as you set off you find yourself in a swamp. You are sinking in the mud and getting tired from the extra effort you need to exert. The choice that needs to be made is to either stop the journey, or continue moving in the direction of the mountain.

The notion behind this metaphor is that the person may not want to go into the swamp, but that they will need to be prepared to go because to do so will move them towards their valued direction. This can then be discussed in terms of pain.

Conclusion

This chapter provides a brief overview of some of the main concepts of ACT as it applies to chronic pain. The techniques presented are largely experiential and serve to steer individuals away from the verbal restraints that, from an ACT perspective, are associated with, and contribute to, psychological distress. Additional techniques are constantly emerging and can be found on the ACT website (http://www.acceptanceandcommit-menttherapy.com) and in ACT textbooks. The application of ACT to chronic pain involves identifying valued directions in life; setting goals in order to achieve these values; identifying barriers; being willing to experience chronic pain, as well as associated cognitions and emotions; and being able to observe and be mindful of unpleasant emotional and cognitive states whilst living according to one's values.

The authors are currently collecting outcome data for the application of ACT to chronic pain within an intensive pain management programme. Although in its' early stages, the data is encouraging, suggesting that clinically significant outcomes are achievable when ACT is applied to chronic pain.

References

Dahl, J., & Lundgren, T. (2006). *Living beyond your pain: Using acceptance and commitment therapy to ease chronic pain.* Oakland, CA: New Harbinger Press.

Freud, S. (1966). *Introductory lectures to psychoanalysis.* London: George Allen and Unwin.

Hayes, S.C., Luoma, J.B., Bond, F.W., Masuda, A., & Lillis, J. (2006). Acceptance and commitment therapy: Model, processes and outcomes. *Behaviour Research and Therapy, 44*, 1–25.

Hayes, S.C., Strosahl, K.D., & Wilson, K.G. (1999). *Acceptance and commitment therapy: An experiential approach to behaviour change.* London: Guildford Press.

McCracken, L.M., & Eccleston, C. (2003). Coping or acceptance: What to do about chronic pain? *Pain, 105*, 197–204.

McCracken, L.M., & Eccleston, C. (2005). A prospective study of acceptance of pain and patient functioning with chronic pain. *Pain, 118*, 164–169.

McCracken, L.M., & Eccleston, C. (2006). A comparison of the relative utility of coping and acceptance-based measures in a sample of chronic pain sufferers. *European Journal of Pain, 10*, 23–29.

McCracken, L.M., Vowles, K.E., & Eccleston, C. (2005). Acceptance-based treatment for persons with complex, long standing chronic pain: A preliminary analysis of treatment outcome in comparison to the waiting phase. *Behaviour Research and Therapy, 43*, 1335–1346.

Perls, F. (1973). *The Gestalt approach and eyewitness to therapy.* Palo Alto, CA: Science and Behaviour Books.

Rogers, C. (1961). *On becoming a person.* Boston: Houghton Mifflin.

CHAPTER 10

From Passive Acceptance to Active Engagement: The Path of CBT for Psychosis

Julia Shearsby, Peter Walker and Zachary Steel

The 20th century saw a series of major shifts in the nature of care available for the seriously mentally ill. Advances in psychopharmacology resulted in progressive improvements in symptom management from the 1950s onwards. Community-based models of care have replaced the large institutions which once dominated the psychiatric landscape. The patients' rights movement has seen consumers and carers play an increasingly important role in advocating for improved services and involvement in key policy making bodies. Despite these changes, the mental health system for the seriously mentally ill in Australia exists in a state of continuing crisis (Mental Health Council of Australia, 2005). The advent of a new generation of atypical antipsychotic medication, while improving effectiveness and reducing adverse reactions, continues to leave many patients with residual symptoms. There is a general consensus that current models of care are not working adequately and that alternative approaches are required (Mental Health Council of Australia, 2005).

In the late 1980s, Marius Romme identified a large number of people who experienced psychotic symptoms, such as hearing voices, without needing to access psychiatric services (Romme & Escher, 1989). He found that not all people who experienced voices found them distressing and suggested that, where distress is experienced, it may come from the meaning the person gives to the voices based on the stigmatisation and misunderstanding by the wider society of such experiences. In response to this, self-help groups such as Foundation Resonance and 'The Hearing Voices Network' were established. These groups argue that consumer-led liberation is necessary in order to change both the assumptions of psychiatry and those of wider society.

Contemporaneously, a number of psychologists, based primarily in the United Kingdom, buoyed by the effectiveness of cognitive–behaviour therapy (CBT) for other disorders, began to apply CBT principles to the treatment of psychosis. The clinical models developed suggested that normal psychological and cognitive principles apply to the psychotic experience. Influenced by the emerging consumer movement, the approach challenged the prevailing view in psychiatry — that delusions and hallucinations represented a major discontinuation from normal experience and that the content and meaning of such experiences was of minimal relevance to treatment. These developments were accompanied by the publication of several clinical manuals and theoretical papers carefully describing how to work with consumers experiencing voices and delusions from a CBT perspective (Birchwood & Tarrier, 1994; Chadwick, Birchwood, & Trower, 1996; Chadwick & Lowe, 1994; Fowler, Garety, & Kuipers, 1998a, 1998b; Garety, Kuipers, Fowler, Freeman, & Bebbington, 2001; Kingdon, 2004; Nelson, 1997). This new psychological paradigm for understanding and intervening in the management of psychosis also provided a major challenge to clinical psychologists who had, until this point, surrendered the treatment of the psychotic spectrum disorders, with few exceptions, to psychiatrists and mental health nurses, restricting their attention to mood, anxiety and eating disorders.

Empirical Findings

The first results from randomised controlled trials (RCTs) emerged during the early 1990s and suggested great promise for the efficacy of CBT for psychosis (Drury, Birchwood, Cochrane, & MacMillan, 1996; Kuipers et al., 1997; Tarrier et al., 1993a; Tarrier et al., 1993b). These trials found significantly greater improvements for those randomised to the CBT conditions compared with the control conditions (generally standard care), both in terms of the frequency and severity of psychotic symptoms.

There was evidence that at 6-, 9- and 12-month posttreatment follow-up, the superiority of CBT was maintained, suggesting that CBT was a durable treatment (Kuipers et al., 1998; Rector, Seeman, & Segal, 2003; Sensky et al., 2000; Tarrier et al., 1999). There was also evidence that CBT could be useful in the acute (Drury et al., 1996) and prodromal phases of psychosis (Morrison et al., 2004).

By the end of the 1990s, a substantial number of RCTs examining the effectiveness of CBT in treating psychotic symptoms across a range of interventions and patient groups had been undertaken. Early meta-analyses suggested that CBT for psychotic symptoms could produce strong effects. Gould and colleagues (2001) reported effect sizes of 0.65 at post-treatment and 0.93 at follow-up. Rector and Beck (2001) reported effect sizes of 1.31 at posttreatment and 1.48 at follow-up.

The overwhelmingly positive results from the initial studies were soon replaced by a more complex set of findings. Jakes and colleagues (1999) reported more modest results, with only one third of their sample responding to cognitive therapy. Doubt about CBT's particular efficacy emerged as comparisons between CBT and a non-specific 'befriending' condition (Sensky et al., 2000) and between CBT and a specialised schizophrenia treatment service (Rector et al., 2003) demonstrated similar outcomes for both conditions at posttreatment. However, CBT seemed to be superior at follow-up. The largest scale study to date indicated that the benefits of CBT were perhaps more modest and circumscribed than the initial RCTs indicated (Lewis et al., 2002). These findings prompted further reviews of the empirical studies, with the aim of determining the magnitude of the effect of CBT for psychosis.

An important meta-analysis conducted by Tarrier and Wykes (2004) attempted to divide the studies into differing patient groups and explore the relationship between methodological rigour and reported effect size. Overall, the effect size for the 20 RCTs identified was 0.37, a more modest result when compared to effect sizes reported by earlier meta-analyses. They also found that there was a negative correlation between the effect size and the measured quality of the RCT, suggesting that studies with poorer methodology may lead to inflated estimates of the effectiveness of CBT for psychosis.

CBT for Psychosis in Sydney and the Voices and Beliefs Project

In the late 1990s, a small group of clinical psychologists in Sydney began to meet bimonthly to discuss the emerging literature on CBT for psychosis, share their practice and provide each other with peer supervision.

In 1999, Campbelltown Mental Health Service, in the south-west of Sydney, profiled a clinical psychology position that worked solely with consumers with chronic schizophrenia within a CBT framework. Brian O'Grady took up this position and developed a CBT for Psychosis Network that included psychologists across the Sydney region who were interested in working with psychotic clients. The aim of the network was to learn from the experience of other clinicians working in the area, as well as widen the availability of these interventions for psychotic populations. A core group of practitioners met every 3 months.

The Voices and Beliefs Project, forming the basis of the current chapter, developed out of this network. Despite the general pessimism within the mental health sector about the application of talking therapies to consumers with psychosis, the authors found the network inspiring and became interested in designing a research project that could test the effectiveness of CBT for psychosis in the Australian context. We set about designing a RCT of CBT across two sites — Bankstown Hospital/Mental Health Service and Prince of Wales Hospital — in the south-west and eastern suburbs of Sydney respectively.

The Voices and Beliefs Project involved consumers with a diagnosis of schizophrenia, who had been on antipsychotic medication for at least 12 months and continued to experience distressing auditory hallucinations and/or delusions. Consumers were randomly allocated to one of two cognitive–behavioural interventions, cognitive therapy (CT; Chadwick et al., 1996) or coping strategy enhancement (CSE; Tarrier et al., 1993a; Tarrier et al., 1993b), or a 2-month waiting list (Waitlist). Treatment consisted of nine individual weekly sessions. Participants were assessed at pre- and posttreatment and at 2-month and 6-month follow-up. All participants continued to receive routine care throughout the study.

A number of standardised measures were used to determine outcomes. Treating psychiatrists completed the Brief Psychiatric Rating Scale (BPRS; Overall & Gorham, 1962) and the nonblind therapists completed the Psychiatric Rating Scale (PSYRATS; Haddock, McCarron, Tarrier, & Faragher, 1999) for both voices and delusional beliefs — which assesses various dimensions of the psychotic experiences including frequency, beliefs about origin, degree of negative content and level of distress. Self-report measures included the Depression, Anxiety and Stress Scales (DASS; Lovibond & Lovibond, 1995); a short questionnaire measuring three dimensions of psychological distress; and the Beliefs about Voices Questionnaire (BAVQ-R; Chadwick, Lees, & Birchwood, 2000), which measures the experience of voices on the dimensions of malevolence/ benevolence, omniscience and resistance/engagement. Further, Likert scales for dimensions of the experience of voices and delusions (avoidance, preoccupation, conviction, distress) were completed each session. These consisted of a 5-point scale, 1 representing *no impact* and 5 representing *severe impact*. Finally, the Similarities subscale of the Wechsler Adult Intelligence Scale—Revised (WAIS-R; Wecshler, 1997) was included at pretreatment as a measure of abstract thinking ability.

The details of the design, methodology and results of the project will be published elsewhere. In brief, the results were mixed, complex and modest. Naturalistic research is difficult even under optimal conditions and completing the RCT was a very difficult process. Attrition rates were particularly high during the initial sessions with participants; it was difficult to gain written consent from participants who were paranoid (in compliance with ethics requirements); referral rates were slow, reflecting the pessimism of mental health clinicians, which resulted in smaller than anticipated sample sizes for the three groups (CT, CSE and Waitlist); and remaining within the randomisation process was difficult when clinical judgment suggested that particular consumers would probably benefit from a broader multimodal intervention. The experience of this RCT accords with the complexity that has emerged in the literature about the benefits and limits of CBT for psychosis. This chapter will present a series of case studies from the CT arm of the study to illustrate key issues that emerged in using CBT with this population, the complexity of treatment and some recommendations to help improve practice.

In the CT arm of the study the aim was to explore the consumer's delusional network and/or the themes associated with their beliefs about their voices (e.g., omnipotence, malevolence). This cognitive therapy model suggests that voices can be seen as activating events (As) about which individuals have certain beliefs or attitudes (Bs) and that such beliefs are in turn responsible for the emotion that the individual experiences (Cs). Consumers are introduced to the cognitive model (ABC) of affective states. Delusional beliefs or beliefs about voices (Bs in the ABC) are conceptualised as hypotheses that have been derived from the consumer's life experiences and their experiences with the delusions and/or hallucinations. As in other forms of cognitive therapy the therapist works with the consumer to collect and examine evidence for and against a certain belief through the application of Socratic questioning and the development of behavioural experiments. In addition, the consumer is taught about the role of automatic thinking and how such automatic thoughts often contain cognitive errors. Logical inconsistencies in the belief system are identified and gently introduced. Behavioural experiments may follow if they allow for clear changes in the belief structure.

Case Studies

Case 1: Rebecca

Rebecca was a 32-year-old female client referred by a private practitioner who had heard about the Voices and Beliefs Project. Rebecca was diagnosed with schizophrenia in 2000 (age 30). She reported that she started to 'imagine things' from the age of 20 and the voices began at age 26.

At this time she also had some grandiose delusions about being a celebrity lawyer. This belief was not without meaning as Rebecca had completed a degree in law prior to becoming unwell but was unable to work in her profession because of her illness. She also experienced ideas of reference from the television and radio and believed that her house was under electronic surveillance.

She went to Cumberland Hospital Emergency Department at age 26, four years prior to diagnosis, but was not diagnosed or prescribed any medication. Rebecca presented as quite intelligent and high functioning. Her self-care was extremely good and her social skills seemed largely intact. She also seemed to have a good capacity for abstract thought as indicated by her high score on the Similarities subtest of the WAIS-R. The authors hypothesised that such ability for abstract thought may assist in responding to cognitive therapy. She reported significant distress related to her auditory hallucinations. The voices made derogatory statements such as 'you're sick', 'you're schizo', 'you suck' as well as non-derogatory statements such as 'Rebecca' or 'hey'. She reported that the voices clouded her thinking and prevented her from doing anything else. She stated that if she heard voices, the rest of her day would be ruined. Rebecca spent substantial amounts of time anticipating the onset of the voices and this would also prevent her from doing normal activities. Her primary coping strategy was to tell people around her what was happening, a strategy that resulted in feelings of rejection or family conflict.

Rebecca's pretreatment scores (Table 1) indicated high levels of depression, anxiety and stress. The profile of her beliefs about her voices indicated that Rebecca perceived them as malevolent and omnipotent, but also that she strongly resisted them rather than engaging with them, consistent with normative data for this clinical population (Chadwick et al., 2000). Rebecca's psychotic symptomatology was moderate as indicated by the BPRS and the PSYRATS.

Rebecca was randomly allocated to the CT condition. She engaged with treatment extremely well. She regularly attended her appointments and completed her homework tasks. She quickly grasped the cognitive model and chose to focus the sessions on exploring the impact of her illness and her experience of stigma within her family and the workplace, her identity and what it meant to be sane. Rebecca opted to discontinue with the research project at the end of the treatment period (which was limited to nine sessions), as she keenly wanted to continue the sessions.

Rebecca started working part-time towards the end of the sessions and she had also begun a new relationship, suggesting an improvement in her

Table 1
Pre- and Posttreatment Scores for Case Studies

	Pretreatment Scores			Posttreatment Scores		
	Rebecca	Richard	Sophie	Rebecca	Richard	Sophie
Depression Anxiety and Stress Scales (DASS)						
DASS Depression[a]	26	20	40	14	14	9
DASS Anxiety[b]	22	12	17	8	12	16
DASS Stress[c]	28	16	23	20	10	17
Brief Psychiatric Rating Scale (min = 0, max = 126)	26	48	52	—	—	—
Psychiatric Rating Scale						
Auditory Hallucinations (AH) (max = 44)	28.5	31	28	28	27	20
AH Distress Amount (max = 5)	4	3	3	4	4	1
AH Distress Intensity (max = 5)	4	4	3	3	2	2
Delusions (max = 24)	—	17	8	—	11	7
Delusions Distress Amount (max = 5)	—	4	1	—	2	1
Delusions Distress Intensity (max = 5)	—	4	1	—	2	1
Beliefs about Voices Questionnaire						
Malevolence (max = 18)	11	12	15	9	7	6
Benevolence (max = 18)	0	5	9	0	6	10
Omnipotence (max = 18)	11	10	17	11	8	10
Resistance (max = 24)	22	18	16	19	19	12
Engagement (max = 24)	0	2	8	0	1	14

Note: [a]Normal (0–9); Mild (10–13); Moderate (14–20); Severe (21–27);Extremely Severe (28–42)
[b]Normal (0–7); Mild (8–9); Moderate (10–14); Severe (15–19); Extrememly Severe (20–42)
[c]Normal (0–14); Mild (15–18); Moderate (19–26); Severe (27–34); Extremely Severe (35–42)

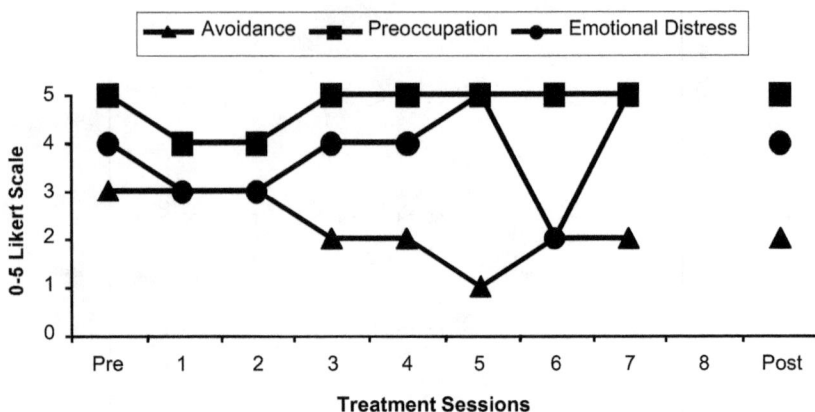

Figure 1
Rebbeca: Likert scores for voices across treatment.

quality of life. Cognitive therapy enabled Rebecca to challenge her internalised stigma in terms of her beliefs about the limitations imposed by her illness. These beliefs were not only challenged at a cognitive level but were translated into behavioural changes in her social and vocational life.

Table 1 provides Rebecca's posttreatment scores and Figure 1 provides her weekly Likert ratings (for voices). Interestingly, at the point of postdata collection Rebecca's levels of depression, anxiety and stress had improved; however, her experience of her psychotic symptoms did not change as can be seen by her scores on the PSYRATS and the BAVQ-R. Additionally, Rebecca's weekly Likert scale ratings (see Figure 1) did not change. Her avoidance stayed in the mild–moderate range and her preoccupation stayed in the severe–very severe range. Her distress fluctuated, ranging from mild to very severe.

Key Lesson 1

We may target the experience of psychotic symptomatology, but that is not necessarily what will change as a result of the intervention. Rebecca's mood, her anxiety levels and her engagement with life improved despite her remaining highly symptomatic with regard to psychotic symptoms. What constitutes a response to therapy needs to be reconsidered. Rebecca's scores on all of the psychosis-specific measures revealed no improvement; however, by the end of treatment Rebecca was more hopeful, confident, active and engaged in life. Rebecca clearly valued therapy despite the lack of change in her psychotic symptoms. This was demonstrated by her decision to opt out of the research project for the follow-up phase, in order to continue weekly therapy sessions.

Case 2: Richard

Richard was a 29-year-old male client referred by the consultant psychiatrist from a medication-based clinic. Richard was diagnosed with schizophrenia at the age of 20 and had been on clozapine (an atypical antipsychotic) for 5 years, after previous trials of other antipsychotic medications. Richard presented with marked avoidance due to persistent paranoid delusions, for example, 'That person is following me', 'They know about my past', 'They are out to get me', and auditory hallucinations. Richard was not engaged in any kind of social or vocational activity as a result of these symptoms and the only times he would leave his home were to attend appointments, visit his mother or to occasionally go to the shops. He had been referred to the vocational training unit by the consultant psychiatrist but was unable to tolerate the anxiety provoked by attending. Richard's life appeared to be devoid of meaningful social relationships outside of his immediate family and he was not engaged in meaningful recreational or occupational activities.

Richard was randomly allocated to the CT condition. The initial clinical impression was that Richard was unlikely to benefit from this intervention. He was difficult to engage in conversation and there seemed to be a degree of cognitive impairment that would impede his comprehension and application of the concepts of cognitive therapy. This was further supported by self-reported poor concentration. Correspondingly, his score on the Similarities subtest of the WAIS-R was low. The authors hypothesised that poor abstract reasoning may reduce responsiveness to cognitive therapy. It was also considered that his high level of anxiety would limit the success of cognitive therapy.

Richard's pretreatment scores (Table 1) on the DASS revealed a moderate to severe level of depressive symptoms, a moderate level of anxiety and a mild level of stress. These scores, particularly the anxiety score, did not match with his clinical presentation. Richard's pretreatment data also indicated moderate to severe psychotic symptoms and concomitant levels of distress (relating to his delusional beliefs and voices). The profile of his beliefs about his voices included perceiving them as malevolent, omnipotent and suggested that he strongly resisted them rather than engaging with them, consistent with normative data for this clinical population (Chadwick et al., 2000).

Richard reliably attended his weekly sessions. Therapy focused mainly on the delusional beliefs rather than auditory hallucinations as Richard reported that his beliefs were more problematic. Richard always completed his homework tasks and was able to see the impact his beliefs were having on his life.

Figure 2 presents the case formulation that was developed collaboratively with Richard. Richard's anxiety was the result of (1) a shy personality, (2) beliefs about people harming him and knowing secret information about him and thoughts that he will do something wrong and (3) avoidance. His beliefs stemmed from prior experiences and were strengthened by the content of the auditory hallucinations. Richard was motivated to try and endure different situations but found this difficult as he was so preoccupied by his thoughts. Over time he had gradually avoided most activities so that his beliefs were never disconfirmed. This formulation helped Richard to understand the way his thinking perpetuated his avoidance, which in turn perpetuated his distress. Richard learnt to identify cognitive distortions, particularly jumping to conclusions and catastrophising. He was able to consider the evidence for and against his automatic thoughts and alternatives to these thoughts. As the sessions progressed Richard became less avoidant and was willing to try various activities such as volunteering at a dog shelter, going to the markets and driving. These changes demonstrated significant progress for Richard. He used a couple of the sessions to discuss issues that he had never spoken about before. However, by the end of treatment, his activity level was starting to reduce. It seemed that Richard had benefited from the intervention but that these benefits would not be sustained. It seemed that as

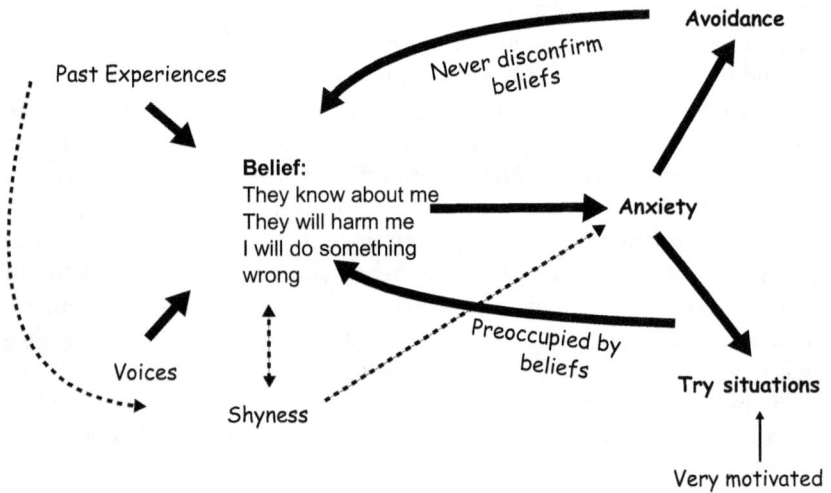

Figure 2
Case formulation for Richard.

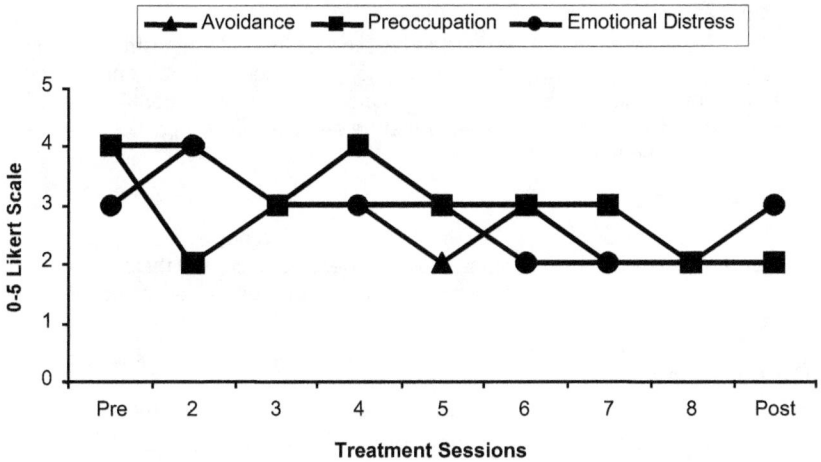

Figure 3
Richard: Likert scores for beliefs across treatment.

the treatment drew to a close, so did his progress and his ability to push himself to make significant changes to his lifestyle diminished.

As can be seen in Table 1, his posttreatment scores revealed some improvement. On the DASS, his depression score reduced, his anxiety level remained the same and his stress score dropped into the normal range. His severity scores for auditory hallucinations and delusions dropped. His distress scores (amount and intensity) dropped for his delusions but only the intensity of distress score for voices dropped.

Richard's beliefs about his voices also changed. He perceived them as less malevolent and slightly less omnipotent. Throughout treatment, Richard's conviction about his delusional beliefs reduced from 60% at the beginning of treatment to 20% by the end of treatment. Richard's weekly Likert scale ratings for avoidance reduced from the severe range to the low–moderate range over the course of treatment. His Likert ratings for distress and preoccupation improved slightly (Figure 3).

Key Lesson 2

Clinical predictions based on cognitive capacity do not always bear out. Despite Richard's apparent illness-related cognitive limitations, he responded to treatment. Poor concentration, cognitive impairment, difficulty with social engagement and high levels of anxiety may not be reliable indicators for potential non-responders.

Key Lesson 3

Cognitive therapy enabled Richard to believe that he could be instrumental in altering the course of his life. Despite ongoing paranoia and associated distress, his symptoms became less disabling. Richard used therapy to identify areas of interest and act on these. It seemed that he saw change as a possibility and a meaningful existence within reach.

Key Lesson 4

Treatment termination can often be associated with a deterioration in clinical gains. The expectation that consumers can become their own therapist once trained in CBT may not be as readily applicable for those experiencing psychosis.

Case 3: Sophie

Sophie was a 46-year-old woman, referred to the study by a women's housing organisation. She was diagnosed with schizophrenia at the age of 32. She lived alone in supported accommodation in a beachside suburb of Sydney.

Sophie engaged easily and had a well-developed sense of humour and insight into her condition. She would often laugh when describing some of her beliefs and said that describing them sometimes allowed her to see that they might not be true.

Sophie reported persistent, distressing voices. She stated that she heard several voices, both male and female of unknown identity. Their clarity was variable. At times she could hear distinct voices telling her that she was 'too soft' and 'unable to get through the battles of life'. At other times the voices were in the background and difficult to comprehend. They were still distracting for her at these times. Sophie stated that she believed the clarity of the voices varied with her menstrual cycle.

Sophie also experienced visual hallucinations, which are relatively rare in schizophrenia. She saw 'invisible people', explaining that they were like friends and she noticed them around her home. She described a boy in blue and a woman aged 23 who had died from leukaemia. This had personal relevance as Sophie's father had died of leukaemia and Sophie was fearful of developing this condition. She explained that they don't talk a great deal but keep her company. Although they caused some anxiety, Sophie stated that she would prefer them to stay.

Sophie's delusions were many and varied. They rarely persisted for significant periods of time although they were often linked by similar themes. For example, Sophie believed that at times she was invisible. She reported being shocked when she was noticed in public by strangers. Although this was a literal belief, she stated that she felt it was related to the feeling of having little to contribute to society as a sufferer of mental illness.

Despite her capacity for social engagement, Sophie's behaviour was at times disinhibited and she displayed lability of mood. She described laughing aloud at jokes that she had made up and singing, when travelling on public transport.

Overall, Sophie had a relatively high level of functioning. She practised yoga daily. She was engaged with community groups, including art classes and women's support groups. Sophie's insight into her illness enhanced her capacity to cope.

Sophie's pretreatment scores (Table 1) suggested a severe level of depression and anxiety and a moderate level of stress. Measures of beliefs about voices revealed that she considered them malevolent and omnipotent and she tended to resist them, consistent with normative data for this clinical population (Chadwick et al., 2000). Sophie's pretreatment data also indicated moderate psychotic symptoms and concomitant levels of distress relating to her voices. Her pretreatment data for delusions was less severe than for auditory hallucinations.

Cognitive therapy targeted the distress associated with the experience of voices. Although Sophie experienced delusions they were quite dynamic, changing from week to week and therefore, it was difficult to systematically challenge them. Further, Sophie's delusions were less distressing to her than the experience of voices.

Sophie was randomly allocated to the CT condition. For the majority of treatment the target of the intervention was the distress associated with the experience of voices. Education on the cognitive model of voices was provided to Sophie. Sophie was encouraged to monitor her voices within the structure of the ABC model. An example is given in Figure 4.

Sophie familiarised herself with the model over several weeks. In the fourth session, gentle cognitive challenging of the thoughts associated with her voices was introduced. Sophie was encouraged to see the voice-related beliefs as theories that could be considered in light of wider evi-

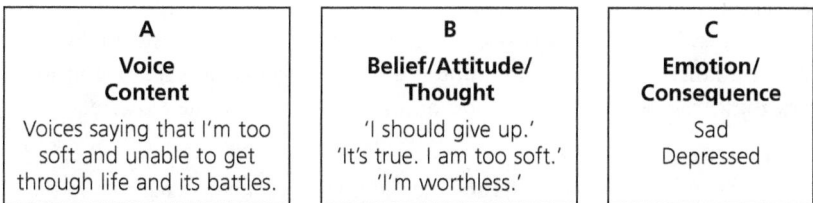

A Voice Content	B Belief/Attitude/ Thought	C Emotion/ Consequence
Voices saying that I'm too soft and unable to get through life and its battles.	'I should give up.' 'It's true. I am too soft.' 'I'm worthless.'	Sad Depressed

Figure 4
Sophie's example of using the ABC model to monitor voices.

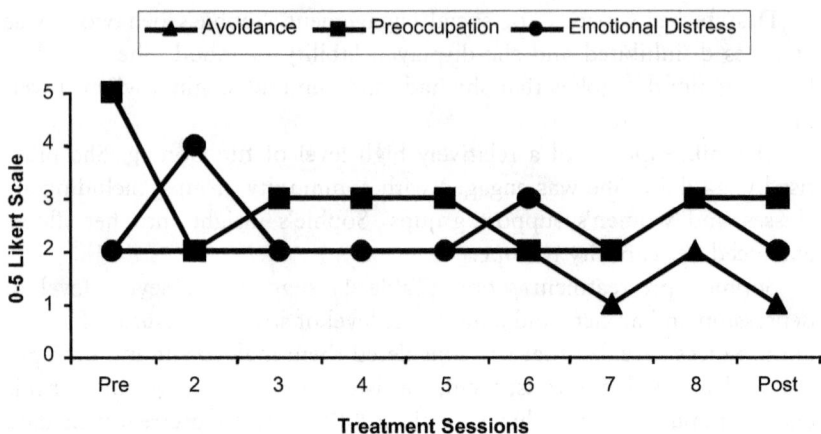

Figure 5
Sophie: Likert scores for voices across treatment.

dence. Alternatives to her beliefs were generated and she started seeing the voices as fallible. The voices were referred to as 'noisy neighbours' that shout abuse intended to deflate her.

As can be seen from Table 1, Sophie demonstrated a large reduction in depression, more moderate reductions in anxiety and stress were observed. There was little change in severity scores for auditory hallucinations and delusions. For auditory hallucinations there were reductions in both the amount of distress experienced and severity of this distress. Weekly Likert scale ratings suggested some reduction in distress, although preoccupation and avoidance showed little change (Figures 5 and 6). The beliefs that Sophie held about her voices changed after treatment. She believed they were less malevolent and omnipotent and spent less time resisting them. Her conviction in her voices also fell, from 80% in the first session to 50% by the last (Figure 7). Treatment improved Sophie's self-image and reduced her belief in the omnipotence of the voices, resulting in less distress. Cognitive therapy for self-esteem and cognitive challenging of the omnipotence of the voices was effective in moderating the severity of depression and anxiety that Sophie experienced.

Key Lesson 5

Within the mental health system, clinical psychologists have almost no role in determining how a client is medicated or whether or not they are admitted into hospital. Although this has some limitations, when consumers understand this it allows for increased trust. Sophie appreciated her concerns being taken

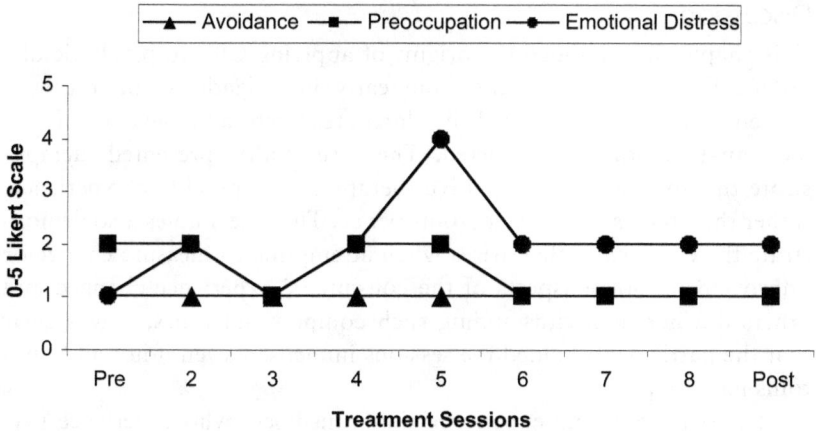

Figure 6
Sophie: Likert scores for beliefs across treatment.

seriously in a nonjudgmental style. Sophie's treatment was truly collaborative and at least part of her success was attributable to improved engagement, as the therapist became a witness to Sophie's distressing experiences without dismissing them.

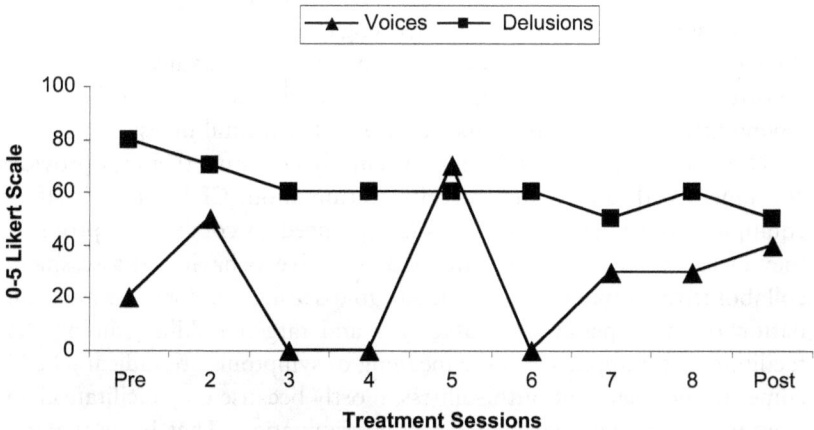

Figure 7
Sophie: Per cent conviction for voices and delusions.

Discussion

This chapter has outlined the origins of applying CBT to psychotic disorders, the promising results from early investigations and the subsequent caution engendered by later research and several of the meta-analytic studies conducted. The case studies presented, demonstrate the application of cognitive therapy to the psychotic experience, rather than the psychotic symptoms per se. The case studies also demonstrate the complexity that arises when attempting to measure change or improvement. Some aspects of the consumers' experience changed and others did not. Notwithstanding such complex outcomes, it was clear that the participants valued the sessions immensely even if not all symptoms had improved.

It is our overriding experience that consumers who experience psychotic symptoms are rendered passive recipients of care by the Australian mental health system. The main role assigned to them is one of compliance as opposed to active engagement. Equally apparent is the extent to which consumers have internalised the dominant societal perspective that stigmatises and degrades the mentally ill, in particular those with schizophrenia. All the participants held beliefs of themselves as worthless, powerless, and socially marginalised or as Sophie put it 'invisible'. The people we worked with were essentially voiceless — silenced by society, the mental health system, and by themselves and their families. Rebecca's targeted cognitions often involved her own self-concept and the negative evaluation of others reflecting the views of her illness held by her family, herself and broader community attitudes. Prior to therapy, Richard's life was extremely limited as he avoided engagement with a world he perceived as hostile. Sophie believed that at times she was invisible and she reported being shocked when she was noticed. She perceived herself as having little to contribute to society due to her mental illness.

Our impression is that CBT (particularly cognitive therapy) provides consumers with an avenue for self-determination. CBT prides itself on equipping consumers with the tools they need to combat the problems they face. The key CBT elements of a cognitive–behavioural assessment, collaborative formulation, individual goal-setting, exploration and validation of the experience of psychosis and targeted skills training that facilitates the reappraisal of the meaning of symptoms are radical when it comes to the treatment of this illness, mostly because they facilitate client empowerment, engagement and self-determination. That is, as the consumers' experiences are heard and validated, a conceptual shift can occur that enables consumers to no longer perceive themselves, or allow others to perceive them, as subhuman and supports them as they refuse to accept society's limits and marginalisation. CBT thus appears to assist in helping consumers approach their illness 'in a way that allows the individual dignity, maximal self-determination, and the highest level of role functioning possible' to be obtained (Cook & Jonikas, 2002).

Many psychologists opt out of working with consumers with psychosis. Psychological interventions remain focused largely on other Axis I disorders. Our hope is that psychologists will recognise the impact they can have by broadening their client base to include this consumer group, even with those who may appear unlikely to benefit (as in the case of Richard). Psychologists often have a unique place in the treating team for consumers with schizophrenia, as seen in the case of Sophie. They can genuinely be a trusted ally and advocate rather than someone who holds coercive power.

Concluding Remarks

The application of CBT principles to the treatment and management of psychotic symptoms represents a unique and important change in the nature of care available to people with a psychotic illness. It offers consumers a therapeutic partnership in which they can share the distress of their illness and actively participate in the process of reclaiming control over their lives. In particular, cognitive therapy facilitates the identification, challenging and restructuring of the internalised prejudice, dehumanisation and worthlessness so often associated with this illness. Perhaps most important of all is the hope that CBT can be a tool to empower consumers experiencing a psychotic illness to claim their right to meaningful work, housing, medical care, mental health services and an active role in civil society — rights that are often noticeably absent.

References

Birchwood, M.J., & Tarrier, N. (1994). *Psychological management of schizophrenia*. Oxford, England: John Wiley and Sons.

Chadwick, P., Lees, S., & Birchwood, M. (2000). The revised Beliefs about Voices Questionnaire (BAVQ-R). *British Journal of Psychiatry, 177*, 229–232.

Chadwick, P.D., Birchwood, M.J., & Trower, P. (1996). *Cognitive therapy for delusions, voices and paranoia*. Oxford, England: John Wiley and Sons.

Chadwick, P.D., & Lowe, C. (1994). A cognitive approach to measuring and modifying delusions. *Behaviour Research and Therapy, 32*(3), 355–367.

Cook, J.A., & Jonikas, J.A. (2002). Self-determination among mental health consumers/survivors: Using lessons from the past to guide the future. *Journal of Disability Policy Studies, 13*(2), 87–95.

Drury, V., Birchwood, M., Cochrane, R., & MacMillan, F. (1996). Cognitive therapy and recovery from acute psychosis: A controlled trial: I. Impact on psychotic symptoms. *British Journal of Psychiatry, 169*(5), 593–601.

Fowler, D., Garety, P., & Kuipers, E. (1998a). Cognitive therapy for psychosis: Formulation, treatment, effects and service implications. *Journal of Mental Health, 7*(2), 123–133.

Fowler, D., Garety, P., & Kuipers, E. (1998b). *Understanding the inexplicable: An individually formulated cognitive approach to delusional beliefs.* In C. Perris & P.D. McGorry (Eds.), *Cognitive psychotherapy of psychotic and personality disorders: Handbook of theory and practice.* NY, US: John Wiley and Sons.

Garety, P., Kuipers, E., Fowler, D., Freeman, D., & Bebbington, P. (2001). A cognitive model of the positive symptoms of psychosis. *Psychological Medicine, 31*(2), 189–195.

Gould, R.A., Mueser, K.T., Bolton, E., Mays, V., & Goff, D. (2001). Cognitive therapy for psychosis in schizophrenia: An effect size analysis. *Schizophrenia Research, 48*(203), 335–342.

Haddock, G., McCarron, J., Tarrier, N., & Faragher, E. (1999). Scales to measure dimensions of hallucinations and delusions: The psychotic symptom rating scales (PSYRATS). *Psychological Medicine, 29*(4), 879–889.

Jakes, S., Rhodes, J., & Turner, T. (1999). Effectiveness of cognitive therapy for delusions in routine clinical practice. *British Journal of Psychiatry, 175*, 331–335.

Kingdon, D. (2004). Cognitive-behavioural therapy for psychosis. *British Journal of Psychiatry, 184*(1), 85–86.

Kuipers, E., Fowler, D., Garety, P., Chisholm, D., Freeman, D., Dunn, G., et al. (1998). London-East Anglia randomised controlled trial of cognitive-behavioural therapy for psychosis: III. Follow-up and economic evaluation at 18 months. *British Journal of Psychiatry, 173*, 61–68.

Kuipers, E., Garety, P., Fowler, D., Dunn, G., Bebbington, P., Freeman, D., et al. (1997). London-East Anglia randomised controlled trial of cognitive-behavioural therapy for psychosis. I: Effects of the treatment phase. *British Journal of Psychiatry, 171*, 319–327.

Lewis, S., Tarrier, N., Haddock, G., Bentall, R., Kinderman, P., Kingdon, D., et al. (2002). Randomised controlled trial of cognitive-behavioural therapy in early schizophrenia: Acute-phase outcomes. *British Journal of Psychiatry, 181* (Suppl. 43), s91–s97.

Lovibond, S.H., & Lovibond, P.F. (1995). *Manual for the Depression Anxiety Stress Scales* (2nd ed.). Sydney, Australia: Psychological Foundation.

Mental Health Council of Australia. (2005). *Not for service: Experiences of injustice and despair in mental health care in Australia.* Deakin West, Australia: Mental Health Council of Australia.

Morrison, A.P., French, P., Walford, L., Lewis, S.W., Kilcommons, A., Green, J., et al. (2004). Cognitive therapy for the prevention of psychosis in people at ultra-high risk: Randomised controlled trial. *British Journal of Psychiatry, 185*(4), 291–297.

Nelson, H.E. (1997). *Cognitive behavioural therapy with schizophrenia: A practice manual.* Cheltenham, England: Stanley Thornes.

Overall, J.E., & Gorham, D.R. (1962). The Brief Psychiatric Rating Scale. *Psychological Reports, 10*, 799–812.

Rector, N.A., & Beck, A.T. (2001). Cognitive behavioral therapy for schizophrenia: An empirical review. *Journal of Nervous and Mental Disease, 189*(5) 278–287.

Rector, N.A., Seeman, M.V., & Segal, Z.V. (2003). Cognitive therapy for schizophrenia: A preliminary randomized controlled trial. *Schizophrenia Research, 63*(1–2), 1–11.

Romme, M., & Escher, A. (1989). Hearing voices. *Schizophrenia Bulletin, 15*, 209–216.

Sensky, T., Turkington, D., Kingdon, D., Scott, J.L., Scott, J., Siddle, R., et al. (2000). A randomized controlled trial of cognitive–behavioral therapy for persistent symptoms in schizophrenia resistant to medication. *Archives of General Psychiatry, 57*(2), 165–172.

Tarrier, N., Beckett, R., Harwood, S., Baker, A., Yusupoff, I., & Ugarteburu, I. (1993a). A trial of two cognitive-behavioural methods of treating drug-resistant residual psychotic symptoms in schizophrenic patients: I. Outcome. *British Journal of Psychiatry, 162*, 524–532.

Tarrier, N., Sharpe, L., Beckett, R., Harwood, R., Baker, A., & Yusupoff, I. (1993b). A trial of two cognitive–behavioural methods of treating drug-resistant residual psychotic symptoms in schizophrenic patients: II. Treatment-specific changes in coping and problem-solving skills. *Social Psychiatry and Psychiatric Epidemiology, 28*(1), 5–10.

Tarrier, N., Wittkowski, A., Kinney, C., McCarthy, E., Morris, J., & Humphreys, L. (1999). Durability of the effects of cognitive-behavioural therapy in the treatment of chronic schizophrenia: 12-month follow-up. *British Journal of Psychiatry, 174*, 500–504.

Tarrier, N., & Wykes, T. (2004). Is there evidence that cognitive behaviour therapy is an effective treatment for schizophrenia? A cautious or cautionary tale? *Behaviour Research and Therapy, 42*(12), 1377–1401.

Wechsler, D. (1997). *Wechsler Adult Intelligence Scale-Third edition. Administration and scoring manual.* San Antonio, TX: Harcourt Brace and Company.

Treatment comparisons

Cognitive Therapy Enhanced With Emotive Techniques in the Treatment of Bipolar Disorder

Jillian Ball, Ashleigh Skillecorn, Justine Corry
and Philip Mitchell

Over the past decade, cognitive therapy (CT) for bipolar disorder has received increasing interest in clinical trials (Lam, Hayward, Watkins, Wright, & Sham, 2005; Perry, Tarrier, Morriss, McCarthy, & Limb, 1999; Scott et al., 2006; Zaretsky, Segal, & Gemar, 1999). The clearest evidence is for the impact of CT on depressive and manic symptoms during active treatment with long-term benefits often fading out once treatment is withdrawn.

An earlier paper published by the present authors (Ball, Mitchell, Malhi, Skillecorn, & Smith, 2003) outlined a biopsychosocial model of chronic illness behaviour highlighting the importance of attitudinal change in treating patients with bipolar disorder. Dysfunctional attitudes associated with sociotrophy and autonomy (Scott & Pope, 2003) and extreme goal striving (Lam, Wright, & Smith, 2004) have been considered characteristic amongst bipolar patients. Newman, Leahy, Beck, Reilly-Harrington and Gyulai (2002) were among the first group of researchers to highlight the role of maladaptive schemas amongst bipolar patients. They suggested that maladaptive schemas originating in childhood may be reactivated in response to bipolar illness, or that the condition itself may cause maladaptive schema to develop, especially during adolescence. This is supported by recent studies indicating that many bipolar patients have distinct cognitive vulnerabilities and negative self-schema associated with poor self-worth, even when euthymic (Winters & Neale, 1985).

The present authors are interested in how best to elicit long lasting attitudinal changes during the psychological treatment of bipolar patients.

Our attention has been drawn to clinical research highlighting the importance of emotive techniques in the construction of new and more adaptive emotional and behavioural responses (Greenberg & Watson, 1998). Such techniques have been used effectively in the treatment of unipolar depression (Greenberg & Watson, 1998) and personality disorders (Leahy & Beck, 1988; Young, 1994). Traditional CT has been shown to have limited success with more complex and chronic presentations, particularly where rigid beliefs systems, self-defeating behaviours and avoidant coping styles are prominent (Scott et al., 2006; Young, 1994). Many of the emotive techniques are drawn from Gestalt therapy and involve accessing emotion and triggering dysfunctional attitudes during the session in order to affect change. Imagery techniques have long been considered powerful means of reconstructing experiences and generating alternative attitudes, not by changing feelings with reason, but through imagining other responses (Greenberg, 2002; Layden, Newman, Freeman, & Morse, 1993). The importance of narratives in helping patients relive their experiences and access feelings is used widely as a means of altering affect and adjusting to chronic illness (Little, Jordens, & Paul, 2001).

Emotive interventions generally involve three initiatives from the therapist: (a) acknowledging and validating the patient's initial experience, (b) activating the emotional memories and any associated dysfunctional beliefs by arousing distressing emotions (such as fear or shame) in response to an imagined scene, and finally (c) activating healthy emotional responses within the patient (such as anger, violation or sadness). Self-validation is then introduced as an alternative response to replace the person's maladaptive emotional, social or behavioural responses (Greenberg, 2002). As these new experiences are repeatedly processed, the traumatic memory or sense of loss is generally reduced. Towards the end of the process, the therapist encourages the development of a new belief system that incorporates modified emotions and attitudes and more adaptive levels of functioning.

In the process of emotive work, core beliefs are brought to consciousness. They may include themes of dependency, vulnerability, inadequacy, failure, or distrust. Whereas underlying assumptions hold out the possibility of beliefs being met (e.g., 'If others approve of me then I am worthwhile'), maladaptive schemas do not (e.g., 'I am inadequate'). When extreme, such maladaptive beliefs are associated with poor psychosocial functioning and behavioural avoidance. Newman et al. (2002) hypothesise that bipolar patients experience a bio-directionality in the expression of their schemas. They suggest that some patients maintain consistent, maladaptive schemas that shift polarity with their mood swings. For example, a patient may think that his ideas are 'universally admired' or 'brilliant' when manic, and yet experience maladaptive schemas of 'failure' or 'inadequacy' when depressed. Therapy aims to reduce these cognitive and emotional swings with the assumption that modification delays relapse and reduces the duration and severity of episodes when they occur.

Some Cautions

Bipolar patients comprise a highly heterogeneous group and each individual's emotional states can shift between sessions. The therapists in our study highlighted the importance of being highly aware of, and flexible to, the patient's individual needs. Since emotive techniques are potentially arousing of affect, it is critical that their use be restricted to times of stable mood. While the treatment program used in our study is presented in modules, it was necessary for the therapists to carefully accommodate techniques to the patient's needs at any point in time.

Modified Cognitive Therapy for Bipolar Disorder

In modifying CT for the needs of bipolar patients, we have highlighted the importance of:
- the biological and genetic components of the illness
- stressors which trigger episodes
- identifying prodromes
- stabilising sleep–wake cycles
- emotional regulation skills
- skills in managing relationships effectively
- managing the high suicide risk often associated with the illness.

The treatment aims not only to equip patients with the skills to manage their symptoms, but to alter their appraisals of self, others and their illness in order to facilitate adjustment and functional recovery In our study, patients participated in 20 to 25 sessions of therapy over a 6-month period.

Treatment Interventions

A range of emotive, cognitive, behavioural and interpersonal techniques are used throughout treatment.

Emotive Techniques

These techniques aimed to change core beliefs through the accessing of affect during the session. Every effort is made to convey empathy and respect for the patient's experiences. Key emotive techniques include:

Imagery. Imagery assists in the process of modifying and restructuring the meaning of the patient's visual memory. Patients are encouraged to observe their images and consider other ways of interpreting events. A common theme raised by bipolar patients involves perceived parental rejection for being moody as a child.

Affect bridge. This technique is used when high levels of affect are expressed either spontaneously during the session or when recalling past events. Patients are encouraged to stay with their emotions and track them back in time, indicating when an earlier memory triggered the same emotional response. Through open-ended questioning the earlier experience is then explored. Once connected with the affect, the patient's distress generally eases.

Narratives. When significantly high levels of affect are experienced, patients are encouraged to write about their feelings and memories between sessions. The objective of narrative writing is to increase awareness of internal dialogues and how meaning is being assigned to life changing experiences. The narratives generally change as the patients' moods and understanding of their illness change. Eventually, other ways of responding can be chosen by the patient.

Cognitive Techniques

Cognitive techniques are used throughout the sessions to systematically test the evidence associated with the schemas. A balance is attempted as the therapist empathises with the patient, while simultaneously confronting and discrediting subjective cognitive biases. This process of thought challenging continues as overvalued ideas are expressed. The process of discounting contradictory evidence is simplified using an exercise called the point–counterpoint technique (Young, 1994). During this intervention the patient plays the negative beliefs and the therapist adopts the role of the positive cognitive set. Debate continues back and forth between therapist and patient with contradictory evidence offered before reversing roles.

Interpersonal Techniques

The importance of the therapeutic relationship has been described by a number of researchers (Greenberg, 2002; Young, 1994). It is considered an important means of identifying and confronting dysfunctional attitudes acted out by the patient during sessions. Through interpersonal techniques, the therapist helps patients directly test the reality of their beliefs and counteract dysfunctional attitudes in a relatively safe environment. This is particularly important when patients have experienced a background of emotional deprivation and need to express themselves in the context of a trusting and caring relationship.

Behavioural Techniques
Throughout therapy, every opportunity is taken to change long-term self-defeating behavioural patterns that continue to reinforce the schemas. The therapist sets tasks in the form of graduated homework exercises. Changes in the patient's environment are also made to reinforce more adaptive behaviours including, for example, more or less contact with families, the reduction or increase of work responsibilities, initiating activities or making new friendships.

Outline of the Treatment Program

Module 1: Assessment
This initial module aims to build rapport and establish a trusting therapeutic relationship. Previous episodes, precipitants and triggers, coping strategies and past and current treatment interventions are reviewed. Given the schema-focused nature of therapy, the assessment also examines the relationship between cognitive vulnerabilities, personality style and unresolved family of origin issues which may be precipitating and maintaining illness episodes and increasing the risk of relapse. The therapist notes the language patients use when describing their illness, how they feel about their diagnosis and the implications of the illness on their sense of self and perceptions of others.

Module 2: Education
These sessions address the biological, social and psychological aspects of bipolar disorder within the context of the stress-diathesis model. The cognitive model is presented, highlighting the role of appraisals and belief systems in managing the illness. Patients are encouraged to become effective and active participants in their own treatment. Questions are asked eliciting details about the patients' perceptions of their illness, how they respond to other people taking control, whether they had reoccurring dreams or nightmares about these experiences and how they are affected by these experiences. Particular attention is given to possible signs of

trauma. Feelings of shame, anger and fear are explored as well as the subsequent effects on the person's interpersonal relationships and attitudes towards work in the present and future.

Therapy proceeds according to the traditional structure of CT with the setting of agendas and a collaborative approach to session content. To help patients become acute observers of their own cognitions, mood and behaviours, strategies promoting self-monitoring and self-regulation are introduced early in the therapeutic process. Homework tasks focusing on problem-solving, cognitive imagery and graduated behavioural tasks further enhance independent coping skills. Feelings of hopelessness and suicidality are addressed with crisis management plans for acute episodes set in place.

Case 1

One of the participants in our program was Mia, a 32-year-old research scientist who had experienced numerous admissions to public hospitals for mania and depression. In the initial interview, she described in detail her first manic episode. She thought at the time that the doctor was involved with the FBI and that this was a conspiracy to imprison her. She subsequently felt trapped, held down and injected against her wishes. Mia described problems integrating her experiences long after the acute manic symptoms had subsided. She was plagued with constant ruminations about what had happened and was constantly trying to piece together the jigsaw to work out why these episodes had occurred. Ever since her hospitalisation, she had experienced severe anxiety at the first sign of depressed or elevated mood. A fear of losing control and having her current life destroyed was never far from her mind. She described how her illness had affected her relationship with her boyfriend and his reluctance to get married or have children with her. He shared her fears of how Mia would cope with the stresses involved and the genetic risks associated with bipolar disorder. Adjustment issues, the traumatic nature of her episodes and the chronic issues associated with mental illness featured in Mia's therapy.

Module 3: Effective Management of Prodromes and Stress

The recurrent nature of bipolar disorder is tackled through effective management of early warning signs and stress. Using information gathered in mood monitoring exercises, triggers from previous episodes are identified and new ways of coping examined. A 'relapse profile' for each patient is developed and lists how the patient should respond. Common triggers for hypomanic or manic episodes are changes to everyday rhythms and an accumulation of stressful life events. Early warning signs for depression can be more difficult to identify as the onset of the mood is often more insidious in nature. Stimulus control measures are considered, for example, keeping attendance at social functions to a minimum, moderating workloads, setting priorities, using distractions and making others responsible for finances.

Case 2
Mia was able to identify a number of signs suggesting her mood was becoming elevated. These included a rise in blood pressure, feeling energised or wired, a flood of great ideas, not being able to sit long enough to watch TV and becoming irritable if anyone tried to stop her carrying out her ideas.

Module 4: Stabilising Routines
Activity scheduling is used to gradually increase the patients' opportunities for pleasurable and achievement-oriented activities while depressed, and to slow down and prioritise current levels of activity during hypomanic/manic states. Emphasis is also placed on sustaining regular sleep–wake cycles to enhance stability of mood.

Module 5: Identifying and Modifying Cognitions
When negative cognitions are identified, traditional thought challenging techniques are used. Common cognitive distortions amongst participants in our study included the tendency to overreact to situational stresses, catastrophise setbacks and disappointments, confuse feelings with facts, and draw irrational conclusions about medications from isolated experiences. Cognitive techniques are also used to enhance problem-solving, mobilise support systems, identify personal strengths, accept limitations and construct a positive view of the future.

Not all the negative cognitions experienced by bipolar disorder patients are distorted, as the patient's illness may have, in fact, ruined relationships, contributed to difficulties at work, jeopardised career paths and so on. To deal with such occurrences, a series of Socratic questions recommended is used (Newman et al., 2002). For example, 'What can I still do with my life despite my past suffering?', 'What can I learn from my past behaviours?', 'How can I present myself in order to maintain my integrity and privacy?', 'How can I rebuild my life with bipolar disorder so that I have things to look forward to in the future?'

Cognitive distortions in mania are considered to mirror the distortions seen in unipolar depression (Leahy & Beck, 1988). As recommended by Lam, Jones, Haywood and Bright (1999), the high personal costs and the damaging effects on others are emphasised. Cognitive interventions also target the extremes of unproductive decision-making and offered mechanisms for problem-solving with patients who were encouraged to make realistic appraisals of the costs and benefits of pursuing their grandiose goals. Strategies also focus on the productive potential versus destructive risk ratings to reduce impulsive and reckless behaviours and delay action for a specific period of time (Newman et al., 2002). Other techniques include differentiating normal good mood from hypomania, collaborative reality testing with trusted others, foreseeing negative consequences of behaviours through imagery, stimulus control and thought monitoring.

Psychotic thoughts experienced by patients with bipolar disorder are approached using similar strategies to those employed with schizophrenic patients (Chadwick & Lowe, 1994; Kingdon & Turkington, 1994). Reality testing (when delusions are present) is considered to improve decision-making thereby breaking the vicious cycle of symptoms. Cognitive distraction techniques include shifting attention and the suppression of unwanted thoughts, while behavioural techniques include distraction through either passive or active diversion and increased or reduced activity levels.

Module 6: Identifying and Modifying Schemas

These sessions focus on identifying and accessing the patients' core beliefs about themselves, others and the world. Such beliefs and associated affect are accessed through imagery, discussion of current events, past memories, dreams and writings by the patient. The Schema Questionnaire (Young, 1994) is more formally used to identify schemas with common themes of emotional deprivation, dependency, defectiveness and incompetence, unrelenting standards, poor self-discipline or emotional inhibition.

Finally, this module focuses on the specific adaptive styles which patients are currently using in dealing with their bipolar disorder. In particular, attention is drawn to how patients are assimilating past and present experiences into their memories and how meaning is assigned to them. Adaptation to new insights, new relationships with partners and family, old and new friends, work colleagues and new perceptions of themselves are examined and special strengths and inner resources formed. The patient is encouraged to write narratives about their experience of living with bipolar disorder and the effects of the illness on their sense of self and relationships with others. Feelings of confusion, loss, guilt, shame, fear and anger are often expressed.

Evaluation of Cognitive Therapy Enhanced With Emotive Techniques

A randomised controlled trial was conducted to evaluate the modified CT program described in this chapter (Ball et al., 2006). Fifty-two patients with bipolar I and II as per the *Diagnostic and Statistical Manual of*

Mental Disorders (4th ed.; DSM-IV; American Psychiatric Association, 1994) were randomly allocated to a 6-month trial of either CT or treatment-as-usual (TAU), with both treatment groups also receiving mood stabilisers. Outcome measures included relapse rates, dysfunctional attitudes, psychosocial functioning, hopelessness, self-control, and medication adherence. Patients were assessed during treatment by independent raters blind to the patients' group status.

The CT group showed significantly longer time to depressive relapse and lower Beck Depression Inventory (BDI; Beck, Steer, & Brown, 1996) and Mania and Depression Rating Scale (MADRS; Montgomery & Asberg, 1979) scores posttreatment compared to TAU. After controlling for the presence of a (mild) major depressive episode at baseline, a strong trend towards longer time to depressive relapse remained. These findings are similar to previous randomised controlled trials evaluating CT for bipolar disorder, which have also demonstrated reduction in depressive symptoms and prolonged time to relapse at post-treatment (Lam et al., 2005; Scott et al., 2006). Since the CT group did not differ from TAU in medication adherence, this outcome could not simply be attributed to compliance effects. At 12-month follow-up, these between-group differences in depressive symptomatology and relapse were no longer significant.

CT demonstrated significantly greater benefits in dysfunctional attitudes at posttreatment than TAU, with similar trends also for social adjustment and social performance. The relative benefits amongst CT participants in these measures were strongest during active treatment with the significance gradually diminishing as the effect of therapy became more distant. Scores on the Social Performance Scale (SPS; Hurry, Sturt, Bebbington, & Tennant, 1983) continued to approach significance at 6- and 9-months follow-up, but had weakened by follow-up at 12 months. Dysfunctional Attitude Scale (DAS; Weissman, 1979) scores in the CT group remained in the normal range for euthymic patients at both posttreatment and follow-up with no loss of treatment benefits occurring over this period ($F = 0.29$, $df = 1, 24$, $p = .88$), although there were no significant differences or trends compared to TAU after the immediate posttreatment assessment. This suggests the sustainability of attitudinal change once active treatment was withdrawn, although it must be acknowledged that this was no longer superior to the TAU group.

At 12-months follow-up, the CT group showed strong trends (although nonsignificant) towards more effective self-control behaviours and a lower Young Mania Rating Scale (YMRS; Young, Biggs, Ziegler, & Meyer, 1978) score than TAU. This improvement in manic symptoms at follow-up is in accordance with the findings of Lam et al. (2005) and Perry et al. (1999) where the latter study employed cognitive–behavioural techniques to help patients detect early warning signs. Given the small sample size of the current study, these trends are considered noteworthy. At posttreatment, the CT group scored in the 'recovery range' for self-control behaviours and gradually improved until eventually reaching the normal range at 12-months follow-up. In our study, cognitive changes demonstrated on the DAS appeared to precede self-regulatory behavioural change. While several previous trials have included follow-up data (Lam et al., 2005; Perry et al., 1999; Scott et al., 2006), this is the first study to demonstrate sustained benefits in dysfunctional attitudes 12 months after therapy has been withdrawn.

Although requiring more substantial evidence, it is possible that the efficacy of CT in eliciting certain benefits at posttreatment and to a lesser degree at follow-up, is partly due to the addition of emotive techniques to the CT armoury. As discussed, emotive techniques are known to be powerful in accessing maladaptive beliefs and constructing more substantial changes. It has been proposed that cognitive and attitudinal changes depend on a certain level of affective experience and emotive techniques are sometimes necessary to help with new learning and unlearning. Emotive techniques may be effecting emotional and cognitive changes leading to enduring changes in the patients' deeper schematic structures and subsequent behaviours. To understand more fully the contribution of these techniques in enhancing cognitive–behavioural techniques, it would be necessary to directly compare CT with and without emotive techniques.

A strength of our study was the use of a clearly defined treatment design which increased internal validity and offered a marked distinction between treatment conditions. The rating of treatment fidelity enabled us to demonstrate high therapist adherence to this particular treatment intervention. However, our study had several limitations. The small sample size and relatively large number of dependent variables restricted the power to demonstrate differences between the groups. Furthermore, no control was made for the nonspecific effects of treatment.

Conclusions

The recurring and often extreme nature of bipolar disorder inevitably affects the individual's capacity to establish a stable life with regard to education, work and long-term relationships. Managing these disruptions and losses, in addition to the stigma of the illness, requires particular therapeutic skills. Cognitive and emotional adjustments which facilitate functional recovery are often overlooked in the traditional treatments of bipolar disorder. CT enhanced with emotive techniques extends beyond traditional cognitive and behavioural interventions to facilitate the expression of emotions, such as anger and grief associated with loss of the healthy self. Results of our randomised controlled trial offer preliminary support to the feasibility of this approach for patients with bipolar disorder.

References

American Psychiatric Association. (1994). *Diagnostic and statistical manual of mental disorders* (4th ed.). Washington, DC: Author.

Ball, J., Mitchell, P., Corry, J., Skillecorn, A., Smith, M., & Malhi, G. (2006). A randomised controlled trial of cognitive therapy for bipolar disorder: Focus on long-term change. *Journal of Clinical Psychiatry, 67,* 277–286.

Ball, J., Mitchell, P., Malhi, G., Skillecorn, A., & Smith, M. (2003). Schema-focused cognitive therapy for bipolar disorder: Reducing vulnerability to relapse through attitudinal change. *Australian and New Zealand Journal of Psychiatry, 37,* 41–48.

Beck, A.T., & Freeman, A. (1990). *Cognitive therapy of personality disorders.* New York, Guilford.

Beck, A.T., Steer, R.A., & Brown, G.K. (1996). *Beck Depression Inventory* (2nd ed.). San Antonio, TX: The Psychological Corporation.

Chadwick, P., & Lowe, C. (1994). A cognitive approach to modifying delusions. *Behavior Research and Therapy, 32,* 355–367.

Greenberg, L.S. (2002). *Emotion focused therapy.* Washington, DC: American Psychological Association.

Greenberg, L.S., & Watson, J. (1998). Experiential therapy of depression; differential effects of client-centered relationships conditions and active experiential interventions. *Psychological Research, 8,* 210–224.

Hurry, J., Sturt, R., Bebbington, P., & Tennant, C. (1983). Sociodemographic associations with social disablement in a community sample. *Social Psychiatry, 18,* 113–121.

Kingdon, D.G., & Turkington, D. (1994). *Cognitive-behavioral therapy of schizophrenia.* New York: Guilford Press.

Lam, D.H., Hayward, P., Watkins, E.R., Wright, K., & Sham, P. (2005). Relapse prevention in patients with bipolar disorder: Cognitive therapy outcome after 2 years. *American Journal of Psychiatry, 162*(2), 324–329.

Lam, D.H., Jones, S.H., Haywood, P., & Bright, J.A. (1999). *Cognitive therapy for bipolar disorder: A therapist's guide to concepts, methods and practice.* Chichester, UK: John Wiley & Sons.

Lam, D.H., Watkins, E.R., & Haywood, P. (2003). A randomized controlled trial of cognitive therapy for relapse prevention for bipolar affective disorder: Outcome at the first year. *Archives of General Psychiatry, 60,* 145–152.

Lam, D., Wright, K., & Smith, N. (2004). Dysfunctional assumptions in bipolar disorder. *Journal of Affective Disorders, 79,* 193–199.

Layden, M.A., Newman, C.F., Freeman, A., & Morse (1993). *Cognitive therapy for borderline personality disorder*. Boston, MA: Allyn and Bacon.

Leahy, R.L., & Beck, A.T., (1988). Cognitive therapy, depression and mania. In A. Georgotas & R. Cancro, *Depression and mania* (pp. 517–537). New York: Elsevoir-Science Publishing.

Little, M., Jordens, C., & Paul, K. (2001). *Surviving survival: Life after cancer*. Sydney, Australia: Choice.

Montgomery, S.A., & Asberg, M. (1979). A new depression scale designed to be sensitive to change. *British Journal of Psychiatry, 134*, 382–389.

Newman, C.F., Leahy, R.L., Beck, A.T., Reilly-Harrington, N.A., & Gyulai, L. (2002). *Bipolar disorder: A cognitive therapy approach*. Washington, DC: American Psychological Association.

Perry, A., Tarrier, N., Morriss, R., McCarthy, E., & Limb, K. (1999). Randomised controlled trial of efficacy of teaching patients with bipolar disorder to identify early symptoms of relapse and obtain treatment. *British Medical Journal, 318*, 49–53.

Scott, J., Paykel, E., Morriss, R., Bentall, R., Kinderman, P., Abbott, R., et al. (2006). Cognitive behavior therapy for severe and recurrent bipolar disorders: A randomized trial. *British Journal of Psychiatry, 188*, 313–320.

Scott, J., & Pope, M. (2003). Cognitive styles in individuals with bipolar disorder. *Psychological Medicine, 33*, 1081–1088.

Weissman, A.N. (1979). The Dysfunctional Attitude Scale: A validation scale. *Dissertation Abstract International, 40*, 1389B–1390B.

Winters, K.C., & Neale, J.M. (1985). Mania and low self-esteem. *Journal of Abnormal Psychology, 94*, 282–290.

Young, J.E. (1994). *Cognitive therapy for personality disorders: A schema-focused approach*. Sarasota, FL: Professional Resource Press.

Young, R.C., Biggs, J.T., Ziegler, V.E., & Meyer, (1978). A rating scale for mania: Reliability, validity and sensitivity. *British Journal of Psychiatry, 133*, 429–435.

Zaretsky, A.E., Segal, Z.V., & Gemar, M. (1999). Cognitive therapy for bipolar depression: A pilot study. *The Canadian Journal of Psychiatry, 44*, 491–494.

CHAPTER 12

Enhancing Outcomes in the Treatment of Generalised Anxiety Disorder

Maree Abbott

Generalised Anxiety Disorder: Overview

Generalised anxiety disorder (GAD) has a lifetime prevalence of 5% (Kessler, McGonagle, et al., 1994; Wittchen, Zhao, Kessler, & Eaton, 1994) and is characterised by excessive and uncontrollable worry about a range of life areas including family, relationships, finances, health problems and world events. Thus, the content of worries for people with GAD can include both social and physical threat themes. Individuals suffering from GAD also report a number of associated symptoms including feelings of irritability, fatigue, muscle tension, sleep problems and concentration difficulties (American Psychiatric Association [APA], 1994). Research has shown that most sufferers do not seek help from mental health professionals and of those that do, the delay in help seeking is marked, being often more than a decade post onset (Olfson, Kessler, Berglund, & Lin, 1998). This is particularly concerning given that GAD has an early age of onset and a chronic course and is unlikely to remit without substantial treatment (Noyes et al., 1992). GAD also presents a significant financial burden to the community, indexed by its high health care costs, and has the unfortunate status of ranking in the top 12 'diseases' for disability adjusted life years lost (Mathers, Vos, & Stevenson, 1999). In fact, in the absence of comorbidity, GAD and major depressive disorder have been shown to be equally disabling (Kessler, Dupont, Berglund, & Wittchen, 1999).

Unfortunately, there has been a growing body of data showing that our treatments for GAD are not as effective as we had hoped. Meta-analyses of cognitive–behavioural interventions for GAD have found that the average effect size for our best evidence-based treatments is 0.7 and the average attrition rate is 11.4% (Gould, Safren, Washington, & Otto, 2004). In fact, a leading researcher in the field recently said that 'after 16 years of concerted effort, applications of behavioral and cognitive therapy techniques for treating this anxiety disorder continue to fail to bring about 50% of our clients back to within normal degrees of anxiety' (Borkovec, 2002, p. 76). In addition, treatment outcomes have not improved by spending more time on individual treatment components (Durham et al., 1994). These data suggest that there is significant scope for the development and evaluation of new approaches for helping people with GAD. Increases in our understanding of the processes underlying and maintaining worry and generalised anxiety has led to the development of new cognitive–behavioural treatment (CBT) programs (e.g., Leahy, 2005; Rygh & Sanderson, 2004). This chapter describes the rationale and content for each of the treatment modules in our cognitive–behavioural treatment for GAD (Abbott & Kemp, 2003). In addition, mindfulness training for GAD is discussed and some results from our randomised controlled trial comparing mindfulness training with CBT for GAD are described.

Cognitive–Behavioural Treatment for Generalised Anxiety Disorder

Our Excessive Worry Program adopts a CBT approach and includes both therapist and client manuals for the treatment of GAD (Abbott & Kemp, 2003). We take a threat expectancy approach to understanding and treating GAD, which means that we attempt to redress the full range of beliefs driving anxiety and associated safety strategy use, which are in place to prevent perceived negative outcomes. We also emphasise the importance of the therapeutic relationship and acknowledge the particular importance of interpersonal engagement in therapy for this client group (Newman, Castonguay, Borkovec, & Molnar, 2004). The program includes eight modules; to date we have conducted the program in a group format of six to eight clients over 12 (3-hour long) sessions. The program is also used to treat individual clients with GAD and some clinical units have adapted the modules to incorporate a session format of 9 half-days. Most notably, we have *not* included some key elements of other 'stress reduction' programs, such as relaxation training, structured problem-solving or time management. Each module in our treatment is specifically designed to address unhelpful maintaining cognitions. The application of these strategies is not to help clients relax per se, but rather to teach that anxiety is not dangerous or intolerable and that the beliefs that trigger and maintain anxiety are unrealistic; anxiety reduction is argued to occur as a necessary consequence of reductions in threat appraisal. Each of the modules is described below, including an additional module outlining mindfulness training techniques.

Module 1a ■ 'I Worry All the Time and I Am So Stressed': Formulating a Collaborative Model

Perhaps the most important aspect of the early phase of any CBT program is psychoeducation regarding worry and anxiety and the collaborative development of an individualised formulation. These areas are covered in the first phase of the program so that clients fully understand the factors maintaining their worry and anxiety, the role and function of anxiety and the ways in which CBT can help impact on beliefs that drive anxiety and associated safety behaviours. The rationale and practice of thought monitoring is introduced, including the phrasing of worries as predictions.

Module 1b ■ 'What Will Happen if I Don't Worry?': The Pros and Cons of Change

Module 1 also addresses issues related to achieving change. Clients are asked to assess their reasons for wanting change and the benefits of achieving changes in worry and anxiety. Clients then examine two alternate futures, one where desired changes have occurred and the other without change. Lastly, potential obstacles to change are considered (e.g., self-expectations, life pressures, motivation), as well as possible drawbacks to change (e.g., change to a relationship).

Module 2 ■ 'My Fear Will Come True, It Will Be Really Bad and I Won't Be Able to Cope': Overestimation of Threat in GAD

People with GAD overestimate both the likelihood of threatening events occurring and the cost (or consequence) of negative outcomes. In addition, people with GAD underestimate their ability to cope should a negative outcome occur. It is adaptive for people to experience fear in the presence of actual threat and to maintain vigilance and experience anxiety in anticipation of danger. However, GAD sufferers are chronically vigilant for threat, find it difficult to realistically appraise perceived danger and doubt their ability to cope with negative outcomes. More typically, people with GAD find themselves engaged in a process of catastrophising that feels out of control.

Module 2 teaches realistic thinking skills to help clients (a) understand the negative predictions that they make (often automatically), and (b) to realistically appraise the probability and consequences of their negative predictions. We encourage clients to realistically evaluate their ability to cope with and 'survive' even distressing events like the diagnosis of a serious disease, the death of a loved one or being alone. While anxiety-provoking and difficult, this is an important skill for clients — they engage with the notion that time continues even after distressing events. Addressing the perceived cost of worries is particularly important for fears that are highly unlikely to occur but that would be objectively diffi-cult (i.e., low probability, high cost fears), such as contracting cancer. These types of fears are common in GAD and while clients can readily acknowledge that the prediction is unlikely to occur, they nonetheless worry excessively about any possibility. The negative predictions made by GAD sufferers can also be multilayered. For example, one client reported trying to stay uninvolved in workplace conflict but reported constant interruptions from colleagues (situation) and worried about not being able to get her work done (negative prediction). She was easily able to challenge this fear as her work was always completed. The use of Socratic questioning was helpful in isolating the nature of her fear and assump-tions more fully — 'I'll lose my temper when provoked ... if I am aggres-sive, then I'll lose my job ... and if I lose my job, then my family and I will be destitute ... I won't be able to cope'. Thus the 'trigger/situation' in this worry scenario is actually the experience of anger, which the client believes she cannot control, and any lack of control over angry emotions is predicted to produce further negative consequences. Realistic thinking skills can then be practised for each aspect of this catastrophising sequence. When helping clients gather evidence regarding their capacity to cope with difficult situations, therapists should be mindful of perfec-tionistic beliefs about coping, that is, the unrealistic belief that one must cope without distress or difficulty. Realistic thinking is an essential foun-dation tool of the program.

Module 3 ■ 'Worry Is Harmful to Me': Negative Meta-Beliefs About Worry

Wells (1995, 1997) highlighted the important role that negative meta-cognitive beliefs play in the maintenance of GAD. In an attempt to mean-ingfully understand their symptoms, sufferers often appraise the process of worry as harmful to themselves or others. For example, beliefs that excessive worrying is harmful, uncontrollable, indicates weakness of character or that one is 'going crazy', typically activates 'worrying about worry'. The net result is that clients increase the frequency and severity of their worrying, as they are now worrying about the process of worry in addition to other negative predictions. In addition, the belief that worry is harmful triggers a range of other unhelpful coping strategies such as monitoring one's thoughts, trying not to worry and safety strategy use.

Module 3 teaches clients to (1) identify their negative beliefs about worry, (2) realistically evaluate these beliefs and (3) to conduct behavioural experiments that directly test their beliefs. Several authors have now suggested a range of behavioural experiments for use with negative beliefs about worry (e.g., Bennett-Levy et al., 2004; Wells, 1997). For example, a test of the prediction that 'my worry is uncontrollable' may include the decision to deliberately worry as much as possible for 10–15 minutes. After this time clients should decide to postpone further worry until later in the day. Clients can then evaluate their experiment; if they were able to put off worry for part or whole of the time, then they are able to control their worry more than they previously believed. This example shares some similarities with 'worry time' but differs from this strategy in that it explicitly reframes the idea of postponing worry as a behavioural experiment. Behavioural experiments are often a powerful means of achieving cognitive change.

Module 4 ■ 'I Can't Stand Thinking About This in Detail ... I Won't Be Able to Cope': Processing Worry Scenarios Affectively

People with GAD worry a lot, but they do not necessarily think through their fears in step-by-step detail, instead preferring to avoid focusing directly on worst case scenarios and associated emotions. Indeed, emotional avoidance and maladaptive processing of emotions is considered central to understanding GAD. For example, Borkovec, Alcaine and Behar (2004) argue that worry acts as a form of cognitive avoidance that inhibits negative affect through the automatic/unconscious inhibition of imaginal processing. This in turn negatively reinforces the use of worry as an emotion regulation strategy, which dampens anxiety in the short term. More recently, Mennin, Heimberg, Turk and Fresco (2002) suggested that people with GAD have difficulties in emotion regulation — including appraising emotions negatively and displaying poor tolerance for, and avoidance of, emotional experience.

Imaginal exposure techniques have been used in the treatment of GAD to help clients redress their fears, to process feared scenarios and their aftermath in detail and to enhance tolerance for difficult emotions (e.g., anxiety, loss). Module 4 addresses emotional avoidance and imaginal exposure to 'high cost' feared outcomes using a variant of Pennebaker's emotional writing technique, which we have called 'worry stories'. There is now a large body of evidence showing the benefits of emotional writing for stress, trauma, health worries and adjustment problems (e.g., Furer, Walker, & Freeston, 2001; Pennebaker, Kiecolt-Glaser, & Glaser, 1988). Clients are asked to write about their fears in sequence as if they were happening, making their story as real and emotional as possible, and to continue their story about how they cope after the feared outcome has occurred. Worry stories may impact in a number of ways — including helping clients to process their fears without avoiding; revising beliefs about the probability, cost and coping with feared outcomes; increasing tolerance of negative affect; improving insight into underlying issues and challenging magical thinking.

Module 5 ■ 'Uncertainty Is Bad ... I Must Stay in Control': Avoidance and Safety Strategy Use

Theoretical models of GAD have posited a central role for intolerance of uncertainty in the maintenance of GAD (Dugas, Buhr, & Lacouceur, 2004, Dugas et al., 2003). People with GAD fear and avoid situations which are perceived as potentially dangerous and attempt to control the occurrence of potential negative outcomes when faced with uncertainty. In addition to maximising control, people with GAD use a range of associated safety strategies like reassurance seeking, perfectionistic behaviour, task avoidance, constant busyness, over planning and preparation, cognitive distraction, emotional suppression and taking too much responsibility, among others. While avoidance and safety strategies use is reinforced in the short term by decreasing anxiety (and increased perceived control), these behaviours only serve to maintain anxiety in the long term by preventing the disconfirmation of negative beliefs and assumptions. Thus, Module 5 first focuses on isolating and addressing the patterns of avoidance and safety strategy use. Clients receive psychoeducation about the role of avoidance in the maintenance of anxiety and learn about the principles and impact of graded exposure as a way of addressing the myriad of avoidance and safety behaviours. These stepladders often resemble exposure and response prevention hierarchies such as stepladders aimed at 'being less controlling'. Exposure stepladders are also used to help clients control their emotions less, face triggers for worry and situations they avoid.

Module 6 ■ 'Worry Helps Me': Positive Meta-Beliefs About Worry

Wells (1997) also suggested that people with GAD adopt worry as a potentially useful strategy for coping with perceived negative outcomes.

People with GAD tend to report three main categories of positive meta-beliefs: (1) beliefs about the worry process (e.g., 'worry helps me prepare for danger', 'worry helps me to get things done', 'worry stops me from making mistakes'), (2) beliefs related to magical thinking tendencies (e.g., 'worry stops bad things from happening') and (3) beliefs that worrying is a positive self-characteristic (e.g., 'worrying about others means I am a caring person'). Clients who hold positive beliefs about worry strongly (either by adopting worry as a strategy or as a post-hoc justification for 'worry behaviour') will find that these beliefs represent an obstacle to change.

Positive metabeliefs about worry are addressed similarly to negative metabeliefs, that is, through the application of realistic thinking skills and behavioural experiments (see Wells, 1997). In our experience, it is most helpful to address these beliefs after the successful completion of earlier modules. In particular, challenging the belief that 'worrying makes me a kind person' too early in treatment is especially difficult for clients, as they identify strongly with worry as a central aspect of themselves and fear who they will be without this trait. Cognitive challenging and behavioural experiments help clients to consider whether characteristics like 'caring' and 'worrier' necessarily co-occur. Therapists also challenge the appraisal that worry is a helpful strategy for solving problems by distinguishing true problem-solving from worry and catastrophising. Behavioural experiments are introduced to test beliefs that 'worry helps me get things done' or 'stops bad things from happening'. These positive predictions can be directly evaluated by deliberately worrying while trying to do a task on one occasion and not worrying at all on another. The outcome of the experiment can then be assessed, that is, did the client work more efficiently on the day they worried or did the feared outcome occur on the day they failed to worry? Clients may also find it helpful to consider the contradiction in holding both positive and negative metabeliefs.

Module 7 ■ 'The World is Dangerous and I Am Bad': Negative Assumptions and Underlying Beliefs About Oneself and the World

Underlying (core) beliefs and schemata are central driving factors in cognitive–behavioural models of anxiety disorders. For example, anxiety is experienced when clients perceive that there is the potential for negative core beliefs to be confirmed (e.g., an exam may be particularly anxiety-provoking if the results have the potential to confirm fears of inadequacy). The negative core beliefs about the self of GAD clients include beliefs that one is worthless, vulnerable, a failure/inadequate and weak or defective. The approach taken to elicit, challenge and shift these assumptions and beliefs closely follows that of Greenberger and Padesky (1995) and is conducted over the last third of the program. This module includes psychoeducation about the role of core beliefs in the development and maintenance of anxiety. The 'downward arrow' technique is used to help clients identify their negative self-belief(s) and these beliefs are then challenged by asking clients to examine contradictory evidence. A series of worksheets is used to help clients link their unhelpful assumptions (e.g., everyone must like me otherwise ...) to their negative core beliefs (e.g., I am unlovable) and unhelpful behaviours (e.g., approval seeking). Clients then examine the ways in which their underlying beliefs impact on their lives (e.g., relationships, career, family, health, self-care). Graded hierarchies, goal setting and behavioural experiments are then designed to help clients 'act as if' their underlying beliefs are untrue with the aim of developing more helpful beliefs and behaviours.

Some preliminary research points to the importance of addressing interpersonal relationships for people with GAD as many perceive their important relationships to be moderately to significantly impaired (Pincus & Borkovec, 1994, as cited in Turk, Heimberg, & Mennin, 2004). In fact, the severity of interpersonal problems predicts poor end state functioning at long-term follow-up (Borkovec, Newman, Lytle, & Pincus, 2002). Interpersonal styles that may feature in GAD include avoidant ways of relating to others, interpersonal coldness and overly nurturant and intrusive styles. Unhelpful ways of relating are also addressed clinically in this module by helping clients to gain insight into the behaviour patterns associated with the activation of negative underlying schemas. New ways of relating are then approached and practised with role plays, assertiveness training, stepladders and behavioural experiments. Further details about interpersonal therapy for GAD can be found in Newman et al. (2004) and relevant strategies are presented in Rygh and Sanderson (2004).

Module 8 ■ 'What If My Worry Feels Out of Control Again': Appropriate Planning for the Future

Module 8 is presented in the final session and includes relapse prevention strategies. Clients are asked to reflect on their progress throughout the program. Each component of the program is summarised and clients are asked to set continuing goals that they would like to achieve over the next months. The nature of progress and setbacks is discussed and normalised, and clients are asked to think about potential setbacks realistically and to plan skills and strategies that would be useful should a setback occur.

Additional Module ■ Addressing Experiential Avoidance and Encouraging Present Focused Attention Using Mindfulness Training

Mindfulness training is a meditation-based practice that advocates approaching one's experience by 'paying attention in a particular way; on purpose, in the present moment, and non-judgmentally' (Kabat-Zinn, 1994, p. 4). The goal is to develop a new relationship with thoughts and feelings through direct experience. Clients are encouraged to be curious about their internal processes, experiences and responses and to gain insight into these as a means of facilitating understanding and choice. Clients practise being aware of their internal experiences without controlling them, such as noting any experience of worry and anxiety without struggling, reacting or engaging with anxious thoughts and feelings. This is a particularly difficult approach for people with GAD, who are often preoccupied with scenarios of future-focused threat or the attempted avoidance of distressing thoughts and feelings.

We have used the mindfulness training program for GAD written by Huxter (2006); see also Rygh and Sanderson (2004) and Segal, Williams, and Teasdale (2002). This program is written from a Buddhist perspective to understanding unhelpful patterns of responding to internal experience (though it is not religious). The program includes a range of meditation exercises and instructions for practising mindfulness of the breath, mindfulness of thoughts and painful emotions as well as lovingkindness meditations, among others. These meditation exercises are practised in session and for homework and the client's experience of these exercises is discussed. Each meditation has a primary object (e.g., breath), which clients return to when they notice that their focus has shifted. Mindfulness training is another approach for addressing avoidance of thoughts and emotions, is a form of response prevention for safety strategies and also indirectly challenges metabeliefs and core beliefs. Meditation practice also promotes the ability to focus and shift attention, improves concentration skills and provides a relaxation response. Mindfulness training has been shown to reduce symptoms of stress and has received support as an intervention for preventing relapse for sufferers of chronic depression (Miller, Fletcher, & Kabat-Zinn, 1995; Segal et al., 2002; Teasdale, Segal, & Williams, 1995). There is also some preliminary case series data to support using mindfulness in the treatment of GAD (Roemer & Orsillo, 2002).

Comparing CBT With Mindfulness Training for GAD

Over the last 3 years we have been conducting a randomised control trial comparing CBT with mindfulness training (MFT) and a waiting list control group for GAD (Abbott, Rapee, & Stapinski, 2007). The two active treatments were led by experienced clinical psychologists in a group format of approximately six clients; sessions were conducted on a weekly basis over 3 months and the treatments did not involve medication. Participants were assessed with structured diagnostic interviews (Anxiety Disorders Interview Schedule for DSM-IV; ADIS-IV; DiNardo, Brown, & Barlow, 1994) and a range of self-report symptom measures at pretreatment/waitlist, posttreatment/waitlist, 6 months after treatment and 18 months after treatment.

Participants and Recruitment

A total of 100 participants were recruited to the project over the 3 years, representing a large sample in the area of GAD research. Participants were referred from general practitioners (GPs) and other mental health professionals, or self-referred from word of mouth and advertisements, articles and interviews about the program. Most participants in the program were female (75%) and the mean age of participants was 37 years. High rates of comorbid psychological disorders were identified among participants, particularly for other anxiety disorders (most notably social phobia) and major depressive disorder.

Treatment Effectiveness

Treatment outcome was assessed across a range of variables, including clinician ratings of diagnostic severity using the ADIS-IV, the proportion of participants in each condition who were diagnosis-free following treatment, and scores on self-report symptoms measures. Only a summary of the full results is presented here (see Abbott et al., 2007, for a full description). Demographic characteristics were comparable across conditions. In addition, attrition rates were remarkably low and consistent across groups, with 10% of participants discontinuing the program. The active treatments were also comparable in terms of participants' view of their relationship with their therapist, cohesion with their group and the level of confidence they had in their allocated treatment program.

Figure 1 shows the ADIS-IV diagnostic severity ratings for GAD (using the 0 to 8 scale) at pretreatment, posttreatment/waitlist and at 6-month follow-up for each group. As expected, the waitlist condition showed no change from pre to posttreatment. The two active treatments showed comparable change with significant reductions in symptomatology from pre- to posttreatment. Most notably, the mean GAD severity score for both active treatments was in the nonclinical range. In addition,

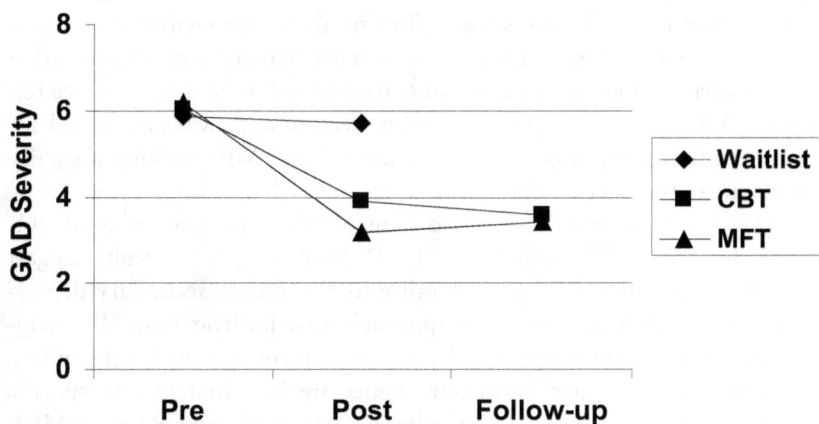

Figure 1
Mean diagnostic severity for GAD at pretreatment, posttreatment and follow-up for the three groups.

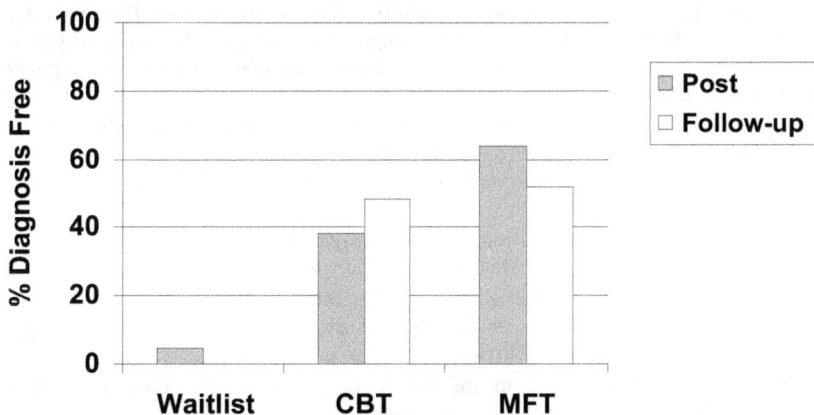

Figure 2
Diagnosis-free rates for WL, CBT and MFT groups at posttreatment and follow-up.

treatment gains were maintained at 6-month follow-up. The same pattern of data was observed from Penn State Worry Questionnaire scores.

Figure 2 shows the proportion of participants who were diagnosis-free for each group at post treatment and at 6-month follow-up for the active treatments. Very few (4.3%) of the waitlist group had diagnosis-free status following their 12-week waiting period. Significantly more participants were shown to be diagnosis-free following treatment relative to waitlist. However, an important difference between active treatments emerged, that is, a greater proportion of participants were found to be diagnosis-free following MFT compared to CBT. This pattern of data was also found for participants' self-reported depression scores, with MFT making a significantly greater impact on depression levels than CBT.

The results of our randomised control trial have shown good outcomes for both CBT and MFT for GAD. Moreover, these results suggest that the effects of MFT may generalise to also reduce secondary depressive symptomatology. These two approaches are far from mutually exclusive and broaden the range and depth of treatment options for therapists. Understanding whether particular clients are best matched to specific treatments, and assessments of the impact of combining CBT with MFT, will help to further enhance evidence-based treatments for the many sufferers of GAD.

References

Abbott, M.J., & Kemp, N. (2003). *Cognitive–Behavioural Group Treatment for Excessive Worry: A Twelve-Session Program — Therapist Manual and Client Workbook*. Macquarie University, Sydney: Macquarie University Anxiety Research Unit.

Abbott, M.J., Rapee, R.M., & Stapinski, L.A. (2007). *Comparing the effectiveness of enhanced cognitive–behavioural therapy with mindfulness training for generalised anxiety disorder: Results from a randomised controlled trial.* Manuscript in preparation.

American Psychiatric Association. (1994). *Diagnostic and statistical manual of mental disorders* (4th ed.). Washington, DC: Author.

Bennett-Levy, J., Butler, G., Fennell, M., Hackmann, A., Mueller, M., & Westbrook, D. (2004). *Oxford guide to behavioural experiments in cognitive therapy*. Oxford: Oxford University Press.

Borkovec, T.D. (2002). Life in the future versus life in the present. *Clinical Psychology: Science and Practice, 9,* 76–80.

Borkovec, T.D., Alcaine, O., & Behar, E. (2004). Avoidance theory of worry and generalized anxiety disorder. In R.G. Heimberg, C.L. Turk, & D.S. Mennin (Eds.), *Generalized anxiety disorder: Advances in research and practice*. New York: Guilford.

Borkovec, T.D., Newman, M., Lytle, R., & Pincus, A. (2002). A component analysis of cognitive–behavioral therapy for generalized anxiety disorder and the role of interpersonal problems. *Journal of Consulting and Clinical Psychology, 70,* 288–298.

DiNardo, P.A., Brown, T.A., & Barlow, D.H. (1994). *Anxiety Disorders Interview Schedule for DSM-IV*. San Antonio, TX: The Psychological Corporation, Harcourt Brace and Company.

Dugas, M., Buhr, K., & Lacouceur, R. (2004). The role of intolerance of uncertainty in etiology and maintenance. In R.G. Heimberg, C.L. Turk, & D.S. Mennin (Eds.), *Generalized anxiety disorder: Advances in research and practice* (pp. 143-163). New York: Guilford.

Dugas, M., Ladouceur, R., Leger, E., Freeston, M., Langlois, F., Provencher, M.D., et al. (2003). Group cognitive–behavioral therapy for generalized anxiety disorder: Treatment outcome and long-term follow-up. *Journal of Consulting and Clinical Psychology, 71*, 821–825.

Durham, R.C., Murphy, T.J., Allan, R., Richard, K., Treliving, L., & Fenton, G.W. (1994). Cognitive therapy, analytic psychotherapy and anxiety management training for generalized anxiety disorder. *British Journal of Psychiatry, 165*, 315–323.

Furer, P., Walker, J.R., & Freeston, M.H. (2001). Approaches to individual and group cognitive-behavioral therapy. In G.J.G. Asmundson, S. Taylor, & B.J. Cox (Eds.), *Health anxiety: Clinical and research perspectives on hypochondriasis and related conditions* (pp. 161-192). New York: Wiley.

Gould, R.M., Safren, S., Washington, D., & Otto, M. (2004). A meta-analytic review of cognitive–behavioural treatments. In R.G. Heimberg, C.L. Turk, & D.S. Mennin (Eds.), *Generalized anxiety disorder: Advances in research and practice* (pp. 248-264). New York: Guilford.

Greenberger, D., & Padesky, C. (1995). *Mind over mood*. Guilford: New York.

Huxter, M. (2006). *Mindfulness and a path of understanding. A workbook for the release from stress, anxiety and depression.* Manuscript submitted for publication. (Available from malhuxter@bigpond.com).

Kabat-Zinn, J. (1994). *Wherever you go, there you are: Mindfulness meditation for everyday life.* London: Piatkus.

Kessler, R.C., McGonagle, K.A., Zhao, S., Nelson, C.B., Hughes, M., Eshleman, S., et al. (1994). Lifetime and 12-month prevalence of DSM-III-R psychiatric disorders in the United States: Results from the National Comorbidity Survey. *Archives of General Psychiatry, 51*, 8–19.

Kessler, R.C., Dupont, R.L., Berglund, P., & Wittchen, H. (1999). Impairments in pure and comorbid generalized anxiety disorder and major depression at 12 months in two national surveys. *American Journal of Psychiatry, 156*, 1915–1923.

Leahy, R.L. (2005). *The worry cure: Seven steps to stop worry from stopping you.* New York: Harmony Books.

Mennin, D., Heimberg, R., Turk, C., & Fresco, D. (2002). Applying an emotional regulation framework to integrative approaches to generalized anxiety disorder. *Clinical Psychology: Science and Practice, 9*, 85–90.

Mathers, C., Vos, T., & Stevenson, C. (1999). *The burden of disease and injury in Australia* (AIHW cat. no. PHE 17). Canberra, Australia: Australian Bureau of Statistics.

Miller, J., Fletcher, K., & Kabat-Zinn, J. (1995). Three year follow up and clinical implications of a mindfulness-based stress reduction intervention in the treatment of anxiety disorders. *General Hospital Psychiatry, 17*, 192–200.

Newman, M., Castonguay, L., Borkovec, T., & Molnar, C. (2004). Integrative psychotherapy. In R.G. Heimberg, C.L. Turk, & D.S. Mennin (Eds.), *Generalized anxiety disorder: Advances in research and practice* (pp. 320-350). New York: Guilford.

Noyes, R., Woodman, C., Garvey, M.J., Cook, B.L., Suelzer, M., Clancy, J., et al. (1992). Generalized anxiety disorder versus panic disorder: Distinguishing characteristics and patterns of comorbidity. *Journal of Nervous and Mental Disease, 180*, 369–370.

Olfson, M., Kessler, R.C., Berglund, P.A., & Lin, E. (1998). Psychiatric disorder onset and first treatment contact in the United States and Ontario. *American Journal of Psychiatry, 155*, 1415–1422.

Pennebaker, J., Kiecolt-Glaser, J., & Glaser, R. (1988). Disclosure of traumas and immune function: Health implications for psychotherapy. *Journal of Consulting and Clinical Psychology, 56*, 239–245.

Roemer, L., & Orsillo, S.M. (2002). Expanding our conceptualization of and treatment for generalized anxiety disorder: Integrating mindfulness/acceptance-based approaches with existing cognitive–behavioral models. *Clinical Psychology: Science and Practice, 9*, 54–68.

Rygh, J., & Sanderson, W. (2004). *Treating generalized anxiety disorder*. New York: Guilford.

Segal, Z., Williams, J.M.G., & Teasdale, J.D. (2002). *Mindfulness-based cognitive therapy for depression*. New York: Guilford.

Teasdale, J.D., Segal, Z., & Williams, J.M. (1995). How does cognitive therapy prevent depressive relapse and why should attentional control (mindfulness) training help? *Behaviour Research and Therapy, 33*, 25–39.

Turk, C., Heimberg, R., & Mennin, D. (2004). Assessment. In R.G. Heimberg, C.L. Turk, & D.S. Mennin (Eds.), *Generalized anxiety disorder: Advances in research and practice* (pp. 219-247). New York: Guilford.

Wells, A. (1995). Meta-cognition and worry: A cognitive model of generalized anxiety disorder. *Behavioural and Cognitive Psychotherapy, 23*, 301–320.

Wells, A. (1997). *Cognitive therapy of anxiety disorders*. Chichester, UK: Wiley.

Wittchen, H.U., Zhao, S., Kessler, R.C., & Eaton, W.W. (1994). DSM-III-R generalized anxiety disorder in the National Comorbidity Survey. *Archives of General Psychiatry, 51*, 355–364.

CHAPTER 13

Can Motivational Enhancement Therapy Improve a Cognitive Behaviourally Based Inpatient Program for Eating Disorders?

Helen Y. Dean, Stephen W. Touyz, Elizabeth Rieger and Christopher E. Thornton

Inpatient Treatment for Eating Disorders

There are currently numerous theories that purport to explain eating disorders in the literature and hence a multitude of treatment strategies and treatment settings (e.g., outpatient, day patient, inpatient) have been proposed. Touyz and Beumont (1991) suggest that patients with anorexia nervosa (AN) may need to be hospitalised for a number of medical reasons including low body weight or an abrupt weight loss, abnormalities in heart and/or liver function, abnormal biochemistry and haematology test results, marked dehydration and hypotension. Patients with bulimia nervosa (BN) may also be hospitalised if there are medical complications, if their bingeing and purging is extremely frequent, or due to concerning psychological comorbidity (e.g., major depression).

There has been a move away from strict and rigid behavioural programs with the suggestion that more flexible inpatient programs can achieve equivalent results (Dalle Grave, Bartocci, Todisco, Pantano, & Bosello, 1993; National Institute for Health and Clinical Excellence [NICE], 2004; Touyz, Beumont, & Dunn, 1987). Despite this endorsement, only a few studies have assessed symptomatic change over short inpatient admissions using more lenient approaches, in which the primary focus is on shaping and positively reinforcing appropriate behaviours, rather than constantly punishing patients for inappropriate behaviours. Difficulties encountered in these studies include a number of patients discharging prematurely against medical advice (Treat et al., 2005), a majority of patients classified as having a 'poor' outcome at 1-year post-hospitalisation (Ro, Martinsen, Hoffart, & Risenvinge, 2004), and more favourable outcome during admission being related to less favourable outcome during the follow-up period (Lowe, Davis, Annunziato, & Lucks, 2003). Thus, conclusions drawn from the current literature suggest that the rates of both short- and long- term recovery and treatment adherence associated with these inpatient programs are unacceptably low.

Cognitive–Behaviour Therapy for Eating Disorders

Most inpatient eating disorder programs include psychological therapy as a major treatment component. The most widespread psychological treatment for eating disorders is cognitive–behaviour therapy (CBT). Generally, this involves a specific form of CBT which focuses on the interaction between overvalued ideas regarding weight and shape, associated maintaining thoughts, and strict dieting practices that result in disordered eating (Fairburn et al., 1991).

This type of CBT is the most comprehensively studied treatment for BN and has been shown to be efficacious across more than thirty clinical trials utilising both outpatient individual (e.g., Fairburn et al., 1991) and group formats (e.g., Chen et al., 2003). Approximately one third to one half of patients make a lasting recovery, with the remainder exhibiting some improvement or no improvement (Lundgren, Danoff-Burg, & Anderson, 2004; Wilson & Fairburn, 2002). Whilst CBT does usually provide statistically significant changes in symptoms in BN, it may not reliably reduce symptoms to within the normative range, despite being the treatment of choice for this population.

Although the method for implementing CBT for AN is well documented (e.g., Garner, Vitousek, & Pike, 1997), only a few controlled studies have examined the use of CBT for this population, with the majority of clients treated on an outpatient basis (e.g., Ball & Mitchell, 2004; Channon, de Silva, Hemsley, & Perkins, 1989; Halmi et al., 2005; McIntosh et al., 2005; Serfaty, Turkington, Heap, Ledsham, & Jolley, 1999).

Conclusions drawn from the current literature suggest that CBT for AN may be moderately effective, but perhaps no more so than alternative therapies (NICE, 2004). Moreover, there is a distinct lack of studies with designs capable of providing evidence for the effectiveness of CBT interventions for a mixed group of eating disorder patients (i.e., with AN, BN or eating disorder not otherwise specified [EDNOS]) with illnesses serious enough to warrant hospitalisation.

Cognitive–Behaviour Therapy in an Inpatient Eating Disorders Unit

The Peter Beumont Centre for Eating Disorders at Wesley Private Hospital in Sydney utilises a CBT framework within its inpatient unit. The program is conducted by a multidisciplinary team and is based on a lenient behavioural modification approach. Patients attend compulsory groups run by either a nurse therapist or a clinical psychologist every weekday. Weekly groups are also conducted by a consultant clinical psychologist, a psychiatrist, intern clinical psychologists and a dietician. These focus on skills taken from CBT (e.g., problem-solving, thought challenging, graded exposure to feared foods, goal setting, and planning), distress tolerance, communication skills, and dietary counselling. Additionally, patients have individual meetings with a dietician, psychiatrist and/or clinical psychologist at least weekly. Meals and snacks are supervised by nurses according to strict guidelines around meal duration and permissible eating behaviour.

Barriers to the Successful Treatment of Eating Disorders

Despite such comprehensive inpatient therapy, eating disorder units continue to be plagued by patient resistance to treatment. The intensity of this problem was highlighted in a study by Rieger, Touyz and Beumont (2002) which reported that approximately 80% of patients with AN within a specialist eating disorder unit were not yet actively working towards change according to the Anorexia Nervosa Stages of Change Questionnaire (ANSOCQ; Rieger et al., 2000). Perhaps even more concerningly, the majority (i.e., 66%) of consenting patients were still not actively engaged in the change process after an average admission length of nearly 3 months. Accordingly, clinicians and researchers concur that difficulties in fostering the patient's motivation to overcome their illness is a major hurdle in the course of treatment (George, Thornton, Touyz, Waller, & Beumont, 2004; Treasure & Schmidt, 2001; Vitousek, Watson, & Wilson, 1998).

Ambivalence About Change

Due to their lack of motivation to change, patients may defy any attempts to alter their weight loss assisting behaviours (Kaplan, 2002; Vitousek et al., 1998). In fact, Kaplan suggests that AN could be reconceptualised as a disorder in which the primary symptom is ambivalence about change. Whilst individuals with BN are typically more motivated to recover, ambivalence about changing attitudes and behaviours that are personally valued (e.g., surrendering the 'thin ideal' and relinquishing purging behaviour) may be evident (Vitousek et al., 1998).

The resistance to treatment experienced within CBT-oriented eating disorder units is not unexpected given that, to date, no trial of CBT for inpatient eating disorders supports the notion that CBT enhances poor motivation amongst eating disorder sufferers. The apparent failure of CBT within the eating disorders field is probably attributable to the ego-syntonic (i.e., highly valued) nature of eating disorder symptoms, as patients will not actively engage in cognitive or behavioural strategies aimed at resolving symptoms they wish to keep. Indeed research has demonstrated that lower levels of motivation to change are associated with less weight gain during admission and during the 6-month period postdischarge for individuals with AN (Rieger, Touyz, & Beumont, 2002).

Given the centrality of low motivation to change amongst patients with eating disorders, focus has turned to therapies developed in the context of other conditions entailing motivational deficits. One such approach is motivational interviewing, a therapeutic style developed for the substance abuse population (Miller & Rollnick, 2002). The inherent assumption of motivational interviewing is that motivation cannot be imposed, but rather lies within each client, who can be assisted to draw upon it, through a collaborative and empathetic therapeutic approach.

Motivational enhancement therapy (MET) is based on the motivational interviewing approach in that the primary therapeutic focus is the manner in which the therapist supports the patient in reaching their own, change focused, conclusions (Miller, 1995; Miller, Zweben, DiClemente, & Rychtarik, 1992). The topics and techniques of therapy are intended to engage ambivalent and change resistant patients in the treatment process. Many authors (e.g., Miller & Rollnick, 2002) advocate that MET should ideally be used at the beginning of treatment.

Only two studies have empirically examined the use of MET for patients suffering from eating disorders. Treasure and colleagues (1999) compared the use of manualised MET (Schmidt & Treasure, 1997) and CBT with 125 female outpatients with BN. Participants were randomly assigned to either four individual sessions of MET or CBT. Whilst both treatments resulted in significant reductions in bulimic behaviours and increases in motivation to change and therapeutic alliance, there were no significant differences between the two interventions. However, the study's design was potentially flawed in assessing MET as an alternative to CBT given that MET is best conceptualised as a preparation for, or adjunct to, cognitive–behavioural approaches. Furthermore, this study may be an unfair assessment of MET due to the patients in the CBT group being significantly more motivated to change than the patients within the MET group at pretreatment.

Feld, Woodside, Kaplan, Olmstead and Carter (2001) conducted an uncontrolled pilot study of a pretreatment MET group program for eating disorder patients. The majority of the 19 participants were diagnosed with AN (12), with the remainder diagnosed with either BN (4) or EDNOS (3). The four sessions of manualised MET were held weekly on an outpatient basis. Participants' motivation to change and self-esteem increased, and their level of depressive symptomatology decreased following the intervention. However, given that this study was uncontrolled, the findings cannot unambiguously be attributed to the specific techniques of MET as opposed to general aspects of the group intervention.

These two studies provide some evidence regarding the use of MET to increase motivation for change, and to decrease eating disorder symptomatology, and/or general psychopathology. The limited research base in this area indicates that the use of motivational interviewing-based techniques in eating disorders clearly requires further investigation. In particular, controlled research assessing preparatory treatment to increase willingness to engage in the process of change and recovery for patients with eating disorders that are serious enough to warrant hospitalisation is essential.

An Inpatient Trial of Brief Motivational Enhancement Therapy for Eating Disorders

The current study attempted to begin to overcome this gap in the literature by implementing a MET group program aimed at fostering engagement with the CBT approach of the Wesley Private Hospital inpatient eating disorder unit. In addition to taking part in the standard hospital program, within the initial 2 weeks of admission patients in the MET group commenced weekly MET sessions, which they attended for four weeks. Assessment measures for the treatment group were taken before and after the patients completed the MET intervention and at 6-week follow-up. A treatment as usual (TAU) control group, who took part in the standard hospital program only, was recruited subsequent to the MET program ending and was assessed at comparable times.

The Motivational Enhancement Therapy Intervention

The four-session MET intervention was developed specifically for the current project. The basic structure was grounded in the intervention developed by Feld et al. (2001); however, changes were made to make it more relevant to the inpatient population (e.g., increases in motivation expressed by patients were linked to the opportunity to make behavioural changes within the unit). The groups were open, and designed to stand alone, with new participants commencing each week as they entered the hospital program and consented to the study.

The intervention aimed to encourage participants to engage in the standard cognitive–behavioural hospital program. Thus participants were asked to comply with the hospital program, whilst concurrently examining their intrinsic motivation to change within the MET sessions. The concurrent nature of the intervention and the general hospital program allowed for an immediacy of practice if a participant decided to make behavioural changes, as ambivalence can best be resolved through direct experience (Vitousek et al., 1998).

The purposes of Session A were to normalise the ambivalence that eating disorder patients feel towards recovery and to increase self-efficacy, particularly amongst those who have relapsed in the past, through an understanding that change is a circular process. The discussion focused on the transtheoretical model of change, which describes how individuals alter problem behaviours of any kind, both within and outside formal treatment (DiClemente & Prochaska, 1998). According to the model, individuals cycle through a series of discrete stages during the course of change. Six stages have been described: precontemplation (not thinking about change), contemplation (thinking about the possibility of change), preparation (getting ready for behavioural change), action (behavioural change), maintenance (working to sustain the behavioural changes that have been achieved), and termination (when the changes are fully incorporated into one's life). This session explained the stages of change model through discussion and clinical vignettes and established the patients' stages of change for various eating disordered behaviours. The possibility of being in different stages of change for different behaviours was discussed. An examination of a problematic behaviour that one had successfully changed in the past was undertaken in an attempt to enhance self-efficacy. Each session finished with a discussion of the homework exercise that built upon the session topic. In the spirit of motivational interviewing, which respects the autonomy of the patient, these exercises were not compulsory, but were encouraged. In this session, the homework exercise consisted of a further examination of each patient's current attitude towards recovery.

The structure of Session B encouraged a discussion of the benefits and costs of maintaining versus relinquishing one's eating disorder (Schmidt

& Treasure, 1997) in an attempt to shift the balance in the direction of change (i.e., whereby the disadvantages of the disorder come to outweigh the perceived advantages). The functional nature of the disorder was discussed. For example, the eating disorder may function as a suppressor of negative emotions, as a way of keeping intimate relationships at bay, and as a method for enhancing self-esteem through a sense of accomplishment. Following a summary of the functions, a discussion about the disadvantages (introduced as the 'not so good things') of the eating disorder was conducted and patients were encouraged to specifically describe events that were negatively affected by the presence of the illness, for example, having to miss their school dance, or feeling disconnected from their friends. Patients were then asked to consider the 'package deal' of the eating disorder, that is, that the disadvantages and advantages are intrinsically linked such that any perceived benefits will be obtained at a cost.

Again in an attempt to shift the balance towards the direction of change, the second aim of Session B was to foster an awareness of the incompatibility between current eating disordered behaviour and more deeply held values. This was undertaken via a card-sorting task adapted from Feld et al. (2001). Patients were asked to write their life's goals and strongly held values on coloured cards and arrange them in order of importance. Patients were then asked to write down the function/s of the eating disorder on another card and instructed to place this amongst the other cards in order of importance. The goal of this session was to determine if the participants' life goals are congruent with having an eating disorder and a group discussion was undertaken about their current value–behaviour consistency (i.e., the patients' evaluations about the role that the eating disorder plays in achieving and/or preventing value–behaviour consistency). The homework exercise consisted of a letter writing task about the effect of the eating disorder on one's life. This involved writing a letter to the eating disorder as a 'friend' and a second letter to the disorder as an 'enemy', as described in Schmidt and Treasure (1997). This exercise served the dual purpose of further enhancing awareness about the benefits and costs of the eating disorder as well as separating the disorder from oneself.

Session C commenced with an exercise adapted from Farrall (2001) designed to encourage an exploration of the origins of the eating disorder behaviour, its current state and likely future presentation in an attempt to gain perspective and to promote an examination into what the eating disorder had stolen from the individual's life. The aim was to further tip the balance towards the burden, rather than the benefits, of the illness.

This task involved asking a volunteer to sit in a chair placed in front of the group, which represented the 'present'. Their understanding of their present situation was elicited through motivational interviewing strategies and group members' input. A second chair was placed alongside the first and the volunteer was invited to move to this chair which represented the 'past' prior to the eating disorder becoming part of their life. The differences between the past and the present were highlighted through discussion. Finally, the volunteer was invited to move to a third chair, the 'future'. They could choose to discuss this in terms of life with or without the eating disorder. Following a facilitated discussion, they were then asked to consider an alternative future (i.e., life with or without the eating disorder). Participants were asked to speak in the present tense and the physicality of the approach appeared to aid perspective. The session finished with a visualisation task in which patients were guided to visualise their life in 12 months' time, focusing on an area that they would like to change. The homework task focused on patients' goals and current barriers to their fruition, and encouraged problem-solving around these difficulties.

Session D included a group exercise about the advantages and disadvantages of recovery, again in an attempt to shift the balance towards change. The discussion examined practical losses and gains for oneself, practical losses and gains for others, self-approval and disapproval, and social approval and disapproval (for details see Schmidt & Treasure, 1997). Finally, patients were asked for their perspectives and comments on the following issue: 'If you were on your death bed thinking about your life, what experiences do you think would stick out as most meaningful to you? Is your eating disorder involved in these experiences?' (Schmidt & Treasure, 1997). This exercise aimed to encourage patients to view their life as a whole, rather than through the filter of the eating disorder, in order to begin to question the impact that the eating disorder has had.

In addition to the particular strategies outlined above, the MET approach relied on the particular therapeutic principles of motivational interviewing described in Miller and Rollnick (2002). These include the expression of empathy and acceptance through the skilled use of reflective listening, the ability to avoid argumentation and instead reframe patients' statements in the direction of change (i.e., 'rolling with resistance'), and supporting the patient's self-efficacy. These fundamentals of the motivational approach underpin the collaborative nature of therapy, in which the therapist elicits, rather than instils, motivation from the patient.

Results and Discussion

Initial results from the entire sample (N = 42) presented at the 12th Annual Meeting of the Eating Disorders Research Society (Port Douglas, September, 2006) suggest that brief hospitalisation effectively increased the mean body mass index (kgm^{-2}) in underweight participants, enhanced readiness to recover from the eating disorder (as measured by the ANSOCQ; Rieger et al., 2000), and perceived self-efficacy to overcome the disorder (all at the $p < .05$ significance level). There were also significant reductions in eating disordered attitudes and behaviours (measured on the Eating Disorders Examination–Questionnaire, EDE–Q; Fairburn & Beglin, 1994) that held at the six-week follow-up. In addition, there was a reduction in the frequency of self-induced vomiting and bingeing. Results on the 'Drive for Thinness', 'Bulimia', 'Ineffectiveness', and 'Social Insecurity' subscales of the Eating Disorders Inventory II (EDI-II; Garner, 1991) improved across the intervention, with these improvements remaining at follow-up.

However, there were no significant differences between the results for patients who completed the MET (n = 19) intervention as well as routine hospital treatment and those who completed routine hospital treatment alone (n = 16) on any of the formal measures. Given the highly significant results of the intensive hospital treatment program, and the relatively small sample size of the current study, it is not surprising that the four-session MET intervention did not significantly improve outcome.

There was, however, an interesting yet nonsignificant trend in the scores on the main motivational measure (ANSOCQ; Rieger et al., 2000) across time points, graphically represented in Figure 1, which indicates that whilst both groups showed an increase in scores from pre- to post-assessment, the patients in the standard treatment arm appeared to show a reduction in readiness to recover between post- and follow-up assessment, whereas those in the MET group continued to report increasing levels of motivation. Given that an increase in motivation should theoretically lead to improvement in behaviour, perhaps differences in eating disorder symptomatology between the two groups would have emerged had there been a longer follow-up period. Future research should consider extending the study with a larger sample of patients and a longer follow-up period, in order to examine such a hypothesis.

Furthermore, whilst there were no overt groups of MET conducted within the standard treatment program during the course of the study, the overall principles and tone (Geller et al., 2001) of the motivational interviewing approach were very much incorporated into the unit.

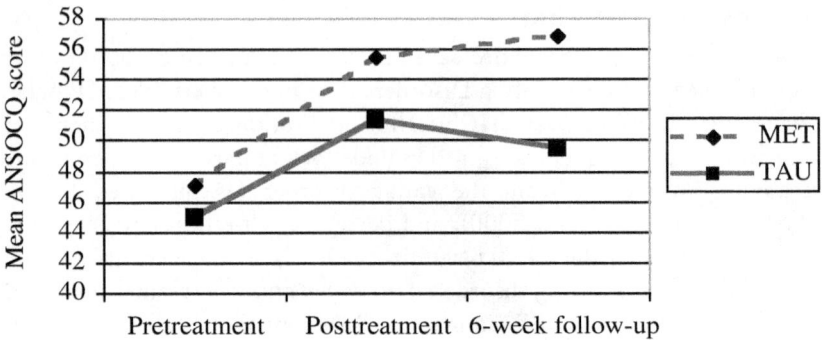

Figure 1
Mean ANSOCQ scores for the motivational enhancement therapy (MET; *n* = 17) and treatment as usual (TAU; *n* = 11) groups across assessments.

Hence, all patients in the study received some sort of motivational interviewing during their interactions with staff, even those in the standard treatment group.

Even though there were no statistically significant differences between the MET and standard treatment groups on formal measures, there were nevertheless possible differences between the groups. In particular, there were several qualitative indications of the effectiveness of the MET intervention. Specifically, patients in the MET group spontaneously reported insights that they had gained from the MET sessions to other staff members. Other clinicians reported that patients who had attended the sessions appeared to have a better understanding of their disorder and were more willing to engage in discussions about change. Moreover, patients reported enjoying attending the groups. Having a treatment in which eating disordered inpatients will participate is noteworthy when one considers that such units are generally a place of high treatment resistance. Suggesting that such interest could not be attributed to the specific therapist effects is the observation that the MET groups appeared to be more effective in engaging group participation than behavioural groups (e.g., goal setting and problem-solving) conducted by the same therapist. While tentative, these qualitative observations suggest that the MET approach in an inpatient setting warrants further investigation.

Conclusion

Whilst being preliminary in nature due to the small sample size, and short follow-up period, the results of the current study suggest that MET could potentially be useful in improving the outcome of brief inpatient hospital-isation within the notoriously difficult eating disorder patient group.

References

Ball, J., & Mitchell, P. (2004). A randomised controlled study of cognitive behaviour therapy and behavioural family therapy for anorexia nervosa patients. *Eating Disorders, 12,* 303–314.

Channon, S., de Silva, P., Hemsley, D., & Perkins, R. (1989). A controlled trial of cognitive-behavioural and behavioural treatment in anorexia nervosa. *Behaviour Research and Theory, 27,* 529–535.

Chen, E., Touyz, S.W., Beumont, P.J.V., Fairburn, C.G., Griffiths, R.G., Butow, P., et al. (2003). Comparison of group and individual cognitive-behavioural therapy for patients with bulimia nervosa. *International Journal of Eating Disorders, 33,* 241–254.

Dalle Grave, R., Bartocci, C., Todisco, P., Pantano, M., & Bosello, O. (1993). Inpatient treatment for anorexia nervosa: A lenient approach. *European Eating Disorders Review, 1,* 166–176.

DiClemente, C.C., & Prochaska, J.O. (1998). Toward a comprehensive, transtheo-retical model of change. In W.R. Miller & N. Heather (Eds.), *Treating addictive behaviours* (2nd ed., pp. 3–24). New York: Plenum Press.

Fairburn, C.G., & Beglin, S.J. (1994). Assessment of eating disorders: Interview or self-report questionnaire? *International Journal of Eating Disorders, 16,* 363–370.

Fairburn, C.G., Jones, R., Peveler, R.C., Carr, S.J., Solomon, R.A., O'Connor, M.E., et al. (1991). Three psychological treatments for bulimia nervosa: A comparative trial. *Archives of General Psychiatry, 48,* 463–469.

Farrall, M. (2001). The use of motivational interviewing techniques in offending behaviour group work. *Motivational Interviewing Newsletter, 8*(1), 8–12.

Feld, R., Woodside, D.B., Kaplan, A.S., Olmstead, M.P., & Carter, J.C. (2001). Pretreatment motivational enhancement therapy for eating disorders: A pilot study. *International Journal of Eating Disorders, 29,* 393–400.

Garner, D.M. (1991). *Eating Disorder Inventory-2. Professional manual.* Odessa Florida: Psychological Assessment Resources.

Garner, D.M., Vitousek, K.M., & Pike, K.M. (1997). Cognitive-behavioural therapy for anorexia nervosa. In D.M. Garner & P.E. Garfinkel (Eds.), *Handbook of treatment for eating disorders* (pp. 94–144). New York: Guildford Press.

Geller, J., Williams, K.D., & Srikameswaran, S. (2001). Clinical stance in the treatment of chronic eating disorders. *European Eating Disorders Review, 9,* 365–373.

George, L., Thornton, C., Touyz, S.W., Waller, G., & Beumont, P.J.V. (2004). Motivational enhancement therapy and schema-focused cognitive behaviour therapy in the treatment of chronic eating disorders. *Clinical Psychologist, 8,* 81–85.

Halmi, K.A., Agras, W.S., Crow, S., Mitchell, J., Wilson, G.T., Bryson, S.W., et al. (2005). Predictors of treatment acceptance and completion in anorexia nervosa: Implications for future study designs. *Archives of General Psychiatry, 62,* 776–781.

Kaplan, A.S. (2002). Psychological treatments for anorexia nervosa: A review of published studies and promising new directions. *Canadian Journal of Psychiatry, 47*(3), 235–242.

Lowe, M.R., Davis, W.N., Annunziato, R.A., & Lucks, D.L. (2003). Inpatient treatment for eating disorders: Outcome at discharge and 3-month follow-up. *Eating Behaviors, 4*, 385–397.

Lundgren, J.D., Danoff-Burg, S., & Anderson, D.A. (2004). Cognitive-behavioural therapy for bulimia nervosa: An empirical analysis of clinical significance. *International Journal of Eating Disorders, 35*, 262–274.

McIntosh, V., Jordan, J., Carter, F.A., Luty, S.E., McKenzie, J.M., Bulik, C.M., et al. (2005). Three Psychotherapies for anorexia nervosa: A randomized, controlled trial. *American Journal of Psychiatry, 162*, 741–747.

Miller, W.R. (1995). *Motivational enhancement therapy with drug abusers.* Unpublished therapist manual, University of New Mexico.

Miller, W.R., & Rollnick, S. (2002). *Motivational interviewing: Preparing people for change* (2nd ed.). New York: Guildford Press.

Miller, W.R., Zweber, A., DiClemente, C.C., & Rychtarik, R.G. (1992). *Motivational Enhancement Therapy Manual: A clinical research guide for therapists treating individuals with alcohol abuse and dependence.* Rockville, MD: National Institute on Alcohol Abuse and Alcoholism.

National Institute for Health and Clinical Excellence [NICE]. (2004). *Eating disorders: Core interventions in the treatment and management of anorexia nervosa, bulimia nervosa and related eating disorders.* London: NICE.

Rieger, E., Touyz, S.W., Schotte, D., Beumont, P., Russell, J., Clarke, S., et al. (2000). Development of an instrument to assess readiness to recover in anorexia nervosa. *International Journal of Eating Disorders, 28*, 387–396.

Rieger, E., Touyz, S.W., & Beumont, P.J.V. (2002) The Anorexia Nervosa Stages of Change Questionnaire (ANSOCQ): Information regarding its psychometric properties. *International Journal of Eating Disorders, 32*(1), 24–38.

Ro, O., Martinsen, E.W., Hoffart, A., & Risenvinge, J.H. (2004). Short-term follow-up of adults with long standing anorexia nervosa or non-specified eating disorder after inpatient treatment. *Eating and Weight Disorders, 9*(1), 62–68.

Schmidt, U.H., & Treasure, J.L. (1997). *Clinician's guide to getting better bit(e) by bit(e).* Hove, England: Psychology Press.

Serfaty, M.A., Turkington, D., Heap, M., Ledsham, L., & Jolley, E. (1999). Cognitive therapy versus dietary counselling in the outpatient treatment of anorexia nervosa: Effects of the treatment phase. *European Eating Disorders Review, 7*, 334–350.

Touyz, S.W., Beumont, P., & Dunn, S.N. (1987). Behaviour therapy in the management of patients with anorexia nervosa: A lenient, flexible approach. *Psychotherapy and Psychosomatics, 48*(1–4), 151–156.

Touyz, S.W., & Beumont, P. (1991). The management of anorexia nervosa in adolescence. *Modern Medicine, 34*, 86–97.

Treasure, J. L., Katzman, M., Schmidt, U., Troop, N., Todd, G., & de Silva, P. (1999). Engagement and outcome in the treatment of bulimia nervosa: First phase of a sequential design comparing motivation enhancement therapy and cognitive behavioural therapy. *Behaviour Research and Therapy, 37*, 405–418.

Treasure, J., & Schmidt, U. (2001). Ready, willing and able to change: Motivational aspects of the assessment and treatment of eating disorders. *European Eating Disorders Review, 9,* 4–18.

Treat, T.A., Gaskill, J.A., McCabe, E.B., Ghinassi, F.A., Luczak, A.D., & Marcus, M.D. (2005). Short-term outcome of psychiatric inpatients with anorexia nervosa in the current care environment. *International Journal of Eating Disorders, 38,* 123–133.

Vitousek, K., Watson, S., & Wilson, G.T. (1998). Enhancing motivation for change in treatment-resistant eating disorders. *Clinical Psychology Review, 18,* 391–420.

Wilson, G.T., & Fairburn, C.G. (2002). Treatments for eating disorders. In P.E. Nathan & J.M. Gorman (Eds.), *A guide to treatments that work* (2nd ed., pp. 559–592). New York: Oxford University Press.

CHAPTER 14

Using Cognitive Processing Therapy for Assault Victims With Acute Stress Disorder

Reginald D.V. Nixon

Acute stress disorder (ASD) is diagnosed in the first month following exposure to significant trauma such as physical and sexual assault, war or combat-related trauma, motor vehicle accidents and natural disasters (American Psychiatric Association, 1994). Approximately 15% of individuals exposed to trauma will develop ASD (Bryant & Harvey, 2000) and the presence of ASD has been shown to predict the later occurrence of posttraumatic stress disorder (PTSD), a chronic and disabling trauma response (Bryant & Harvey, 1998). Cognitive–behavioural treatments have consistently been found to be the most empirically supported psychological intervention for PTSD (Foa, Keane, & Friedman, 2000), and CBT has demonstrated effectiveness for ASD and acute trauma response (Bryant, Harvey, Dang, Sackville, & Basten, 1998; Bryant, Moulds, Guthrie, & Nixon, 2003; Bryant, Sackville, Dang, Moulds, & Guthrie, 1999; Foa, Zoellner, & Feeny, 2006).

One therapy that has not been rigorously tested as an acute intervention is cognitive processing therapy (CPT). Cognitive processing therapy was designed as a cognitive–behavioural treatment for PTSD following sexual assault, and has been well supported empirically (Resick, Nishith, Weaver, Astin, & Feuer, 2002; Resick & Schnicke, 1992). Indeed, Resick et al. (2002) demonstrated that CPT was just as effective as prolonged exposure (PE; Foa, Dancu, Hembree, Jaycox, Meadows, & Street, 1999), which is often considered the current gold standard for the treatment of PTSD. CPT has also been shown to be effective for PTSD following other trauma such as nonsexual assault and combat-related trauma (Monson et al., 2005; Resick et al., 2005). At this time, the only published use of CPT for the treatment of ASD has been a single case study (Kaysen, Lostutter, & Goines, 2005).

The importance of developing more effective interventions for acute interpersonal trauma is underscored by the personal and social costs if ASD is left untreated, since it typically results in the development of chronic PTSD. The possibility of reducing rates of chronic PTSD in such victims has obvious benefits to the victims themselves in terms of reduced psychological distress, but also has significant benefits for the community in regard to reduced spending on treatment, reducing health service utilisation, and increasing job productivity (Alonso et al., 2004; Jaycox & Foa, 1999).

CPT is a logical protocol to test for early intervention since it has been developed to target the core belief systems that are theorised to be responsible for the development and maintenance of maladaptive trauma responses, as outlined in recent cognitive conceptualisations of post-traumatic stress (e.g., Ehlers & Clark, 2000). Given its strong cognitive restructuring component, CPT is also likely to be beneficial for a range of comorbid problems associated with trauma (e.g., depression, other anxiety disorders, chronic pain). In the following pages, a description of CPT will be given, followed by preliminary results from a randomised controlled trial of CPT for assault-related ASD.

Cognitive Processing Therapy for Acute Stress Disorder

In its original form (Resick et al., 2002; Resick & Schnicke, 1992, 1993), CPT is delivered individually over 12 sessions, with therapist and client meeting for 1-hour sessions twice a week. Given that ASD interventions typically do not require as many sessions as those conducted for PTSD (a more chronic trauma response), the original CPT protocol was modified for delivery in six weekly sessions of 90 minutes duration. Although CPT is a cognitive–behavioural intervention, it differs from other cognitive–behavioural treatments for ASD and PTSD in several critical ways. First, rather than using imaginal exposure to promote habituation of anxiety to memories of the traumatic event, clients produce a written account of the trauma. This is read aloud in session, and is re-written and re-read as homework. The reading of the account in session is shorter than an imaginal exposure account (which is typically 45–60 minutes in duration), and the account is also used to identify cognitive distortions (labelled 'stuck points' in therapy) that are challenged in later sessions. Second, CPT does not use formal in vivo exposure. The importance of reducing avoidance behaviours is addressed in terms of psychoeducation at the beginning of therapy, and clients are not discouraged from modifying avoidant behaviours, but formal exposure hierarchies are not constructed in therapy or set as homework. Instead, the rest of therapy consists of cognitive restructuring. Where CPT differs from other therapies that use cognitive restructuring or cognitive therapy techniques lies in the specific targeting of cognitive 'themes'. During the course of therapy, five key themes are targeted with cognitive restructuring — unhelpful beliefs regarding safety, trust, power–control, esteem and intimacy. Self-blame is also addressed. Although CPT was initially developed to specifically treat PTSD following sexual assault, most clients with ASD or PTSD will have distorted beliefs in a number of these domains irrespective of trauma type. A brief summary of each session of the ASD protocol follows which is derived from the CPT treatment manual and treatment fidelity checklist (Nishith & Resick, 1994; Resick & Schnicke, 1993).

Session 1

Clients are educated about the results of the pretreatment assessment and ASD symptoms. The rationale and components of treatment are presented based on information processing theory, and the ways in which the client's beliefs may have been affected by the trauma are discussed. The early phases of cognitive restructuring are introduced, starting with discussion of the relationship between thoughts and feelings, and a handout with a series of questions that can be used to challenge unhelpful beliefs (stuck points) is then used in session. Given this is the first session, only a mild level of challenging is utilised. The client is then set two homework tasks for the following session — monitoring and challenging unhelpful thoughts, and writing a one-page impact statement summarising how the trauma has affected the client's beliefs regarding safety, trust and so on. They are explicitly asked not to write an account of the trauma at this time.

Session 2

The therapist checks in with the client regarding their week and their homework, especially in relation to avoidance or noncompliance. Concepts from the first session are reviewed and the client is then asked to read out his/her impact statement, and the meaning of this narrative is discussed. Alternative ways of interpreting situations is introduced, and the issue of whether the client has self-blame surrounding the trauma is examined. Identifying faulty thinking patterns is undertaken, for example, whether the client tends to exaggerate the meaning of events or undertake emotional reasoning (i.e., reasoning from how they feel). Finally, these separate cognitive techniques are put together in a single sheet (Challenging Beliefs

Worksheet). This sheet also has space for the client to reframe their beliefs or interpretations after challenging stuck points. Homework is again set, with clients asked to continue to record their thoughts during the week, and to identify faulty thinking patterns and to challenge these stuck points. The client is also asked to write an account of their trauma, with as much detail as possible, and to read over this account daily before the next session. The therapist discusses potential hurdles with this homework (avoidance, extreme distress) and sets up safety plans if necessary.

Session 3

Homework is reviewed, and the client reads their trauma account to the therapist. The therapist discusses with the client the meaning of expression of affect (or lack of) to identify significant stuck points. For example, a client who shows little emotion may be holding back in fear of being judged by the therapist, or in the belief that they cannot handle the strong emotions. Faulty thinking and challenging in relation to self-blame is reviewed again, before the first two of the five themes (safety, trust) to be targeted for specific examination is undertaken. The client is given a handout on how beliefs regarding safety and trust can change following trauma, and the client is asked to confront these beliefs for homework. The client is also asked to rewrite their trauma account, with a view to provide additional detail compared with the first attempt. The client is asked to re-read this new account daily before the next session.

Session 4

After reviewing the homework, the client reads his/her second trauma account aloud and, with the therapist, identifies any differences between the first and second account. Time is also spent in session discussing trauma-related safety and trust stuck points, with a focus on challenging unhelpful appraisals and exploring alternative interpretations. The client's social support system often is relevant, especially if the client experienced rejection or felt let down by people close to them either at the time of the trauma, or as a result of unsupportive reactions following the trauma. The third and fourth of the five problem areas — power/control and esteem, are then introduced with handouts, and potential stuck points in these domains are identified. A sheet of possible assumptions that the client might hold (e.g., 'I always have to be loved') is reviewed also. The client is set several assignments for the week: to continue reading their trauma account, to challenge stuck points regarding power/control and esteem, and to challenge unhelpful assumptions. In regard to esteem, pleasant events are scheduled.

Session 5

The previous week is reviewed and stuck points regarding power/control are discussed, especially in the context of self-blame. For example, clients often mistakenly overestimate the degree of control they may have had in a traumatic situation, thus can engage in self-blame, believing they should have been able to control or prevent the traumatic situation. Any esteem issues that arose during the week are also identified, and if necessary, challenged. The final domain to be covered is intimacy. Thus stuck points around intimacy with partners, as well as general friendships are explored, and the client is asked to continue identifying and challenging unhelpful beliefs over the next week. The client is also asked to rewrite their impact statement for homework, focusing on how their belief systems are now, compared with when they first started therapy. Finally, pleasant event scheduling is continued.

Session 6

In the final session, homework is reviewed, and continued discussion of intimacy stuck points is carried out. The client and therapist also identify any remaining stuck points that would benefit from continued challenging after treatment has ended. The therapist and client review therapy progress, and the second impact statement is read out, and compared with the one completed at the beginning of therapy. Goals for the future are identified, and the therapist and client work together to set out strategies for achieving these goals. Finally, the treatment rationale and principles are reviewed, and relapse prevention is discussed. The importance of continuing to challenge unhelpful thinking is emphasised.

Preliminary Findings

The aim of this ongoing project is to test the effectiveness of CPT as an early intervention. Participants are randomised to either CPT or supportive counselling (SC). In SC, participants received psychoeducation regarding posttraumatic stress, general problem-solving skills and nondirective unconditional supportive counselling. It serves as a control for any possible nonspecific therapeutic effects due to contact with an empathic therapist. The project is following established recommendation for conducting treatment trials (Altman et al., 2001; Foa & Meadows, 1997). Although participants are being followed up at 6-months posttreatment, only pre- and posttreatment data are presented.

Table 1
Sample Characteristics

Variable	CPT		SC		Statistic
	M	*SD*	*M*	*SD*	
Age (years)	43.73	13.18	41.44	9.15	*t*(18) = 0.44
Gender	7M, 4F		4M, 5F		Fisher's Exact Test = 0.65
Education (years)	12.90	4.13	13.06	3.53	*t*(18) = 0.08
Days since trauma	31.82	8.82	19.56	10.42	*t*(18) = 2.85*
ASDS	70.09	8.79	69.89	7.15	*t*(18) = 0.06
Comorbid depression	*n* = 7		*n* = 5		Fisher's Exact Test = 1.00
Treatment logical	8.30	0.82	7.20	0.84	*t*(13) = 2.43*
Treatment confidence	7.70	1.25	6.40	1.52	*t*(13) = 1.77

Note: *$p < .05$; ASDS = Acute Stress Disorder Scale; Treatment logical and Treatment confidence rated on 1–9 scale, where higher values reflect greater confidence and higher logical ratings.

Participants

At the time of writing, 20 assault victims have entered the study (19 physical assault, 1 sexual assault). Participants are excluded if they have suffered a moderate to severe traumatic brain injury, have uncontrolled psychosis, are currently substance dependent, or are at-risk for self-harm. Table 1 details the demographic and trauma characteristics of the two groups.

Measures

To determine diagnosis at pretreatment (including comorbidity), the Acute Stress Disorder Interview (ASDI; Bryant, Harvey, Dang, & Sackville, 1998) and Structured Clinical Interview for DSM-IV-TR (SCID; First, Spitzer, Gibbon, & Williams, 2002) are administered. The Clinician-Administered PTSD Scale (CAPS; Blake et al., 1995) is used at posttreatment to determine PTSD caseness. The Acute Stress Disorder Scale (ASDS; Bryant, Moulds, & Guthrie, 2000) is given at pretreatment to assess ASD severity, and the Posttraumatic Diagnostic Scale (PDS; Foa, Cashman, Jaycox, & Perry, 1997) and Beck Depression Inventory–II (BDI-II; Beck, Steer, & Brown, 1996) are used to assess changes post-traumatic stress and depression symptoms over treatment, as is the Posttraumatic Cognitions Inventory (PTCI; Foa, Ehlers, Clark, Tolin, &

Orsillo, 1999) which measures trauma-related cognitions. The acceptability and credibility of treatment is determined in Session 1 in order to ensure comparable expectancy effects between the two groups (Resick et al., 2002).

Therapists
The majority of therapy is being delivered by either senior clinical PhD students or recently graduated master's level therapists. All therapists have been trained in the respective treatment conditions by the author, and attend weekly clinical supervision to discuss ongoing cases.

Results
Although the CPT group rated the treatment rationale as more logical than the SC group (see Table 1), both groups were comparable in terms of their confidence that the treatment would be successful in helping them with their symptoms. In terms of drop-out, 3 of the 11 CPT participants (27%) and 4 of the 9 SC participants (44%) did not complete therapy. Drop-outs were invited to complete the posttreatment assessment, and their data were used accordingly for intent-to-treat purposes. Two CPT and 1 SC drop-out were unavailable for posttreatment assessment, thus their pre-treatment scores were carried forward.

To examine the effect of treatment, a series of 2 (Group: CPT, SC) × 2 (Time: pretreatment, posttreatment) repeated measures ANOVAs were conducted. As summarised in Table 2, a consistent pattern of findings was observed for both intent-to-treat and treatment completer analyses. In summary, these analyses demonstrated that both groups experienced significant reductions of PTSD symptoms, depression and trauma-related beliefs over the course of treatment and that although the main effect of time was significant on these measures, the Group × Time interactions were not. This latter finding possibly reflects limited power due to the small sample size. Although the CPT group started treatment later and rated the therapy rationale as more logical than the SC group, controlling for these variables did not alter the pattern of findings.

Effect sizes (Cohen's d) are reported in Table 3. In terms of pre–post differences, the CPT and SC showed similar amounts of change (intent-to-treat samples). However, examination of effects sizes for the completer samples suggest that larger reductions in symptomatology were obtained with the CPT group, and it is likely that this will be observed statistically with increased sample size. When the two groups are compared at post-treatment, the effect sizes again favour CPT; not surprisingly, these differences are most noticeable in the treatment completer group. Although

Table 2
Means, Standard Deviations and Statistics for Self-Report Symptom Measures of Intent-to-Treat and Treatment Completer Analyses

Measures	CPT		SC		Statistics		
	Pre	Post	Pre	Post	ME Group	ME Time	Interaction
Intent-to-treat sample							
PDS	35.55 (5.22)	17.36 (14.02)	36.89 (7.34)	20.00 (11.68)	$F(1, 18) = 0.27$	$F(1, 18) = 48.18$***	$F(1, 18) = 0.07$
BDI-II	20.09 (11.45)	11.82 (13.64)	22.78 (9.23)	16.00 (11.00)	$F(1, 18) = 0.52$	$F(1, 18) = 13.53$**	$F(1, 18) = 0.13$
PTCI	112.55 (27.91)	84.00 (34.44)	123.44 (34.44)	92.44 (38.75)	$F(1, 18) = 0.49$	$F(1, 18) = 17.25$**	$F(1, 18) = 0.03$
Completer sample							
PDS	35.13 (5.28)	12.88 (9.16)	37.60 (5.86)	19.60 (15.08)	$F(1, 11) = 0.98$	$F(1, 11) = 73.75$***	$F(1, 11) = 0.82$
BDI-II	18.50 (10.88)	7.00 (9.02)	24.40 (11.70)	13.40 (14.10)	$F(1, 11) = 1.13$	$F(1, 11) = 17.85$**	$F(1, 11) = 0.01$
PTCI	109.12 (29.67)	73.88 (33.03)	117.40 (45.58)	87.40 (46.47)	$F(1, 11) = 0.32$	$F(1, 11) = 12.96$**	$F(1, 11) = 0.08$

Note: *$p < .05$, **$p < .01$; ***$p < .001$; ME = main effect; PDS = Posttraumatic Diagnostic Scale; BDI-II = Beck Depression Inventory (2nd ed.); PTCI = Posttraumatic Cognitions Inventory (total score).

Table 3

Effect Sizes (Cohen's *d*) for Self-Report Symptom Measures of Intent-to-Treat and Treatment Completer Analyses

Measures	CPT Pre–Post	SC Pre–Post	CPT versus SC[a] Post
Intent-to-treat sample			
PDS	1.89	1.78	0.20
BDI-II	0.66	0.67	0.33
PTCI	0.87	0.85	0.22
Completer sample			
PDS	3.08	1.72	0.58
BDI-II	1.16	0.85	0.57
PTCI	1.12	0.65	0.35

Note: PDS = Posttraumatic Diagnostic Scale; BDI-II = Beck Depression Inventory (2nd ed.); PTCI = Posttraumatic Cognitions Inventory (total score).

[a] Mean difference divided by the average of the two standard deviations (Dunlop, Cortina, Vaslow, & Burke, 1996).

Cohen's *d* can be somewhat inflated when calculated with small samples, Hedges's unbiased estimates (*g*) were only marginally smaller (e.g., 0.54, 0.53, and 0.33 instead of 0.58, 0.57, and 0.35 for the CPT versus SC comparison with treatment completers). For those who completed treatment, 1 of the 8 CPT and 2 of the 5 SC participants met criteria for PTSD (minus the timeframe).

Discussion

The preliminary data from this trial testing the effectiveness of CPT in the treatment of ASD are encouraging. Clearly the results need to be interpreted with caution due to the small sample sizes; however, the findings suggest that CPT may be just as effective as CBT used in published ASD trials. For example, approximation of effect sizes (pre–post) for CBT from ASD treatment studies of Bryant and colleagues (Bryant et al., 1998, 1999, 2003) range between 1.83–2.45 for posttraumatic stress and 0.56–1.25 for depression, with the current data showing effect sizes of 3.08 for reductions in posttraumatic stress and 1.16 for depression. Similarly, approximation of effect sizes (pre–post) from Resick et al.'s (2002) study of chronic PTSD following rape range between 2 to 3 for posttraumatic and depressive symptom reduction following CPT (completer sample).

Interestingly, the difference between CPT and SC is not as marked in the present data as CBT versus SC comparisons in previous ASD trials.

Approximations of effect sizes for posttraumatic stress from these studies (Bryant et al., 1998, 1999, 2003) range between 0.81–1.89, favouring CBT over SC, whereas smaller effects have been obtained between CPT and SC (0.58 for posttraumatic stress, 0.57 for depression). This may reflect differences in sample (assault-related ASD versus assault and MVA clients in the Bryant et al., studies), or be a function of therapist experience (a mixture of student and more experienced therapists in the present study, compared with experienced therapists in Bryant et al. trials). Again, the issue of small sample size cannot be ruled out.

Similarly, caution needs to be exercised with interpreting drop-out data due to the sample size, but the present rate of 27% for CPT is the same as that reported by Resick et al. (2002) for chronic PTSD, and somewhat higher than the 20% reported by Bryant et al. (1999). The marked drop-out of SC (44%) is somewhat surprising given that this is typically a nonconfronting counselling modality, and not usually associated with drop-out. Clearly further data need to be collected before reaching firm conclusions about this.

In summary, CPT is showing promise as a useful intervention for ASD. These preliminary findings suggest that significant reductions in posttraumatic and depressive symptoms can be obtained, as well as a reduction in trauma-related cognitions that are thought to maintain posttraumatic responses. Increased sample size and follow-up data are now required to test these propositions more stringently.

References

Alonso, J., Angermeyer, M., Bernert, S., Bruffaerts, R., Brugha, T., Bryson, H., et al. (2004). Disability and quality of life impact of mental disorders in Europe: Results from the European Study of the Epidemiology of Mental Disorders (ESEMeD) project. *Acta Psychiatrica Scandinavica, 109*(Suppl. 420), 38–46.

Altman, D.G., Schulz, K.F., Moher, D., Egger, M., Davidoff, F., Elbourne, D., et al. (2001). The revised CONSORT statement for reporting randomized trials: Explanation and elaboration. *Annals of Internal Medicine, 134*, 663–694.

American Psychiatric Association. (1994). *Diagnostic and statistical manual of mental disorders* (4th ed.). Washington, DC: Author.

Beck, A.T., Steer, R.A., & Brown, G.K. (1996). *Beck Depression Inventory — Second Edition: Manual*. San Antonio, TX: Psychological Corporation.

Blake, D.D., Weathers, F.W., Nagy, L.M., Kaloupek, D.G., Gusman, F.D., Charney, D.S., et al. (1995). The development of a clinician-administered PTSD scale. *Journal of Traumatic Stress, 8*, 75–90.

Bryant, R.A., & Harvey, A.G. (1998). Relationship of acute stress disorder and posttraumatic stress disorder following mild traumatic brain injury. *American Journal of Psychiatry, 155*, 625–629.

Bryant, R.A., & Harvey, A.G. (2000). *Acute stress disorder: A handbook of theory, assessment, and treatment*. Washington, DC: American Psychological Association.

Bryant, R.A., Harvey, A.G., Dang, S.T., & Sackville, T. (1998). Assessing acute stress disorder: Psychometric properties of a structured clinical interview. *Psychological Assessment, 10*, 215–220.

Bryant, R.A., Harvey, A.G., Dang, S.T., Sackville, T., & Basten, C. (1998). Treatment of acute stress disorder: A comparison of cognitive behavior therapy and supportive counseling. *Journal of Consulting and Clinical Psychology, 66*, 826–866.

Bryant, R.A., Moulds, M., Guthrie, R., & Nixon, R.D.V. (2003). Treating acute stress disorder following mild traumatic brain injury. *American Journal of Psychiatry, 160*, 585–587.

Bryant, R.A., Moulds, M.L., & Guthrie, R.M. (2000). Acute stress disorder scale: A self-report measure of acute stress disorder. *Psychological Assessment, 12*, 61–68.

Bryant, R.A., Sackville, T., Dang, S.T., Moulds, M., & Guthrie, R. (1999). Treating acute stress disorder: An evaluation of cognitive behavior therapy and supportive counseling techniques. *American Journal of Psychiatry, 156*, 1780–1786.

Dunlop, W.P., Cortina, J.M., Vaslow, J.B., & Burke, M.J. (1996). Meta-analysis of experiments with matched groups or repeated measures designs. *Psychological Methods, 1*, 170–177.

Ehlers, A., & Clark, D.M. (2000). A cognitive model of posttraumatic stress disorder. *Behaviour Research and Therapy, 38*, 319–345.

First, M., Spitzer, R.L., Gibbon, M., & Williams, J.B.W. (2002). *Structured Clinical Interview for DSM-IV-TR Axis I Disorders — Patient Edition (SCID-I/P, 11/2002 revision)*. New York: Biometric Research Department, New York State Psychiatric Institute.

Foa, E.B., & Meadows, E.A. (1997). Psychosocial treatments for posttraumatic stress disorder: A critical review. *Annual Review of Psychology, 48*, 449–480.

Foa, E.B., Cashman, L., Jaycox, L., & Perry, K. (1997). The validation of a self-report measure of posttraumatic stress disorder: The Posttraumatic Diagnostic Scale. *Psychological Assessment, 9*, 445–451.

Foa, E.B., Ehlers, A., Clark, D.M., Tolin, D.F., & Orsillo, S.M. (1999). The Posttraumatic Cognitions Inventory (PTCI): Development and validation. *Psychological Assessment, 11*, 303–314.

Foa, E.B., Keane, T.M., & Friedman, M.J. (2000). *Effective treatments for PTSD: Practice guidelines from the International Society for Traumatic Stress Studies*. New York: Guilford Press.

Foa, E.B., Dancu, C.V., Hembree, E.A., Jaycox, L.H., Meadows, E.A., & Street, G.P. (1999). A comparison of exposure therapy, stress innoculation training, and their combination for reducing posttraumatic stress disorder in female assault victims. *Journal of Consulting and Clinical Psychology, 67*, 194–200.

Foa, E.B., Zoellner, L.A., & Feeny, N.C. (2006). An evaluation of three brief programs for facilitating recovery after assault. *Journal of Traumatic Stress, 19*, 29–43.

Jaycox, L.H., & Foa, E.B. (1999). Cost-effectiveness issues in the treatment of posttraumatic stress disorder. In N.E. Miller & K.M. Magruder (Eds.), *Cost-effectiveness of psychotherapy: A guide for practitioners, researchers, and policymakers* (pp. 259–269). New York: Oxford University Press.

Kaysen, D., Lostutter, T.W., & Goines, M.A. (2005). Cognitive processing therapy for acute stress disorder resulting from an anti-gay assault. *Cognitive & Behavioral Practice, 12*, 278–289.

Monson, C.M., Schnurr, P.P., Resick, P.A., Friedman, M.J., Young-Xu, Y., Stevens, S.P., et al. (2005, November). *Cognitive processing therapy for military-related PTSD.* Paper presented at the annual meeting of the Association for Behavioral and Cognitive Therapies, Washington, DC.

Nishith, P., & Resick, P.A. (1994). *Cognitive processing therapy (CPT): Therapist adherence and competence protocol.* Unpublished manuscript, University of Missouri-St. Louis.

Resick, P.A., Galovski, T., Phipps, K., Uhlmansiek, M., Ansel, J., & Griffin, M. (2005). A *dismantling study of the components of cognitive processing therapy.* Paper presented at the annual meeting of the Association for Behavioral and Cognitive Therapies, Washington, DC.

Resick, P.A., Nishith, P., Weaver, T.L., Astin, M.C., & Feuer, C.A. (2002). A comparison of cognitive-processing therapy with prolonged exposure and a waiting condition for the treatment of chronic posttraumatic stress disorder in female rape victims. *Journal of Consulting and Clinical Psychology, 70*, 867–879.

Resick, P.A., & Schnicke, M.K. (1992). Cognitive processing therapy for sexual assault victims. *Journal of Consulting and Clinical Psychology, 60*, 748–756.

Resick, P.A., & Schnicke, M.K. (1993). *Cognitive processing therapy for rape victims: A treatment manual.* Newbury Park, CA: Sage.

CHAPTER 15

A CBT Internet Program for Depression in Adolescents (MoodGYM): Effects on Depressive Symptoms, Attributional Style, Self-Esteem and Beliefs About Depression

Richard O'Kearney, Kanwal Kang, Mal Gibson, Helen Christensen and Kathy Griffiths

Depression in adolescence is a major public health concern because of its high prevalence (Boyd, Kostanski, Gullone, Ollendick, & Shek, 2000; Kessler, Avenevoli, & Merikangas, 2001) and the strong continuity between depression in adolescence and adult major depressive disorder. There is good longitudinal data that adolescents who have a depressive episode or show sub-threshold depressive symptoms are between 2 and 7 times more likely to experience a major depressive episode in adulthood compared to nondepressed youth (Rutter, Kim-Cohen, & Maughan, 2006). These findings, together with youths' reluctance to engage with mental health services, present significant challenges to public health interventions for depression in this group.

One of the strategies developed to meet this challenge has been the use of school-based approaches that provide traditional group delivery of interventions such as cognitive–behaviour therapy (CBT) and psychoeducation into the school curriculum (Cardemil, Reivich, & Seligman, 2002; Clarke et al., 1995; Lowry-Webster, Barrett, & Dadds, 2001; Shochet et al., 2001). Such approaches are effective (Merry, McDowell, Hetrick, Bir, & Muller, 2004) in reducing self-reported depressive symptoms (pooled effect size of .26, CI .36 to .15) as well as for influencing cognitive vulnerabilities for depression, particularly attributional style (Cardemil et al., 2002). As even mild depressive symptoms can impact significantly on functioning in this age group (Harrington, Whittaker, & Shoebridge, 1998), the results offer some encouragement for reducing morbidity associated with depression in adolescents at a population level.

There are, however, limitations to these school-based programs that may have impacts both on how broadly they can be applied and on their sustainability. For the most part, they are face-to-face group programs where specialist mental health workers such as psychologists (Cardemil et al., 2002; Shochet et al., 2001), trained schoolteachers, or facilitators (Clarke et al., 1995; Lowry-Webster et al., 2001) deliver the sessions. The need for appropriately trained professionals and for continuing training and support for the schools' staff presents considerable organisation obstacles to the delivery of these programs. They are seen as not only resource intense and costly, but also difficult to sustain with the levels of staff mobility that are usual for high schools. Because of the low availability of relevant professions in some areas these issues impact particularly on lower socioeconomic status schools and those in rural and remote locations.

These types of considerations have led to the development of nontraditional modes of delivery of effective intervention strategies for depression in this age group. There are good reasons to believe that the Internet could be an effective and appropriate mode of delivery for helping youth, with, or vulnerable to, depression. Adolescents report more positive attitudes and engagement with computers and the Internet than other groups (Colley & Comber, 2003). There is also accumulating evidence that Internet delivery of self-directed CBT programs can be effective for a range of problems in adults including depression (Berstrom et al., 2003; Clarke et al., 2002; Clarke et al., 2005). In Clarke's recent randomised controlled trial (Clarke et al., 2005) 225 adult participants were allocated to one of two Overcoming Depression on the Internet (ODIN) groups or to a control condition. Intervention participants reported greater reduction in depressive symptoms than the control participants ($ES = .28$) with a stronger effect for participants with higher depressive symptoms at baseline ($ES = .54$).

MoodGYM

An Australian-developed Internet intervention for depression (MoodGYM) has also shown to be effective in reducing self-report of depressive symptoms in nontreatment-seeking adults (Christensen, Griffiths, & Jorm, 2004; Christensen, Griffiths, Mackinnon, & Brittliffe, in press). MoodGYM is an interactive Internet-based program (www.moodgym.anu.edu.au) which aims to help people identify problems with anxiety and depression, to help overcome these problems and to develop good coping skills. It is strongly based on standard evidence-based cognitive–behavioural programs. It contains information about depression, demonstrations, questionnaires (e.g., about depression and anxiety levels) and skill practice exercises (e.g., relaxation, problem-solving, cognitive restructuring, assertiveness, self-esteem training, interpersonal problem-solving, and coping with relationships). These techniques are illustrated with particular characters who show specific types of adaptive and maladaptive thinking and coping styles. Users of MoodGYM sample alternative ways of thinking about specific events and means of solving problems which the characters face in these events. At various stages the program asks a series of questions about the user's own feelings and thoughts. Users are able to proceed through the program at their own pace and automatically resume at the point they finished at the end of a previous session. MoodGYM comprises five modules: Feelings, Thoughts, Changing thoughts, Destressing, and Relationships. It also contains two supplementary sections: Introduction/getting started and Final exercises. As well as reducing depressive symptoms, MoodGYM may be helpful in changing vulnerabilities to depression because of its impact on underlying thinking styles and its inclusion of information about depression proneness.

While there are randomised control studies (Christensen et al., 2004; Christensen et al., in press) which provide evidence of the benefits of MoodGYM for adults, it is not yet known whether the benefits apply for adolescents or whether it is suitable for school-based delivery. The program appears promising because the illustrative characters and examples are based on experiences relevant to adolescents and younger adults and it was originally developed with these age groups in mind. The inclusion of interpersonal problem-solving strategies, for example, enhances its suitability to adolescents as interpersonal conflict and role transition are prominent triggers to emotional distress in this age group. As well, the Internet format makes it transportable and, together with its self-directed approach, may overcome some of the resource obstacles that limit the sustainability and overall effectiveness of face-to-face school-based programs.

School-Based Applications of MoodGYM

While originally designed and shown to be helpful as an individually accessible community-based website, MoodGYM may serve as a resource in school settings to supplement the ongoing class curriculum or as an adjunct to face-to-face contact with specific individuals or groups, for example, in psychological care or support. The initial focus of our examination of the effectiveness of MoodGYM in school-based applications has been its usefulness as a universal prevention. In particular, we investigate its ability to facilitate pathways to lower levels of depressive symptoms and vulnerability to depression in adolescents generally. Its applications in school settings to date have been in the context of personal development activities as part of the school curriculum. This approach addresses MoodGYM's impact on the ongoing mental health of the group as a whole rather than its capacity to treat individuals with depression, or those at high risk of depression becoming depressed. As well, we believe that this initial strategy can overcome the recruitment and negative labelling problems that selective mental health programs commonly experience.

The aim of the school studies conducted so far has been to evaluate whether MoodGYM implemented in the classroom reduces depressive symptoms, impacts on vulnerability to depression by enhancing self-esteem and reducing negative attributional style, and improves negative attitudes to and beliefs about depression in adolescents. Two controlled trials involving 75 Year 9 boys and 157 Year 10 girls at two single-sex private schools in the Australian Capital Territory have been completed (O'Kearney, Gibson, Christensen, & Griffiths, 2006; O'Kearney, Kang, Christensen, & Griffiths, 2006). These studies were conducted independently and because of differences in curriculum, timetabling and resources there were some procedural differences between them. For each of the studies, however, students were assigned to either a MoodGYM group or a control condition. MoodGYM participants completed one module a week in a computer laboratory at the school during their personal development class time. MoodGYM modules were open for two weeks. One of the researchers attended the first module session to answer questions and to ensure that all participants successfully logged on. The class teachers were present at all times. Participants in the control group undertook the school's normal personal development activities which were about women's nutrition during the MoodGYM trial for the girls and various topics not related to depression for the boys. All participants completed questionnaires measuring depression (The Centre for Epidemiological Studies Depression Scale [CESD]), self-esteem (Rosenberg Self-Esteem Scale), attributional style (The Revised Children's Attributional Style Questionnaire) and attitudes to depression (the personal attitudes subscale of the Depression Stigma Scale) before beginning the program, after finishing the program and once more 20 weeks after completion of the program. At the completion of the program participants in both groups resumed the normal personal development activities.

Overall, the direction of change from pre-intervention to post-intervention in depressive symptoms and attributional style in the two studies favoured MoodGYM users. The relative degree of change, however, was not strong enough to provide the necessary degree of confidence for concluding that MoodGYM is an effective school-based program for reducing depressive symptoms and negative attributional style in adolescent boys or girls. The analysis for those who completed three or more sessions showed small to moderate effect sizes on depression (girls $ES = .11$ [pre to post], $ES = .25$ [pre to follow-up]; boys $ES = .34$ [pre to post], $ES = .12$ [pre to follow-up]) and inconsistent, weak effects for attributional style (for girls $ES = -.26$ [pre to post], $ES = .05$ [pre to follow-up]; for boys $ES = .17$ [pre to post], $ES = .01$ [pre to follow-up]). None of these were significant within a 95% confidence band. A potentially important finding was that MoodGYM was found to reduce the relative risk of adolescents reporting depressive symptoms above the CESD cut off for 'depressed' status compared to the control by 5% at post-intervention and by 13% at follow-up for girls, and by 13% at post-intervention and by 16% at follow-up for boys. This finding is particularly promising given that half of the girls and 35% of the boys scored above this cut off before intervention and support applications of MoodGYM as an indicated program. At the same time, there were inconsistent results about the sustainability of the MoodGYM effects. At the 20-week follow-up, female MoodGYM users demonstrated significantly lower levels of self-reported depressive symptoms relative to controls while the improvements in depression for boys disappeared over time. The observed improvements in attributional style in the MoodGYM boys were not sustained. There were no benefits for MoodGYM users relative to controls in the measures of self-esteem or beliefs about depression at post-intervention or follow-up.

There were also a number of implications from these studies for attempts to apply MoodGYM and other CBT Internet programs as school-based interventions. Of the MoodGYM users 65% of the boys and 70% of the girls completed only one or two modules out of five. This rate of completing is disappointing in view of the supervised nature of the activity. While not out of keeping with previous studies in adults (Christensen et al., 2004; Clarke et al., 2002), the reasons for these low rates of adherence in a curriculum-based application need to be identified if Internet-delivered CBT is to be considered a useful school resource. Female MoodGYM users with initially more positive beliefs about depression, lower vulnerability and depressive symptoms were more likely to complete three or more MoodGYM modules. The low usage of

MoodGYM by participants with elevated depressive symptoms may be due to the impact of depression on an individual's motivation and their ability to concentrate. MoodGYM is comprehensive and requires active engagement in practical exercises. Those with poor concentration and low motivation due to depression may find it difficult to complete. The lack of engagement might also be related to participants receiving feedback about their depressive symptoms after completing a brief online survey of depressive symptomatology as part of the MoodGYM program. Wisdom and Green (2004) found that for some adolescents receiving information about their depression confirmed part of their identity and consequently, they did not try different symptom relief techniques, were sceptical about the effectiveness of treatment and felt hopeless about their prognosis. It could be that receiving such feedback via MoodGYM elicited a similar response. It is important to note that the MoodGYM program recommends that individuals with elevated scores on the depression scale seek the advice and help of a health professional, such as a general practitioner.

A further reason for the modest findings may be reduced appropriateness and attractiveness of the material for this age group. While CBT principles have been shown to apply to adolescents with or vulnerable to depression (Curry, 2001; Lewinsohn, Clarke, Hops, & Andrews, 1990; Shochet et al., 2001), the context, sequence and emphasis, which MoodGYM gives to the various CBT components, may require adjustments. These could include additional information on the rationale of the cognitive techniques and slower pace of delivery. Additionally, MoodGYM was used in the trials in a time-limited format. Users in the community are able and encouraged to access MoodGYM as many times as desired, while in the school-based studies there was an implicit understanding to use MoodGYM only during class. Those who missed the class were not able to make up the module. These considerations suggest that the intervention may need to be modified into a simpler, possibly shorter session format so that adolescents, including those with poor concentration and motivation, find it easier to engage in the exercises. Nevertheless, the finding that the intervention is appealing to girls with fewer depressive symptoms and lower vulnerability to depression lends support to the use of MoodGYM as a means of engaging adolescents and using cognitive–behavioural techniques to promote resilience. Because of its structure MoodGYM also offers considerable scope in providing a menu of intervention modules and strategies focused on and available to specific populations.

In sum, so far the preliminary results of evaluations of a school-based delivery of MoodGYM with relatively small samples of adolescents are encouraging but modest and provide inconsistent evidence of its long-term benefits. Its impact is strongest on self-report of depressive symptoms and not evident for putative vulnerabilities to depression such as attributional style or self-esteem. The ability of Internet CBT programs like MoodGYM to provide booster and catch-up sessions, and to offer targeted menus of modules provide potential remedies to the sustainability, usage and applicability problems. As both studies had methodological problems that may have favoured a null outcome, it is important to continue evaluations of Internet applications of CBT in school settings. A larger study of MoodGYM that involves 20 schools across Australia with 1500 Year 9 and 10 students is currently underway. The results of this multi-school trial will clarify the effectiveness of MoodGYM as an innovative program for reducing depression in adolescence.

References

Berstrom, J., Hollandare, F., Carlbring, P., Kaldo-Sandstrom, V., Ekselius, L., & Andersson, G. (2003). Treatment of depression via the Internet: A randomised trial of a self-help programme. *Journal of Telemedicine & Telecare, 9*(Suppl. 2), 85.

Boyd, C.P., Kostanski, M., Gullone, E., Ollendick, T.H., & Shek, D.T. (2000). Prevalence of anxiety and depression in Australian adolescents: Comparisons with worldwide data. *Journal of Genetic Psychology, 161*(4), 479–492.

Cardemil, E.V., Reivich, K.J., & Seligman, M.E.P. (2002). The prevention of depressive symptoms in low-income minority middle school students. *Prevention & Treatment, 5*(1).

Christensen, H., Griffiths, K.M., & Jorm, A.F. (2004). Delivering interventions for depression by using the internet: Randomised controlled trial. *British Medical Journal, 328*, 265–268A.

Christensen, H., Griffiths, K.M., Mackinnnon, A.J., & Brittliffe, K. (in press). Online randomised controlled trial of brief and full cognitive behaviour therapy for depression. *Psychological Medicine.*

Clarke, G., Hawkins, W., Murphy, M., Sheeber, M., Lewinsohn, P., & Seeley, J. (1995). Targetted prevention of unipolar depression disorder in an at-risk of high school adolescents: A randomised trial of group cognitive intervention. *Journal of the American Academy of Child and Adolescent Psychiatry, 34*, 312–321.

Clarke, G., Reid, E., Eubanks, D., O'Connor, E., DeBar, L.L., & Kelleher, C. (2002). Overcoming depression on the Internet (ODIN): A randomised controlled trial of an Internet skills intervention program. *Journal of Medical Internet Research, 4*, e14.

Clarke, G., Reid, E., Eubanks, D., Kelleher, C., O'Connor, E., DeBar, L.L., et al. (2005). Overcoming Depression on the Internet (ODIN) (2): A randomised trial of a self-help depression skills program with reminders. *Journal of Medical Internet Research, 7*, e14.

Colley, A., & Comber, C. (2003). Age and gender differences in computer use and attitudes among secondary school students: What has changed? *Educational Research, 45*, 155–165.

Curry, J. (2001). Specific psychotherapies for childhood and adolescent depression. *Biological Psychiatry, 49*, 1091–1100

Harrington, R., Whittaker, J., & Shoebridge, P. (1998). Psychological treatment of depression in children and adolescents. *British Journal of Psychiatry, 248*, 32–45.

Kessler, R.C., Avenevoli, S., & Merikangas, K.R. (2001). Mood disorders in children and adolescents: An epidemiological perspective. *Biological Psychiatry, 49*, 1002–1014.

Lewinsohn, P.M., Clarke, G.N., Hops, H., & Andrews, J. (1990). Cognitive-behavioural treatment for depressed adolescents. *Behaviour Therapy, 21*, 385–401.

Lowry-Webster, H.M., Barrett, P.M., & Dadds, M.R. (2001). A universal prevention trial of anxiety and depressive symptomatology in childhood: Preliminary data from an Australian study. *Behaviour Change, 18*(1), 36–50.

Merry, S., McDowell, H., Hetrick, S., Bir, J., & Muller, N. (2004). Psychological and/or educational interventions for the prevention of depression in children and adolescents. *The Cochrane Database of Systematic Reviews* (2) Art. No.: CD003380. DOI: 10.1002/14651858.CD003380.

O'Kearney, R., Gibson, M., Christensen, H., & Griffiths, K.M (2006). Effects of a cognitive–behavioural Internet program on depression, vulnerability to depression and stigma in adolescent males: A school-based controlled trial. *Cognitive Behaviour Therapy, 35*(1), 43–54.

O'Kearney, R., Kang, K., Christensen, H. & Griffiths, K.M (2006). *A self-directed Internet program for depressive symptoms and vulnerability to depression in adolescent girls: Results of a school-based controlled trial.* Manuscript under review.

Rutter, M., Kim-Cohen, J., & Maughan, B. (2006). Continuities and discontinuities in psychopathology between childhood and adult life. *Journal of Child Psychology and Psychiatry, 47*, 276–295.

Shochet, I.M., Dadds, M.R., Holland, D., Whitefield, K., Harnett, P.H., & Osgarby, S.M. (2001). The efficacy of a universal school-based program to prevent adolescent depression. *Journal of Clinical Child Psychology, 30*(3), 303–315.

Wisdom, J., & Green, C. (2004). 'Being in a funk': Teens' efforts to understand their depressive experiences. *Qualitative Health Research, 14*, 1227–1238.

Clinical implications of empirical research

CHAPTER 16

Maladaptive Schemas and Eating Disorders: Therapeutic Considerations

Sandi Hill and Stephen Touyz

It is well known that eating disorders are characterised by severe distur-bances in eating behaviour and cognitions regarding food, weight and shape. While there is different distinguishing pathology involved in anorexia nervosa (AN) an d bulimia nervosa conditions (BN), cognitive–behavioural treatment (CBT) models applied to the eating disorders have been established on food, weight and shape cognitions maintaining eating disorder pathology (Garner & Bemis, 1982; Fairburn, 1981; Fairburn & Cooper, 1989). CBT studies only provide indirect evidence of cognitive–behavioural models (Byrne & McLean, 2002), and its limited effectiveness to adequately treat eating disorders is problematic for the cognitive–behavioural theory from which it is derived.

It is now common opinion in the literature that while disturbances in cognition regarding eating, weight and shape are necessary for under-standing eating disorders, they are not sufficient explanatory constructs (Fairburn, Cooper, & Shafran, 2003; Waller & Kennerley, 2003; Waller, 2006). More important, it is now recommended that cognitive–behav-ioural models of eating disorders include a focus on the role of 'deeper' schema-level representations unrelated to food, eating, weight and shape in eating disorders as indicated by recent empirical research (e.g., Cooper, 1997; Hughes, Hamill, van Gerko, Lockwood, & Waller, 2006; Leung, Waller, & Thomas, 1999; Waller, Ohanian, Meyer, & Osman, 2000). In fact, some authors have indicated that unless core schemas are identi-fied and ameliorated, eating disorders cannot be treated successfully (Fairburn et al., 2003; Hughes et al., 2006).

Advances in theoretical models have refined the early definitions of schema (Beck, Rush, Shaw, & Emery, 1979) and suggest schemas are interlocking multimodal structures, encapsulating more than a single belief, and comprising memories, emotions, bodily sensations and cognitions (Waller & Kennerley, 2003; Young, Klosko, & Weishaar, 2003). Schemas, in general, are difficult to assess and access in treatment and are more resistant to change than conditional beliefs (Layden, Newman, Freeman, & Byers Morse, 1993). Young (1994) posits that three processes are involved in perpetuating schema: maintenance, avoidance and compensation (Young, 1994). Any clinical assessment of schema and schema processes may be supplemented by questionnaires (Cooper, Cohen-Tovee, Todd, Wells, & Tovee, 1997; Young, 1994). The most utilised and psychometrically validated instrument to identify schemas is the Young Schema Questionnaire (Young, 1994) that comprises 75 statements referring to 15 underlying schemas including emotional deprivation, abandonment, mistrust/abuse, social isolation, defectiveness/shame, failure, dependence/incompetence, vulnerability to harm, enmeshment, subjugation, social sacrifice, emotional inhibition, unrelenting standards, entitlement, and insufficient self-control.

Schema theorists and researchers argue that maladaptive schemas develop early in childhood from the interplay between the child's innate temperament, and the child's ongoing toxic interpersonal experiences with parents, siblings, or peers. Young et al. (2003) suggest schemas that develop early in life are the most powerful and pervasive and typically originate in the family. Young et al. (2003) suggest that maladaptive schemas develop from a frustration of needs, if the child is traumatised or victimised, if the child's needs are overindulged, or there is a selective internalisation of the parents' unhealthy schemas. In eating disorders, the development of maladaptive schemas has been understood from anecdotal evidence and scientific research on family functioning.

Early clinical accounts of family functioning in the development of AN (e.g., Minuchin, Rosman, & Baker, 1978) described the anorexic family as having a characteristic style of interaction, including rigidity, enmeshment, conflict avoidance, and overprotectiveness. In contrast, there is little known of family functioning in BN, due to its emergence in the late 20th century in westernised societies (Russell, 1979), possibly suggesting a significant cultural influence (Ward, Ramsay, Turnball, Benedettini, & Treasure, 2000b). Research suggests that profiles of bulimic and anorexic (binge–purging subtype) families appear quite different from restricting families and, as such, are characterised as being unsupportive, detached, conflictual, hostile, enmeshed but disengaged, and non-nurturant (Humphrey, Apple, & Kirschenbaum, 1986; Johnson & Flach, 1985).

Early observations of family functioning in eating disorder aetiology have been explained in terms of attachment theory (O'Kearney, 1996). The central premise of attachment theory is that the attachment relationship impacts on the development of an infant's beliefs and competencies about interpersonal functioning, on the emergence of the 'self', on motivation, on self-esteem, and on the capacity to regulate affect. Sequelae associated with disturbances in attachment include significant impairments in these areas of functioning and the possibility of profound disruption or delay in the individual's psychological development (Cicchetti, 1993).

In her seminal work, Bruch (1973) postulates early disturbances in the mother–child relationship as links to the aetiology and dynamic issues in AN. Specifically, Bruch describes a mother who superimposes on her infant daughter her own concept of the child's needs so that the child's needs and impulses remain poorly differentiated (Ward, Ramsay, & Treasure, 2000a). The resultant product of this dynamic for the child is a lack of a sense of separateness and a pervasive sense of ineffectiveness, which is posited as underlying the development of an eating disorder (Ward et al., 2000a). A number of Young's (1994) postulated schemas may develop in the child from this form of early maternal relationship such as enmeshment, defectiveness, emotional inhibition, worthlessness and social sacrifice. In order to defer experiencing painful schema, the individual engages in eating disorder thoughts and behaviours, which temporarily aids in avoiding schema contact. Other cognitive strategies used to avoid schema activation include developing compensatory schemas such as unrelenting standards or entitlement. Such schemas may be evident in those who demonstrate obsessive tendencies such as clinical perfectionism.

Eating disorders generally develop in adolescence during the individuation process that constitutes a sensitive period for the attachment system (Holmbeck & Hill, 1986). Armstrong and Roth (1989) argue that eating disorder symptoms persist as a way of maintaining connectedness while avoiding rejection from an insecurely perceived caregiver (Ward et al., 2000a). The authors propose that where restricting food provides a form of controlling interpersonal attachments in a safe nonthreatening way, bingeing fills a need for nurturance and self-soothing for individuals that believe others cannot be trusted to meet these needs. Ward et al.'s (2000b) study on attachment patterns found patients scored significantly higher than controls on compulsive care-seeking and compulsive self-reliance attachment styles. The authors suggest that these patterns of attachment are seen therapeutically where eating disorder patients often display contradictory messages in treatment such as a covert 'help me' together with the overt message 'leave me alone'. This ambivalence toward treatment highlights the possibility of continuing attachment difficulties and the presence of underlying maladaptive schemas (e.g., emotional deprivation and mistrust/abuse) affecting treatment progress.

Additional empirical evidence demonstrates unhealthy patterns of attachment in the development and maintenance of eating disorder pathology (see O'Kearney, 1996). Studies using the Parental Bonding Instrument (PBI; Parker, Tupling, & Brown, 1979) have found unhealthy levels of recalled parental care and overprotection among women with AN and BN (e.g., Calam, Waller, Slade, & Newton, 1990; Rhodes & Kroger, 1992).

Recent empirical research is beginning to highlight the importance of maladaptive schemas (e.g., Cooper, 1997; Dingemans, Spinhoven, & van Furth, 2006; Leung et al., 1999; Leung, Thomas, & Waller, 2000, Waller & Kennerley, 2003; Waller et al., 2000; Waller, Dickson, & Ohanian, 2002) in the aetiology and maintenance of eating disorders. The hypothesised early origin of maladaptive schemas indicates that a disturbed attachment relationship would be closely associated with the development of such schemas. Early research is suggesting significant mediating and moderating relationships of several maladaptive schemas on parental styles and eating disorder psychopathology (Jones, Harris, & Leung, 2005; Meyer & Gillings, 2004; Turner, Rose, & Cooper, 2004).

Leung et al. (2000) explored the postulated link between perceived parental bonding and the development of maladaptive schemas in eating disordered women. The findings indicated a strong link between perceived poor parental attachment behaviour and maladaptive schemas. In particular, low maternal and paternal care was highly predictive of unhealthy core beliefs in anorexic women, but only weak links were found in the bulimic and comparison groups. The only schema reliably predicted by low levels of maternal care in all groups was 'emotional deprivation'. Emotional deprivation schema has been described as a sense that one's emotional needs have not been met, and the individual has not experienced caring and nurturing relationships. Emotional deprivation schema has been associated with bingeing, vomiting, and lower body mass indices in models attempting to explain the link between cognition and behaviour in eating disorders (Hughes et al., 2006).

Hill et al.'s (2006) study examining aspects of the primary caregiver–child relationship in eating disorders found that the eating disorder group had perceived low levels of maternal care compared to a nonclinical control group. In addition, this study demonstrated that in the eating disorder group the only schema significantly correlated for mothers and daughters was emotional deprivation, and this schema in daughters was predicted by both mothers' emotional deprivation schema and daughters' perceived low levels of maternal care. A finding possibly indicating that the development of emotional deprivation schema in eating disorders may be related to the resultant maternal caregivers' difficulty in forming secure relationships due to their own un-nurturing felt experiences. A result that may inform therapists attempting to build healthy therapeutic alliances with eating disorder patients.

In conclusion, the significance of deeper level maladaptive schemas in eating disorder psychopathology is gaining considerable empirical support. There is now general empirical evidence for treatment of eating disorders to include the assessment and treatment of maladaptive schemas. The attendance of clinicians to clients underlying schemas appears important in the amelioration of both eating disorder behaviours and cognitions relating to food, weight and shape. Understanding the implications of holding an 'emotional deprivation' schema may be important in the therapeutic relationship and, thus, treatment efficacy. Clinically, along with traditional CBT framework and techniques, treatment efficacy may be enhanced by considering a client centred approach to the therapeutic relationship to facilitate modelling of a secure attachment relationship and to promote schema healing.

References

Armstrong, J.G., & Roth, D.M. (1989). Attachment and separation difficulties in eating disorders: A preliminary investigation. *International Journal of Eating Disorders, 8*, 141–155.

Beck, A.T., Rush, A.J., Shaw, B.F., & Emery, G. (1979). *Cognitive therapy of depression*. New York: Guildford Press.

Bruch, H. (1973). *Eating disorders: Obesity, anorexia nervosa and the person within*. New York: Basic Books.

Byrne, S.M., & McLean, N.J. (2002). The cognitive-behavioural model of bulimia nervosa: A direct evaluation. *International Journal of Eating Disorders, 31*, 17–31.

Calam, R., Waller, G., Slade, P., & Newton, T. (1990). Eating disorders and perceived relationships with parents. *International Journal of Eating Disorder, 9*, 479–485.

Cicchetti, D. (1993). Developmental psychopathology: Reactions, reflections, projections. *Developmental Review, 13*, 471–502.

Cooper, M. (1997). Cognitive theory in anorexia nervosa and bulimia nervosa: A review. *Behavioural and Cognitive Psychotherapy, 25*, 113–145.

Cooper, M.J., Cohen-Tovee, E., Todd, G., Wells, A., & Tovee, M. (1997). A questionnaire to assess assumptions and beliefs in eating disorders: Preliminary findings. *Behaviour Research and Therapy, 35*, 381–388.

Dingemans, A.E., Spinhoven, P.H., & van Furth, E.F. (2006). Maladaptive core beliefs and eating disorder symptoms. *Eating Behaviors, 7*, 258–265.

Fairburn, C.G. (1981). A cognitive behavioural approach to the treatment of BN. *Psychological Medicine, 11*, 707–711.

Fairburn, C.G., & Cooper, P. (1989). Eating disorders. In K. Hawton, P.M. Salkovskis, J. Kirk, & D.M. Clark (Eds.), *Cognitive behaviour therapy for psychiatric problems* (pp. 227–314). New York: Oxford University Press.

Fairburn, C.G., Cooper, Z., & Shafran, R. (2003). Cognitive behaviour therapy for eating disorders: A "transdiagnostic" theory and treatment. *Behaviour Research and Therapy, 41*, 509–528.

Garner, D.M., & Bemis, K.M. (1982). A cognitive–behavioural approach to AN. *Cognitive Therapy and Research, 6*(2), 123–150.

Hill, S., Touyz, S., Thornton, C., Clarke, S., Kohn, M., George, L., et al. (2006). *An investigation of family factors and schema in mother-daughter dyads with and without an eating disorder.* Manuscript in preparation.

Holmbeck, G.N., & Hill, J.P. (1986). A path-analytic approach to the relations between parental traits and acceptance and adolescent adjustment. *Sex Roles, 14*, 315–334.

Hughes, M.L., Hamill, M., van Gerko, K., Lockwood, R., & Waller, G. (2006). The relationship between different levels of cognition and behavioural symptoms in the eating disorders. *Eating Behaviors, 7*, 125–133.

Humphrey, L.L., Apple, R.F., & Kirschenbaum, D.S. (1986). Differentiating bulimic-anorexic from normal families using interpersonal and behavioral observational systems. *Journal of Consulting and Clinical Psychology, 54*, 190–195.

Johnson, C., & Flach, A. (1985). Family characteristics of 105 patients with bulimia nervosa. *American Journal of Psychiatry, 142*, 1321–1324.

Jones, C., Harris, G., & Leung, N. (2005). Parental rearing behaviours and eating disorders: The moderating role of core beliefs. *Eating Behaviors, 6*, 355–364.

Layden, M.A., Newman, C.F., Freeman, A., & Byers Morse, S. (1993). *Cognitive therapy of borderline personality disorder.* Boston, MA: Allyn and Bacon.

Leung, N., Waller, G., & Thomas, G.V. (1999). Core beliefs in anorexic and bulimic women. *Journal of Nervous and Mental Disease, 187*, 736–741.

Leung, N., Thomas, G.V., & Waller, G. (2000). The relationship between parental bonding and core beliefs in anorexic and bulimic women. *British Journal of Clinical Psychology, 39*, 205–213.

Meyer, C., & Gillings, K. (2004). Parental bonding and bulimic psychopathology: The mediating role of mistrust/abuse beliefs. *International Journal of Eating Disorders, 35*, 229–233.

Minuchin, S., Rosman, B.L., & Baker, L. (1978). *Psychosomatic families: AN in content.* Cambridge, MA: Harvard University Press.

O'Kearney, R. (1996). Attachment disruption in anorexia nervosa and bulimia nervosa: A review of theory and empirical research. *International Journal of Eating Disorders, 20*(2), 115–127.

Parker, G., Tupling, H., & Brown, L. (1979). A parental bonding instrument. *British Journal of Medical Psychology, 52*, 1–10.

Rhodes, B., & Kroger, J. (1992). Parental bonding and separation-individuation difficulties among late adolescent eating disordered women. *Child Psychiatry and Human Development, 22*, 249–263.

Russell, G.F.M. (1979). Bulimia nervosa: An ominous variant of anorexia nervosa. *Psychological Medicine, 9*, 429–448.

Turner, H.M., Rose, K.S., & Cooper, M.J. (2004). Parental bonding and eating disorder symptoms in adolescents: The mediating role of core beliefs. *Eating Behaviors, 6*, 113–118.

Waller, G. (2006). *A schema-based cognitive behavioural model of the aetiology and maintenance of restricting and bulimic pathology in the eating disorders.* Manuscript submitted for publication.

Waller, G., & Kennerley, H. (2003). Cognitive-behavioural treatments: Current status and future directions. In J. Treasure, U. Schmidt, C. Dare, & E. van Furth (Eds.), *Handbook of eating disorders: Theory, treatment and research* (pp. 233–251). Chichester, UK: Wiley.

Waller, G., Dickson, C., & Ohanian, V. (2002). Cognitive content in bulimic disorders: Core beliefs and eating attitudes. *Eating Behaviors, 3*, 171–178.

Waller, G., Ohanian, V., Meyer, C., & Osman, S. (2000). Cognitive content among bulimic women: The role of core beliefs. *International Journal of Eating Disorders, 28*, 235–241.

Ward, A., Ramsay, R., & Treasure, J. (2000a). Attachment research in eating disorders. *British Journal of Medical Psychology, 73*, 35–51.

Ward, A., Ramsay, R., Turnball, S., Benedettini, M., & Treasure, J. (2000b). Attachment patterns in eating disorders: Past in the present. *International Journal of Eating Disorders, 28*, 370–376.

Young, J.E. (1994). *Cognitive therapy for personality disorders: A schema-focused approach* (2nd ed.). Sarasota, FL: Professional Resource Exchange.

Young, J.E., Klosko, J.S., & Weishaar, M.E. (2003). *Schema therapy: A practitioner's guide.* New York: The Guildford Press.

CHAPTER 17

The Nature and Role of Avoidance in Depression

Michelle L. Moulds and Eva Kandris

Avoidance is fundamental to the conceptualisation and diagnosis of anxiety disorders, but has received less attention in the context of depression. As noted in recent commentaries (Martell, Addis, & Jacobson, 2001; Ottenbreit & Dobson, 2004), Ferster (1973) proposed the key role of avoidance in depression, positing that not only do depressed individuals engage in less positively reinforced behaviours, they also demonstrate avoidance and escape behaviours (e.g., rumination, complaining). Ottenbreit and Dobson (2004) note that recently the literature has evidenced a revived interest in avoidance in depression. The development of behavioural activation (BA; Jacobson, Martell, & Dimidjian, 2001) as a treatment for depression reflects this renewed focus. The theoretical basis of BA is that depression is characterised by dysfunctional avoidance, withdrawal and inactivity. Accordingly, the emphasis of BA is on identifying and replacing problematic behavioural patterns.

Understanding the role of avoidance in depression is one focus of our research group. Below is an outline of some of the projects we have conducted to explore the nature, impact and manifestation of behavioural, cognitive and emotional avoidance.

Avoidance and Rumination

In the BA model, rumination is conceptualised as '... an escape or avoidance behavior. It keeps the individual separated from others and prevents true problem solving' (Martell et al., 2001, p. 121). Although rumination is distinctive from more overt examples of avoidant behaviour (e.g., social withdrawal), the BA framework proposes that they share an avoidant function. That is, rumination promotes avoidance of engagement with the environment and, as a result, limits active problem-solving. According to this model, rumination is reinforced in two ways; first, complaints about life circumstances may be reinforced, and/or second, by operating as an alternative to addressing problems, thereby avoiding dealing with difficult circumstances and associated distress (Martell et al., 2001).

In accord with a renewed focus on avoidance in depression, Ottenbreit and Dobson (2004) developed the Cognitive-Behavioral Avoidance Scale (CBAS) to index avoidance across four key domains: behavioural–social, behavioural–nonsocial, cognitive–social, and cognitive–nonsocial. In their validation study, Ottenbreit and Dobson (2004) called for follow-up investigations of the interrelationship of avoidance and established cognitive correlates of depression such as rumination.

Nolen-Hoeksema's response styles theory (Nolen-Hoeksema, 1991) holds that individuals who ruminate about the causes/implications of symptoms are more likely to become depressed and remain depressed for longer. Prospective studies support the role of rumination in depression onset (Nolen-Hoeksema, Morrow, & Fredrickson, 1993) and maintenance (Nolen-Hoeksema, 2000). Experimental work has linked rumination to depression-related deficits, including impoverished problem-solving (Watkins & Moulds, 2005), negative cognition (Lavender & Watkins, 2004) and overgeneral autobiographical memory retrieval (Watkins, Teasdale, & Williams, 2000).

A recent development in this field is the differentiation between two functionally distinct modes of rumination (Treynor, Gonzalez, & Nolen-Hoeksema, 2003; also Watkins, 2004; Watkins & Moulds, 2005). For example, a factor analysis of the Ruminative Response Scale (RRS; Nolen-Hoeksema & Morrow, 1991) — the gold standard self-report measure of rumination — identified two distinct factors: reflection and brooding (Treynor et al., 2003). Treynor et al. (2003) proposed that the brooding factor indexes a tendency toward moody pondering (e.g., *Think about a recent situation, wishing it had gone better*), while reflection captures a tendency to contemplate/reflect (e.g., *Go someplace alone to think about your feelings*). Supporting this conceptual distinction, these factors have differential relationships with depression — brooding is most strongly associated with depression concurrently and longitudinally (Breakspear & Moulds, 2006; Treynor et al., 2003).

We examined the association between rumination and avoidance (Moulds, Kandris, Starr, & Wong, in press). We hypothesised that rumination would be associated with behavioural avoidance, and that brooding would be more strongly correlated with avoidance than reflection. As predicted, participants with higher levels of depression were more likely to ruminate and engage in avoidance, even after controlling for anxiety. Brooding was positively correlated with depression and anxiety, as well as behavioural and cognitive avoidance. Avoidance predicted unique variance in depression, over and above anxiety and rumination, supporting the suggestion that '... avoidance may deserve more consideration in the conceptualization of depressive disorders' (Ottenbreit & Dobson, 2004, p. 308).

Emotional Avoidance and Rumination

Another possibility is that rumination functions to avoid the emotional impact of negative material. On the basis that rumination and worry share common features (Segerstrom, Tsao, Alden, & Craske, 2000; Watkins, Moulds, & Mackintosh, 2005), Watkins and Moulds (2004) proposed that the avoidance theory of worry (Borkovec, Ray, & Stober, 1998; Stober & Borkovec, 2002) may similarly account for the maintenance of rumination. On the grounds that worry is verbal rather than visual/image-based, this model holds that worry impedes the activation of somatic/physiological arousal (Vrana, Cuthbert, & Lang, 1986). Stober (1998) and Borkovec et al. (1998) hypothesised that the abstractness, or reduced concreteness, of worry is the cognitive mechanism that limits activation of imagery. A number of studies have demonstrated that reduced concreteness is a feature of chronic worry (Stober & Borkovec, 2002; Stober, Tepperwien, & Staak, 2000).

Watkins and Moulds (2004) found that depressed individuals generated more abstract descriptions of problems about which they were ruminating, compared to recovered depressed and never depressed participants. These findings concur with the proposal that rumination, like worry, is associated with reduced concreteness, and that this may serve a cognitive avoidant function. In a sense, this may appear counter intuitive; by definition, rumination is a repetitive, recyclic thinking style. Rather than avoid, rumination exacerbates focus on negative material. However, it may be that the abstract style of thinking about the causes/meanings/consequences of problems that characterises rumination facilitates the avoidance of imagery and emotion (Watkins & Moulds, 2004).

To test this possibility, we investigated the relationship between rumination and emotional avoidance (Cribb, Moulds, & Carter, 2005). Experiential avoidance has been the focus of increasing research attention in the past decade (Hayes et al., 2004). Preliminary evidence indicates that depressed individuals engage in experiential avoidance (Hayes et al., 2004; Tull, Gratz, Salters, & Roemer, 2004). Hayes, Strosahl and Wilson

(1999) specify that emotion is the primary internal event that individuals avoid. Thus, experiential avoidance represents a useful construct with which to investigate the avoidant function of rumination. Accordingly, we measured depression, rumination, avoidance and mood state in a non-clinical sample, and presented a sad mood emotion eliciting film clip. Participants' written summary of the clip was rated for degree of abstractness/concreteness. As expected, participants with higher depression levels were more likely to ruminate and engage in experiential avoidance (after covarying for anxiety). Further, greater experiential avoidance and rumination correlated with more abstract film clip descriptions.

Tempting temporal accounts of these findings are that dysphoric and depressed individuals ruminate (a) rather than engage in activities, to limit the discomfort potentially evoked by them (possible behavioural pathway), and/or (b) to limit the distressing affect associated with concrete, image-based thought content (possible cognitive pathway). However, the correlational designs preclude causal or mediational interpretations. Future experimental and longitudinal investigations will clarify the direction of these associations.

Cognitive Avoidance Strategies in the Management of Intrusive Memories

Intrusive memories of negative events are the core diagnostic marker of posttraumatic stress disorder (PTSD). Recent evidence has demonstrated that intrusive memories are also common in depression (Carlier, Voerman, & Gersons, 2000; Kuyken & Brewin, 1994). Kuyken and Brewin (1994) found a positive relationship between depression severity, intrusion and avoidance of memories, and that depressed individuals with more intrusive memories of abuse report lower self-esteem and a more negative attribution style (Kuyken & Brewin, 1999). Intrusive memories also play a role in the course of depression; at 6-month follow-up, baseline intrusion and avoidance of distressing memories predict depression (Brewin, Reynolds, & Tata, 1999) and anxiety (Brewin, Watson, McCarthy, Hyman, & Dayson, 1998). Little research has investigated the cognitive mechanisms employed by depressed individuals in response to intrusive memories.

By contrast, cognitive models of PTSD have implicated a range of avoidant processes in the maintenance of intrusions. Ehlers and Steil (1995) proposed that individuals who possess dysfunctional appraisals of their intrusive symptoms are more likely to rate their intrusions as distressing. This distress prompts the use of avoidance strategies such as rumination, dissociation and suppression. These strategies maintain

PTSD by impeding emotional processing and preventing changes in the meaning of the trauma and/or intrusions, ultimately increasing intrusion frequency (Ehlers & Steil, 1995). This model is well-supported by cross-sectional and longitudinal studies (e.g., Clohessy & Ehlers, 1999; Dunmore, Clark, & Ehlers, 2001; Steil & Ehlers, 2000). Despite evidence of shared features of intrusive memories in depression and PTSD (Reynolds & Brewin, 1999), the role of avoidant strategies in managing intrusive memories in depression has not been explored.

Accordingly, we applied Ehlers and Steil's (1995) model to investigate intrusive memories in depression (Starr & Moulds, 2006). Participants who reported an intrusive memory in the previous week completed questionnaires that indexed cognitive and affective responses to the memory. Negative interpretations of intrusive memories were the strongest predictor of depression, explaining variance over and above intrusion frequency. Negative meanings were associated with depression severity, intrusion-related distress and, as predicted, cognitive avoidance strategies (particularly rumination). These relationships remained significant afater controlling for intrusion frequency and the severity of memory content.

Another characteristic of intrusive memories linked to avoidance is the vantage point from which memories are recalled. Memories recalled in the first person are referred to as 'field' memories, while those recalled in the third person, from a detached perspective, are described as 'observer' memories. Field memories are emotion-laden, while observer memories contain more descriptive but less affective information (McIsaac & Eich, 2002; Nigro & Neisser, 1983). McIsaac and Eich (2004) postulated that an observer perspective may represent a means by which individuals with PTSD avoid the affect associated with recollecting their trauma. Consistent with this proposal, they found that observer perspective PTSD trauma memories contained more physical and peripheral details, while field memories were comprised of more affective information, and were rated as more anxiety-eliciting (McIsaac & Eich, 2004).

We examined whether adopting an observer perspective on the content of intrusive memories is linked to additional cognitive avoidance strategies in depression (Williams & Moulds, 2006). As predicted, in a sample of mildly depressed participants, an observer vantage point was associated with (a) numbness and detachment when recalling the memory and (b) attempts to suppress the memory. Participants who adopted an observer perspective reported higher levels of rumination, suppression and detachment/numbness when recalling the memory (Williams & Moulds, 2006).

Beyond an observer vantage point and the forms of cognitive avoidance outlined by Ehlers and Steil (1995), depressed individuals may employ additional strategies to avoid intrusive memories and their associated affect. We are currently exploring this possibility in an investigation of cognitive and behavioural safety behaviours that depressed individuals adopt in an attempt to avoid the affect elicited by the experience of intrusive memories.

How Do the Findings Inform Clinical Practice?

Our convergent findings have key implications for the assessment, formulation and treatment of depression. First, they highlight the importance of clinicians conducting a thorough evaluation of cognitive, behavioural and emotional avoidance in the assessment of depressed clients. For instance, to assess for the presence of emotional avoidance, a clinician might explore beliefs about the experience of negative emotions and look out for indications of intolerance (e.g., 'I am afraid of my emotions' or 'I just wish I could stop having emotions'). Second, in line with BA, our findings underscore the importance of thoroughly assessing the content of rumination, as well as the potential range of avoidant functions (e.g., promoting avoidance of active problem-solving, limiting the experience of emotion) of this cognitive process. Finally, they highlight the importance of exploring the avoidant cognitive strategies that clients utilise to manage cognitive phenomena such as intrusive memories, as avoidant processes are linked not only to the persistence of these memories, but more broadly, to the maintenance of depression.

In terms of treatment delivery, our outcomes underline the importance of therapists being alert to and anticipating emotional avoidance, in light of its potential capacity to reduce engagement in treatment and thereby limit the effectiveness of interventions (e.g., during cognitive challenging). Consistent with this idea, recently developed therapeutic paradigms aimed explicitly at reducing avoidance have gained popularity, including BA (Martell et al., 2001), mindfulness-based cognitive therapy (Segal, Williams, & Teasdale, 2002) and acceptance and commitment therapy (Hayes et al., 1999). Our findings also highlight the importance of developing treatment strategies that reduce avoidance of intrusive memories. Leading commentators have proposed the utility of addressing intrusive memories as part of CBT protocols for depression (e.g., Brewin et al., 1999; Kuyken & Brewin, 1994). Outcome trials that evaluate the efficacy of cognitive interventions that target avoidance of intrusive memories in depression will be a key development in the field.

Unresolved Questions and Future Directions

Despite recent conceptual and clinical developments, a number of outstanding issues remain. Central to these is the question of whether the tendency to avoid is a trait that confers vulnerability to depression, or rather, is epiphenomenal. We are currently exploring this issue in a large-scale prospective study of a high-risk sample. The findings of this and other longitudinal research will clarify whether possessing a disposition to avoid activities, cognitions and/or emotions is a vulnerability factor that increases the likelihood of experiencing depressive symptoms, intrusive memories and/or additional psychopathological responses following exposure to negative life events.

Acknowledgments

This research was supported by a grant from the Australian Research Council awarded to the first author. The studies reported were conducted with our collaborators Alishia Williams, Gemille Cribb, Sally Carter, Susannah Starr and Amanda Wong. We are grateful for the contribution of their research and for their input into many of the ideas presented in this chapter.

References

Borkovec, T.D., Ray, W.J., & Stober, J. (1998). Worry: A cognitive phenomenon intimately linked to affective, physiological, and interpersonal behavioral processes. *Cognitive Therapy and Research, 22,* 561–576.

Breakspear, S., & Moulds, M.L. (2006). *Is brooding the maladaptive component of depressive rumination?* Manuscript submitted for publication.

Brewin, C.R., Reynolds, M., & Tata, P. (1999). Autobiographical memory processes and the course of depression. *Journal of Abnormal Psychology, 108,* 511–517.

Brewin, C.R., Watson, M., McCarthy, S., Hyman, P., & Dayson, D. (1998). Intrusive memories and depression in cancer patients. *Behaviour Research and Therapy, 36,* 1131–1142.

Carlier, I.V.E., Voerman, B.E., & Gersons, B.P.R. (2000). Intrusive traumatic recollections and comorbid PTSD in depressed patients. *Psychosomatic Medicine, 62,* 26–32.

Clohessy, S., & Ehlers, A. (1999). PTSD symptoms, response to intrusive memories and coping in ambulance service workers. *British Journal of Clinical Psychology, 38,* 251–265.

Cribb, G., Moulds, M.L., & Carter, S. (2005). *Rumination and experiential avoidance in depression.* Manuscript submitted for publication.

Dunmore, E., Clark, D.M., & Ehlers, A. (2001). A prospective study of the role of cognitive factors in persistent PTSD after physical or sexual assault. *Behaviour Research and Therapy, 39,* 1063–1984.

Ehlers, A., & Steil, R. (1995). Maintenance of intrusive memories in PTSD: A cognitive approach. *Behavioural and Cognitive Psychotherapy, 23,* 217–249.

Ferster, C.B. (1973). A functional analysis of depression. *American Psychologist, 28,* 857–870.

Hayes, S.C., Strosahl, K., & Wilson, K.G. (1999). *Acceptance and commitment therapy: An experiential approach to behaviour change.* New York: Guilford Press.

Hayes, S.C., Strosahl, K., Wilson, K.G., Bissett, R.T., Pistorello, J., Toarmino, D. et al. (2004). Measuring experiential avoidance: A preliminary test of a working model. *Psychological Record, 54,* 553–578.

Jacobson, N.S., Martell, C.R., & Dimidjian, S. (2001). Behavioral activation treatment for depression: Returning to contextual roots. *Clinical Psychology: Science and Practice, 8,* 255–270.

Kuyken, W., & Brewin, C.R. (1994). Intrusive memories of childhood abuse during depressive episodes. *Behaviour Research and Therapy, 32,* 525–528.

Kuyken, W., & Brewin, C.R. (1999). The relation of early abuse to cognition and coping in depression. *Cognitive Therapy and Research, 23,* 665–677.

Lavender A., & Watkins, E. (2004). Rumination and future thinking in depression. *British Journal of Clinical Psychology, 43,* 129–142.

Martell, C.R., Addis, M.E., & Jacobson, N.S. (2001). *Depression in context: Strategies for guided action.* New York: Norton.

McIsaac, H.K., & Eich, E. (2002). Vantage point in episodic memory. *Psychonomic Bulletin and Review, 9,* 146–150.

McIsaac, H.K., & Eich, E. (2004). Vantage point in traumatic memory. *Psychological Science, 15,* 248–253.

Moulds, M.L., Kandris, E., Starr, S., & Wong, A.C.M. (2007). The relationship between rumination, avoidance and depression in a non-clinical sample. *Behaviour Research and Therapy, 45,* 251–261.

Nigro, G., & Neisser, U. (1983). Point of view in personal memories. *Cognitive Psychology, 15,* 467–482.

Nolen-Hoeksema, S. (1991). Responses to depression and their effects on the duration of depressive episodes. *Journal of Abnormal Psychology, 100,* 569–582.

Nolen-Hoeksema, S. (2000). The role of rumination in depressive disorders and mixed anxiety/depressive symptoms. *Journal of Abnormal Psychology, 109,* 504–511.

Nolen-Hoeksema, S., & Morrow, J. (1991). A prospective study of depression and posttraumatic stress symptoms after a natural disaster: The 1989 Loma Prieta earthquake. *Journal of Personality and Social Psychology, 61,* 115–121.

Nolen-Hoeksema, S., Morrow, J., & Fredrickson, B.L. (1993). Response styles and the duration of episodes of depressed mood. *Journal of Abnormal Psychology, 102,* 20–28.

Ottenbreit, N.D., & Dobson, K.S. (2004). Avoidance and depression: The construction of the Cognitive-Behavioral Avoidance Scale. *Behaviour Research and Therapy, 42,* 293–313.

Reynolds, M., & Brewin, C.R. (1999). Intrusive memories in depression and PTSD. *Behaviour Research and Therapy, 37,* 201–215.

Segal, Z.V., Williams, J.M.G., & Teasdale, J.D. (2002). *Mindfulness-based cognitive therapy for depression.* New York: The Guilford Press.

Segerstrom, S.C., Tsao, J.C.I., Alden, L.E., & Craske. M.G. (2000). Worry and rumination: Repetitive thoughts as a concomitant and predictor of negative mood. *Cognitive Therapy and Research, 24,* 671–688.

Starr, S., & Moulds, M.L. (2006). The role of negative interpretations of intrusive memories in depression. *Journal of Affective Disorders, 93,* 125–132.

Steil, R., & Ehlers, A. (2000). Dysfunctional meaning of posttraumatic intrusions in chronic PTSD. *Behaviour Research and Therapy, 38,* 537–558.

Stober, J. (1998). Worry, problem elaboration and suppression of imagery: The role of concreteness. *Behaviour Research and Therapy, 36,* 751–756.

Stober, J., & Borkovec, T.D. (2002). Reduced concreteness of worry in generalized anxiety disorder: Findings from a therapy study. *Cognitive Therapy and Research, 26,* 89–96.

Stober, J., Tepperwien, S., & Staak, M. (2000). Worrying leads to reduced concreteness of problem elaborations: Evidence for the avoidance theory of worry. *Anxiety, Stress and Coping, 13,* 217–227.

Treynor, W., Gonzalez, R., & Nolen-Hoeksema, S. (2003). Rumination reconsidered: A psychometric analysis. *Cognitive Therapy and Research, 27,* 247–259.

Tull, M.T., Gratz, K.L., Salters, K., & Roemer, L. (2004). The role of experiential avoidance in posttraumatic stress symptoms and symptoms of depression, anxiety, and somatization. *Journal of Nervous and Mental Disease, 192,* 754–761.

Vrana, S.R., Cuthbert, B.N., & Lang, P.J. (1986). Fear imagery and text processing. *Psychophysiology, 23,* 247–253.

Watkins, E. (2004). Adaptive and maladaptive ruminative self-focus during emotional processing. *Behaviour Research and Therapy, 42,* 1037–1052.

Watkins, E., & Moulds, M.L. (in press). Reduced concreteness of rumination in depression. *Personality and Individual Differences.*

Watkins, E., & Moulds, M. (2005). Distinct modes of ruminative self-focus: Impact of abstract versus concrete rumination on problem solving in depression. *Emotion, 5,* 319–328.

Watkins, E., Moulds, M., & Mackintosh, B. (2005). Comparisons between rumination and worry in a non-clinical population. *Behaviour Research and Therapy, 43,* 1577–1585.

Watkins, E., Teasdale, J.D., & Williams, R.M. (2000). Decentering and distraction reduce overgeneral autobiographical memory in depression. *Psychological Medicine, 30,* 911–920.

Williams, A.D., & Moulds, M.L. (2006). *Vantage point of intrusive memories in depression.* Manuscript submitted for publication.

CHAPTER 18

Modelling the Depressive Disorders: A Subtyping Strategy

Gordon Parker

....

'The wise man does not investigate the source of his wellbeing.'
(Smith, Glass & Miller, 1980, p. 273)

'Declaring that the flawed [Randomised Controlled] studies meet the "gold standard" of clinical research is a marketing rather than research strategy.' (Bolsover, 2002, p. 294)

While depressive disorders have a high lifetime prevalence, constitute the most disabling set of disorders in public health evaluations, are generally responsive to appropriate treatments and are being rapidly destigmatised in the Australian community, we suggest that their modelling is jeopardising aetiological and treatment research, as well as significantly compromising clinical management. The 'evidence based' treatment literature has limited meaningfulness, while those who rely on such material evoke images of the drunk who leant on the lamppost more for support than for illumination. These provocative introductory statements are not intended to criticise practitioners — who are often constrained by the published 'evidence' — but more to criticise underlying models of the depressive disorders and the ways in which treatments are evaluated and consequently proselytised.

Currently, studies pursuing cause and treatment tend to use a reference diagnostic group of 'major depression'. 'Major depression' was a concept (and disorder) introduced in the *Diagnostic and Statistical Manual of Mental Disorders* (3rd ed.; DSM-III; American Psychiatric Association, 1980) in 1980. It reflected a move to a dimensional model for the depressive disorders, which initially contrasted major and minor expressions, but which was subsequently extended to even less severe sets of conditions (e.g., 'subclinical' and 'subsyndromal' depressions). Reading the descriptions of clinical symptoms associated with major depression in

DSM-III suggests an attempt to capture the more gravid biological depressive disorders. However, a diagnosis of major depression could be achieved — and remains so in the fourth edition of the *Diagnostic and Statistical Manual of Mental Disorders* (DSM-IV; American Psychiatric Association, 1994) criteria set — by the presence of a relatively small set of symptoms. In addition, the DSM-III architects adopted a guiding principle that clinical criteria were to be 'described at the lowest order of inference necessary to describe the characteristic features of the disorder', a policy continuing in DSM-IV. Thus, the diagnostic criteria bar for individual items and for an overall diagnosis of major depression are set relatively low, risking overdiagnosis and a number of other predictable problems. While major depression is viewed by me as more an approximate of the probability of 'clinical depression', it has progressively transubstantiated to become an 'entity', and presumed to have explanatory properties beyond its station (Parker, 2005). It adds a stamp of authority to medico-legal reports, in the United States it assists admission to hospital and insurance reimbursement, while to many practitioners it is sufficient in and of itself to shape management plans. I will argue, however, that it is not an entity, and more a 'pseudo-entity'.

In advancing that argument, let me use an analogy of a breast lump. Any equivalent diagnosis of a 'major lump' is unlikely by itself to satisfy a practitioner or a patient. It might subsume a benign and spontaneously remitting cyst (a common and relatively 'normal' condition) or a range of pathologies, ranging from benign to malignant. Any woman attending a practitioner would expect the lump to be diagnosed and subtyped (usually by clinical examination but, if in doubt, by more detailed investigations) — for then treatment (if required) becomes rational and logical. For instance, the individual with a benign lump might be encouraged to wait for a spontaneous remission, while those with a malignant lump might require chemotherapy, radiotherapy, surgery or some combination. Thus, an overall 'class' diagnosis (be it major breast lump or major depression) tells us only about the reference domain, and invites subtyping, consideration of relevant causes and the introduction of a rational management plan that respects the diagnostic subtype.

Staying with that analogy, let me illustrate how reference to major depression has compromised aetiological and treatment research. Nonrepresentative sampling of broad 'domain' diagnoses risks either overrepresentation or underrepresentation of constituent conditions. For example, collecting a sample from breast-feeding mothers might ensure overrepresentation of mastitis-associated lumps, a community sample might quantify a high rate of lumps associated with fibrocystic disease and a low rate of cancerous tumours, while the converse might be anticipated in a surgical ward for women with breast tumours.

The prevalence of the constituent conditions in any treatment trials sample might also influence identification — and appropriate quantification of — effective treatments. Imagine if a very effective chemotherapy agent was trialled against a placebo in a sample of those with a major breast lump. If there was a high prevalence of those with a malignant tumour in the sample, chemotherapy might be demonstrated to be highly efficacious. By contrast, if most subjects had benign fibroadenomas associated with a high recovery rate (reflecting spontaneous remission), the chemotherapy agent might not differentiate from the placebo, and be judged invalidly as an 'ineffective' treatment.

The deference to major depression as a reference condition has therefore predictably led to such logical errors (Parker, 2005). In our earlier monograph (Parker & Hadzi-Pavlovic, 1996) we reviewed evidence to suggest that research had failed to identify any consistent biological correlate or neurobiological marker in relation to major depression. This is hardly surprising if major depression subsumes a number of constituent disorders with differing aetiological factors.

Turning to treatment studies, there have been more randomised control trials (RCTs) of treatments for major depression than for any other psychiatric condition or disorder, with meta-analyses involving datasets from hundreds of thousands of subjects. Results are desultory. In relation to drug trials, Kirsch, Moore, Scoboria and Nicholls (2002) analysed efficacy data for all six antidepressants approved by the Federal Drug Authority (FDA) in the United States between 1987 and 1999. Of the 47 trials, drug–placebo differences were small — if present at all. A similar analytic strategy by Khan, Khan and Brown (2002), quantified that the antidepressant was indistinguishable from placebo in 50% of the 52 trials.

Similar results are evident in relation to cognitive–behaviour therapy (CBT) and interpersonal psychotherapy (IPT). The commonly referenced meta-analysis by Gloaguen, Cottraux, Cucherat and Blackburn (1998) concluded that CBT was superior to (i) no therapy, (ii) all other psychotherapies apart from behaviour therapy, and (iii) antidepressant drugs. However, when Wampold, Minami, Baskin and Tierney (2002) undertook a reanalysis of that dataset, after removing non bona fide therapies (e.g., relaxation), CBT did not differ from other psychotherapies. The only published meta-analysis of IPT by de Mello et al. (2005) quantified only a nonsignificant trend for IPT to be superior to placebo in terms of remission rates. Further, there is now considerable evidence (Westen, Novotny, Thompson-Brenner, 2004) that, when meta-analyses removed inappropriate comparators (e.g., waitlist assignment) or implausible control strategies (now termed 'intent-to-fail' or 'non bona fide' therapies), CBT and IPT are not superior to other psychotherapies. In fact, and as we have overviewed elsewhere (Parker & Manicavasagar, 2005), RCTs of treatments for major depression show that all old and new antidepressants have comparable response rates, St John's Wort is comparable to formal antidepressant drugs, the psychotherapies each have comparable response rates, psychotherapies are comparable to drug therapies, and that all such active treatments differ marginally from placebo — in RCTs it should be emphasised. While there are sufficient RCTs for practitioners of principal modalities to claim that their treatment is efficacious, minimal differentiation of active treatment from placebo invites criticism that many antidepressant treatments strategies (especially antidepressant drugs) are not truly superior to placebo — or that they are placebos.

There are other major implications for treatment. As all such antidepressant treatment modalities appear equipotent in relation to the homogenised reference diagnosis of major depression, treatment (for any particular disorder) is less likely to be less influenced by disorder characteristics and more by the professional's background, discipline, training or preference. This is a nonrational eclectic model that is out of kilter with the rest of medicine (e.g., the management of a major lump) and, as has been argued, is illogical.

While there are a number of reasons for such desultory and sterile findings (and which guide many desultory and meaningless treatment guidelines), two principal ones will be noted (Parker, 2004). Firstly, there are major limitations to the design and undertaking of RCTs, most evident for the trials of antidepressant drugs. Here, screening tends to exclude those with psychotic and melancholic depression, inpatients, those who are suicidal, and those with anxiety, personality problems or alcohol and drug conditions, effectively resulting in pristine samples where members bear little correspondence to clinical reality. In addition, incentives to take part in such studies tend to encourage those with less severe and transient conditions. Once the trial commences, a high rate of spontaneous remission in both groups obscures any true treatment effect, with studies having shown that the 'placebo response rate' has increased 8% per decade, resulting now in a much higher 'number needed to treat' (NNT) required to sufficiently power studies to demonstrate any effect — even if one is capable of being identified.

The second major confounder of RCTs is the model for the depressive disorders. In essence, we argue against the dimensional model for conceptualising the depressive disorders, as evident in both the DSM (with major and minor expressions) and *International Classification of Mental and Behavioural Disorders* (10th Rev., ICD-10; World Health Organization, Geneva 1992) systems, the latter which lists 'severe', 'moderate' and 'mild' conditions. Such a model is intrinsically illogical and leads to simplistic treatment strategies, where quite varying treatment options (e.g., electroconvulsive therapy or ECT, antidepressant drug, psychotherapy) are recommended merely or largely on the basis of the 'severity' of the depressive disorder.

How then might the depressive disorders best be modelled? A binary model essentially contrasting endogenous depression or melancholia (as a genetically underpinned quintessential categorical condition) with a 'neurotic' or 'reactive' depressive class was long favoured. We have detailed (Parker & Hadzi-Pavlovic, 1996) a number of methodological and analytic issues that resulted in failure to 'prove' this model convincingly. Further, we have suggested (Parker, 2005) that it was not inappropriate at the time that the DSM-III system was being designed — in the absence of clear support for a binary model — for the DSM architects to weight a unitary model (i.e., depression as an 'it', principally varying by severity, but also varying dimensionally by persistence and recurrence). However, there is now sufficient 'evidence' to suggest that such dimensional models have failed us.

It was also regrettable that the earlier classificatory debate was restricted to arguing the merits of exclusive binary and unitary models, when we suggest that there is wisdom in invoking multiple models. In essence, if depression can exist as a disease, a syndrome, an existential crisis and a normal reaction, why should one model be explanatory?

Components to our contrasting subtyping model will be briefly overviewed. It is a hierarchical 'structural' one (Parker, 2000), relying on the presence or absence of specific features to define three principal depressive 'classes' — psychotic depression, melancholic depression and a heterogeneous residue of nonmelancholic depressive disorders. A central 'depressed mood' component is ubiquitous (for all three are depressed mood states) but, as it varies dimensionally across the three classes, it is not used to differentiate the three classes (unlike the DSM and ICD models). Melancholia is defined by the presence of observable psychomotor disturbance (PMD), which we have operationalised and quantified diagnostically by the CORE measure (Parker & Hadzi-Pavlovic, 1996).

In psychotic depression, the PMD is more severe than in melancholia, so that we incorporate psychotic features (i.e., delusions, hallucinations and overvalued ideas) as the specific class-defining characteristic. Broad diagnostic decisions can then operationalise those components. Thus, those with melancholic depression report concentration problems during episodes, show psychomotor retardation and/or agitation, and are more likely to report symptom correlates of those signs (e.g., profound anergia, anhedonia, mood nonreactivity — often with such features showing a distinctive diurnal variation). Those with psychotic depression have, in addition to severe PMD, delusions or hallucinations or overvalued ideas.

Observable PMD is viewed by us (Parker & Hadzi-Pavlovic, 1996) as a surface (or recordable) marker of an underlying neuropathological process, and which interestingly is strikingly constant in its phenotypic expression, seemingly independent of language or culture. Its consistency and specificity point to the likely site of a neurobiological perturbation, and we postulate dysregulation of certain neurocircuits linking the basal ganglia and the prefrontal cortex inducing a triad of features (i.e., cognitive disturbance, psychomotor disturbance and depression). In the same monograph we detailed how such disruption can be primarily and essentially 'functional' (and where response to appropriate physical treatments usually ensures a smooth recovery) or reflect 'structural brain' changes presaging a subsequent subcortical dementia (and where more assertive treatment is required along with a diminishing response to such treatment).

Developing appropriate models for the nonmelancholic disorders is more difficult in the absence of any class-specific phenotypic features, and we have therefore proceeded (see Parker & Manicavasagar, 2005) by seeking to identify and measure two salient 'causal drivers' (stress, and temperament or personality style) and model their interaction. This model allows an acute stress-weighted disorder (akin to the historical concept of 'reactive depression'), although our studies have indicated that the salience (i.e., certain 'mirroring' events activating latent cognitive schemas) of the event is more influential than its severity, allowing a 'key and lock' explanatory model for these reactive disorders. For the chronic nonmelancholic depressive disorders, we allow that prolonged and significant life event stressors can be depressogenic, but again weight their salience in driving a sense of 'learned helplessness'.

In terms of any personality contribution to the nonmelancholic depressive disorders, we developed (Parker, Manicavasagar, Crawford, Tully, & Gladstone, 2006) a self-report questionnaire (the Temperament and Personality Measure, available at www.blackdoginstitute.org.au) capturing eight 'styles' observed clinically and/or described from theoretical perspectives. An imposed eight-factor solution confirmed the a priori model of 'anxious worrying', 'self-criticism', 'personal reserve', 'social avoidance', 'perfectionism', 'sensitivity to rejection', 'irritability' or externalised anxiety, and a 'self-focused' or 'hostile' style. However, we also 'tracked' how these facets emerged (and progressively arborised) from a higher-order Eysenckian two-factor solution comprising 'neuroticism' and 'introversion', with imposed solutions allowing any personality contribution to cause and treatment differentiation to be tracked from the two-tier to the eight-tier solution.

Identification of candidate at-risk personality styles has allowed us to progressively develop a 'spectrum model' for many nonmelancholic personality-based disorders, a model presupposing that personality style increases risk to depression and shapes the clinical picture or phenotype. For instance, those with a personality style of anxious worrying tend, when exposed to a stressful event, to have that personality style amplified (as if through a magnifying glass) to develop a depressive syndrome infiltrated with components of worrying, autonomic arousal, tension and catastrophising. Those with an externalising anxious-based 'irritable' personality style tend, by contrast when depressed, to be more irritable and crabby. Those who have a 'self-focused personality style' tend, when depressed, to externalise their frustration, aggression and hostility, and create considerable collateral damage. This leads to partial phenotypic definition (Parker & Manicavasagar, 2005) but, as the nonmelancholic disorders reflect an interaction between dimensional constructs (i.e., life event stress and personality style), such clinical patterns have degrees of interdependency and do not form 'pure types'.

Any model of depression is best judged in terms of its utility. Here, utility is viewed as providing explanations about cause and also having treatment implications. How does our model relate to such issues? It firstly assumes that psychotic depression and melancholic depression are essentially categorical conditions, phenotypically definable and, being underpinned by perturbed biological processes, requiring physical treatments as the primary modality. In comparison to the efficacy data for major depression, when this subtyping model is respected, differential results emerge. For example, analyses indicate that those with psychotic depression have a 5% response to placebo, a 25% response to an antidepressant drug, a 30% response to an antipsychotic drug, an 80% response to combination antidepressant and antipsychotic drug, and an

80% response to ECT (Parker & Manicavasagar, 2005). This is a striking gradient and quite at variance with the 'equipotency' findings quantified for major depression. For melancholic depression, there is again reasonable evidence suggesting that those with this disorder have a low placebo response rate, do poorly with psychotherapy, and require an antidepressant medication. Our application studies (Parker et al., 1999; Parker, Roy, Wilhelm, & Mitchell, 2001) have shown that differing antidepressant classes have differing efficacies for those with melancholia. For instance, merely comparing response rates for those receiving narrow-action selective serotonin reuptake inhibitors (or SSRIs) and broad-action tricyclic antidepressants (or TCAs) demonstrated that the broader-action antidepressants were distinctly more effective than the narrow-action antidepressants for those with melancholia. This is a deceptively important finding in that the narrow-action antidepressants are the most commonly prescribed antidepressants for melancholia, risking a low response rate.

For the stress/personality driven nonmelancholic disorders (and which principally constitute the RCT database for those with major depression), then our application studies referenced in the previous paragraph indicate that antidepressants of all classes show similar levels of efficacy, and we suspect that response rates (for the overall nonmelancholic class) are comparable for all principal drug and nondrug treatment modalities — as noted in relation to major depression. The task then is to determine the relevance of pluralistic — albeit differing — management strategies for the differing constituent stress-related and personality-related conditions, and we have pursued this in great detail in a recent monograph (Parker & Manicavasagar, 2005). For example, for those who have a personality style of anxious worrying, we recommend a trial of an SSRI drug for the high levels of autonomic arousal experienced by such patients — however, we also recommend nondrug strategies such as relaxation, meditation techniques and exercise. For the associated disordered thinking, we recommend cognitive therapy strategies. For the low self-efficacy and problem-solving skills, we recommend a number of behavioural strategies, and for the individual's reliance on others for reassurance, we recommend goal setting and other techniques. For some of the nonmelancholic disorders we favour counselling as the principal modality, for others CBT, IPT, mindfulness therapy or narrative therapy, and, for others, an antidepressant drug. For all of these disorders, we argue for a pluralistic approach, but we also recommend prioritising a therapeutic strategy that is most likely to correct the causal (and ideally primary) contributor. For example, this might be counselling to neutralise a life event stressor, CBT to modify a predisposing personality style, or an SSRI to mute emotional dysregulation. While the model is plausible and clearly respects the heterogeneity of the nonmelancholic disorders, it requires evaluation of its overall effectiveness — our current research priority.

We clearly seek to reawake consideration of the relevance of a subtyping model for the depressive disorders that has greater causal explanatory power than a dimensional nonspecific model. We argue against any therapy (drug or psychotherapy) as having universal application and argue, in essence, for a 'horses for courses' approach to the management of disparate depressive disorders.

Acknowledgments

This chapter reflects research supported by the NHMRC (Program Grant 222708) and an Infrastructure Grant from the NSW Department of Health, the assistance of many colleagues over the last 20 years who have contributed to the many referenced studies, and manuscript assistance by Yvonne Foy.

References

American Psychiatric Association (1980). *Diagnostic and statistical manual of mental disorders* (4th ed.). Washington, DC: Author:

American Psychiatric Association (1994). *Diagnostic and statistical manual of mental disorders* (3rd ed.). Washington, DC: Author:

Bolsover, N. (2002). Commentary: The evidence is weaker than claimed. *British Medical Journal, 324,* 294.

de Mello, M.F., de Jesus Mari, J., Bacaltchuk, G., Verdeli, H., & Neugebauer, R. (2005). A systematic review of research findings on the efficacy of interpersonal therapy for depressive disorders. *European Archives of Psychiatry and Clinical Neuroscience, 225,* 75–82.

Gloaguen, V., Cottraux, J., Cucherat, M., & Blackburn, I.M. (1998). A meta-analysis of the effects of cognitive therapy in depressed patients. *Journal of Affective Disorders, 49,* 59–72.

Khan, A., Khan, S., & Brown, W.A. (2002). Are placebo controls necessary to test new antidepressants and anxiolytics? *International Journal of Neuropsychopharmacology, 5,* 193–197.

Kirsch, I., Moore, T.J., Scoboria, A., & Nicholls, S.S. (2002). The Emperor's new drugs: An analysis of antidepressant medication data, submitted to the US Food and Drug Administration. *Prevention and Treatment, 5,* 1–11.

Parker, G. (2000). Classifying depression: Should paradigms lost be regained? *American Journal of Psychiatry, 157,* 1195–1203.

Parker, G. (2004). Evaluating treatments for the mood disorders: Time for the evidence to get real. *Australian and New Zealand Journal of Psychiatry, 38,* 408–414.

Parker, G. (2005). Beyond major depression. *Psychological Medicine, 35*, 467–474.

Parker, G., & Hadzi-Pavlovic, D. (Eds.). (1996). *Melancholia: A disorder of movement and mood. A phenomenological and neurobiological review.* New York: Cambridge University Press.

Parker, G., & Manicavasagar, V. (2005). *Modelling and managing the depressive disorders.* Cambridge, UK: Cambridge University Press.

Parker, G., Manicavasagar, V., Crawford, J., Tully, L., & Gladstone, G. (2006). Assessing personality traits associated with depression: The utility of a tiered model. *Psychological Medicine 36*, 1–9.

Parker, G., Mitchell, P., Wilhelm, K., Menkes, D., Snowdon, J., Schweitzer, I., et al. (1999). Are the newer antidepressant drugs as effective as established physical treatments? Results from an Australasian clinical panel review. *Australian and New Zealand Journal of Psychiatry, 33*, 874–881.

Parker, G., Roy, K., Wilhelm, K., & Mitchell, P. (2001). Assessing the comparative effectiveness of antidepressant therapies: A prospective clinical practice study. *Journal of Clinical Psychiatry, 62*, 117–125.

Smith. M.L., Glass, G.V., & Miller, T.I. (1980). *The benefits of psychotherapy.* Baltimore: Johns Hopkins University Press.

Wampold, B.E., Minami, T., Baskin, T.W., & Tierney, S.C. (2002). A meta-(re)analysis of the effects of cognitive therapy versus 'other therapies' for depression. *Journal of Affective Disorders, 68*, 159–165.

Westen, D., Novotny, C.M., & Thompson-Brenner, H. (2004). The empirical status of empirically supported psychotherapies, findings, and reporting in controlled clinical trials. *Psychological Bulletin, 130*, 631–663.

CHAPTER 19

Autobiographical Memory in the Development, Maintenance, and Resolution of Posttraumatic Stress Disorder After Trauma

Richard A. Bryant, Kylie Sutherland
and Rachel M. Guthrie

Depressed people display a difficulty in retrieving specific memories of personal experiences (for a review, see Williams, 1996). Much research over the past two decades has studied how depressed people retrieve personal autobiographical memories, and this research has focused on the level of specificity of these memories. In most research, autobiographical memories are indexed by providing participants with cue words and requesting recall of a specific personal memory in response to the cue. A specific memory is defined as the participant being able to recall a particular event, something that happened at a specific place and time, not exceeding a day (Williams, 1996). Less specific memories include categoric memories, in which a summary of a memory or a category of repeated memories is reported. Another form of nonspecific memory is an extended memory, which is a memory of an event that lasted longer than a day. Alternately, patients may not report any memory (omitted memories). Table 1 describes examples of these memory types. In response to cue words, depressed individuals tend to retrieve personal memories that comprise generic summaries of events rather than specific memories. This pattern has been observed across suicidal (Williams & Broadbent, 1986) and depressed (Kuyken & Brewin, 1995; Williams & Scott, 1988) populations.

There is also convergent evidence that people who survive trauma and develop posttraumatic stress disorder (PTSD) have difficulty in retrieving specific memories about their personal past. McNally and colleagues have reported two studies that found that Vietnam veterans with PTSD had

Table 1
Examples of Memory Types

Memory type	Example
Specific	'The first day of school when I cried' 'When my boyfriend proposed to me on my 20th birthday'
Categoric	'The times I got annoyed' 'Every time I failed my family'
Extended	'My summer holiday in France' 'When I was sick for a week with bronchitis'

overgeneral retrieval of autobiographical memories (McNally, Lasko, Macklin, & Pitman, 1995; McNally, Litz, Prassas, Shin, & Weathers, 1994). Patients with acute stress disorder (ASD) after cancer diagnosis also display more overgeneral retrieval than those without ASD (Kangas, Henry, & Bryant, 2005). Harvey and colleagues (1998) found that acute stress disorder (ASD) participants generated fewer specific memories to positive cue words than did non-ASD participants (Harvey, Bryant, & Dang, 1998). Furthermore, impaired retrieval of specific traumatic memories in the acute trauma phase was predictive of PTSD at a 6-month follow-up, suggesting that poor posttrauma adjustment is associated with impaired access to trauma memories and overgeneral memory retrieval.

One important issue that has yet to be clarified is the extent to which overgeneral retrieval is a function of PTSD or is a vulnerability factor that renders people high risk for developing a psychiatric disorder after a traumatic event. It has been suggested that overgeneral retrieval may represent a risk factor for adverse responses to stressful life events (Williams, 1996). One mechanism that may contribute to overgeneral retrieval (and rendering an individual susceptible to an adverse reaction to a negative life event) is poor problem-solving. Numerous studies have linked overgeneral retrieval to poor problem-solving (Evans, Williams, O'Laughlin, & Howells, 1992; Goddard, Dritschel, & Burton, 1996, 2001), and also to difficulties in imagining future events (Williams et al., 1996). Problem-solving entails both the ability to draw on past experiences and to use these experiences to imagine future outcomes. It is possible that deficits in retrieving specific memories limit problem-solving and the ability to facilitate management of current stressors.

There is reasonable evidence to suggest that overgeneral retrieval may be a trait that is not dependent on current mood state. Williams and Dritschel (1988) found that individuals who were previously suicidal still retrieved overgeneral memories. Further, a number of studies have found no relationship between self-reported mood and overgeneral recall (Kuyken & Brewin, 1995; Merckelbach, Muris, & Horselenberg, 1996; Sidley, Whitaker, Calam, & Wells, 1997; Williams & Dritschel, 1988). There are prospective studies that have found overgeneral retrieval prior to treatment predicts residual depressive symptoms after treatment (Brittlebank, Scott, Williams, & Ferrier, 1993; Peeters, Wessel, Merckelbach, & Boon-Vermeeren, 2002). A study of seasonal affective disorder found that overgeneral retrieval to positive cues during winter (when participants were depressed) was associated with more depressive symptoms during summer (when symptoms remitted; Dalgleish, Spinks, Yiend, & Kuyken, 2001). Two studies conducted in medical settings have reported that overgeneral retrieval prior to childbirth (Mackinger, Loschin, & Leibetseder, 2000) and commencing in vitro fertilisation (van Minnen, Wessel, Verhaak, & Smeenk, 2005) predicted subsequent depressive symptoms. Contrary to these findings, Brewin, Reynolds and Tata (1999) found that overgeneral retrieval in depressed patients did not predict depression 6 months later after controlling for the effects of initial depression.

There is a need for prospective research assessing autobiographical memory retrieval prior to trauma exposure and calculating the relationship between prior overgeneral retrieval and subsequent posttraumatic stress. There is an equally important need to study the extent to which overgeneral retrieval remains stable over the course of recovery from PTSD. The current project investigated these two issues. First, we tested the extent to which overgeneral retrieval prior to trauma exposure predicts PTSD and depression in people exposed to trauma. To this end, we administered the autobiographical memory test to a cohort of firefighters during their cadet training (prior to trauma exposure), and subsequently assessed them for PTSD and depression after trauma exposure. We hypothesised that deficits in retrieving specific positive memories prior to trauma would predict posttraumatic stress and depression after trauma. Second, we assessed autobiographical memory prior to and following therapy for PTSD, and predicted that retrieval of specific memories would improve as PTSD symptoms remitted.

Across both studies, participants were told to report the first specific personal memory triggered by a series of stimulus words. Responses were audiotaped. The experimenter read each word as the card was shown to the participant. If participants did not give a specific memory, the experimenter prompted them with 'can you think of a specific time — one particular event?' If participants did not retrieve a specific memory within 60 seconds the next word was presented. The cue words comprised five positive and five negative words selected from the 1000 most frequent English words (Carroll, Davies, & Richman, 1971; Robinson, 1976) and were matched on frequency of usage. The positive words were happy, brave, safe, love, and special. The negative words were hurt, tense, angry, fear, and stress. The two practice words were egg and chocolate. Each word was printed on a white card (12×8 inch). Order of presentation was randomised except that positive and negative words were alternated. Memories were coded as specific if they incorporated a particular event occurring on a discrete day (Williams, 1996). A rater coded audiotaped responses for (1) latency to retrieve the memory (in seconds), (2) specificity of the memory (an event that occurred on a specific day), (3) categoric memories (a summary or category of repeated memories) and (4) extended memories (an event that lasted longer than a day).

Study 1

Procedure

Eligible participants were 60 successive male recruits (mean age = 29.55 years, SD = 4.97) to the New South Wales Fire Brigades who were receiving class-based instruction at the time of recruitment. Participants were initially evaluated prior to commencing active fire-fighting duties (Time 1), and then attempts were made to reassess all participants 4 years after initial assessment, during which time all participants had been exposed to multiple traumatic events.

Forty-six (77%) participants were reassessed at an average 48.98 (SD = 1.59) months after initial assessment. Nonparticipation occurred because 1 participant had moved to a rural area, 1 participant was on physical injury-related workers compensation, and 12 refused to be reassessed. Those participants who participated in the follow-up assessment did not differ from nonparticipants on age or initial psychometric responses.

Following written informed consent, a master's-level clinical psychologist administered the Structured Clinical Interview for DSM-IV (SCID-IV; Spitzer, Gibbon, & Williams, 1996) to assess for current Axis I disorders, and the Clinician Administered PTSD Scale (CAPS; Blake et al., 1995) to index current posttraumatic stress symptoms. Participants were also administered the Traumatic Events Questionnaire (TEQ; Vrana & Lauterbach, 1994) to assess exposure to prior traumatic events, and the Beck Depression Inventory—II (BDI-II; Beck & Steer, 1987) to index depressive symptoms. At Time 1, participants responded to the CAPS interview in relation to a 'very distressing event' that they had experienced.

Approximately 4 years after the initial assessment, participants were mailed a package that instructed participants that the current survey was intended to index current coping levels within the Fire Brigades. Participants were asked to indicate the number and type of incidents that they had attended, and whether they had been threatened or witnessed others being threatened or harmed. Participants also completed the Posttraumatic Stress Disorder Scale (PDS; Foa, Cashman, Jaycox, & Perry, 1997), which comprises a 12-item checklist of traumatic stressors; a question that targets the most distressing event; four questions regarding injury, fear, helplessness, and horror about the event; questions about the 17 symptoms of PTSD; and nine questions regarding functional impairment. The PDS allows for diagnostic decisions about PTSD and a severity score of posttraumatic stress. Participants also completed the BDI-II.

Results

Preliminary Analyses

No participants had PTSD at the initial assessment, and 7 (16%) participants met criteria for PTSD at the follow-up assessment. Table 2 presents the mean participant characteristics according to PTSD status at the follow-up assessment. PTSD participants had higher scores on the PDS and BDI-II at follow-up than no-PTSD participants. In terms of memory coding, the Kappa coefficient of reliability was good for specific (0.87), categoric (0.90), and extended (0.91) memories. Participants with PTSD reported fewer specific memories to positive cues at the initial assessment than participants without PTSD.

Prediction of Posttraumatic Stress

A hierarchical regression was conducted to examine the pretrauma variables that predict PDS total score at follow-up. We initially entered variables that we believed would be likely to contribute to subsequent posttraumatic stress, including lifetime history of traumatic events, traumatic events since active fire-fighting service, pre-existing levels of posttraumatic stress, and pre-trauma deficits in autobiographical memory. Accordingly, we entered (a) TEQ total score and number of traumatic events as a firefighter, (b) pre-trauma CAPS score and (c) pretrauma retrieval of specific memories. Subsequent regressions were conducted with the same variables, but in the last step we entered either pretrauma retrieval of categoric memories, extended memories, or omissions. Pretrauma deficits in retrieving specific memories to positive cues accounted for 20% of the variance ($\beta = -3.52$, $SE = 0.98$, $t = -3.58$, $p < .001$). Pretrauma retrieval of categoric, extended, or omitted memories did not significantly predict PTSD severity.

Table 2
Study 1: Participant Characteristics and Memory Retrieval Patterns

	PTSD (N = 7)	No PTSD (N = 39)	t(44)	p
Age	33.00 (6.81)	29.68 (4.37)	168	ns
Years of education	13.50 (2.51)	13.39 (1.85)	0.21	ns
BDI-II (Time 1)	3.00 (2.80)	2.79 (5.60)	0.77	ns
CAPS (Time 1)	0.00 (0.00)	0.50 (0.21)	0.91	ns
TEQ	2.48 (1.87)	2.46 (2.22)	1.28	ns
Specific memories to positive cues	2.28 (1.25)	4.02 (1.22)	3.45	.001
Specific memories to negative cues	3.80 (0.90)	4.20 (0.83)	1.00	ns
Latency to positive cues (secs)	28.83 (9.74)	21.62 (12.47)	1.45	ns
Latency to negative cues (secs)	19.40 (7.21)	17.54 (10.53)	0.44	ns
Categoric memories to positive cues	0.14 (0.38)	0.81 (1.08)	0.12	ns
Categoric memories to negative cues	0.43 (1.13)	0.58 (0.96)	0.72	ns
Extended memories to positive cues	0.00 (0.00)	0.10 (0.30)	0.41	ns
Extended memories to negative cues	0.00 (0.00)	0.39 (0.49)	0.05	ns
Omissions to positive cues	0.00 (0.00)	03 (0.18)	0.64	ns
Omissions to negative cues	0.00 (0.00)	0.06 (0.25)	0.50	ns
Initial assessment — follow-up interval (months)	48.71 (1.52)	48.72 (2.36)	0.01	ns
Traumatic events as fire-fighter	23.86 (15.38)	40.64 (47.38)	0.91	ns
PDS (follow-up)	21.57 (10.73)	1.87 (3.25)	25.78	.001
BDI-II (follow-up)	14.42 (8.01)	5.87 (7.04)	2.90	.01

Note: CAPS = Clinician Administered PTSD Scale, TEQ = Traumatic Events Questionnaire, BDI-II = Beck Depression Inventory, PDS = Posttraumatic Stress Disorder Scale. Standard deviations appear in parentheses.

Prediction of Posttraumatic Depression

A comparable hierarchical regression was conducted to predict BDI-II score at follow-up. We entered (a) TEQ total score and number of traumatic events as a firefighter, (b) pretrauma BDI-II score, (c) pretrauma retrieval of specific memories to positive cues and (d) pretrauma retrieval of specific memories to negative cues. In terms of predicting BDI-II scores at follow-up, pretrauma BDI-II scores accounted for 8% of the variance ($\beta = .83$, $SE = 0.32$, $t = 2.56$, $p < .05$), and pretrauma deficits in retrieving specific memories to positive cues accounted for an additional 4% of the variance ($\beta = -1.79$, $SE = 0.92$, $t = -1.95$, $p < .05$). Pretrauma retrieval of categoric, extended, or omitted memories did not significantly predict depression severity.

Discussion

Deficits in retrieving specific memories to positive cues before trauma exposure were a key predictor of posttraumatic stress. This finding is consistent with evidence that deficits in retrieving memories to positive cues prior to medical procedures predict subsequent depression (Mackinger et al., 2000). It is possible that an adaptive response to a traumatic event requires retrieving positive experiences from one's past because this allows the traumatic experience to be considered in the context of more positive experiences. Alternately, it is possible that people who have difficulty in retrieving memories to positive cues have poorer problem-solving skills, and this is associated with more posttraumatic stress. There is a relationship between impaired specific retrieval and impaired problem-solving in PTSD (Sutherland & Bryant, 2006). Participants who are exposed to trauma and who have deficient problem-solving skills may develop more severe PTSD reactions because they are less able to problem-solve their posttraumatic problems.

Study 2

Procedure

Participants comprised 20 PTSD (11 female, 9 male) participants of mean age 35.74 years ($SD = 9.84$) who commenced therapy for PTSD following nonsexual assault ($n = 10$) or a motor vehicle accident ($n = 10$). Diagnostic status was determined using the Clinician Administered PTSD Scale—2 (CAPS-2; Blake et al., 1995). Fifteen (75%) of the participants were reassessed at an average of 15.06 months ($SD = 6.31$) after the initial assessment.

Following written informed consent and administration of the CAPS-2 and BDI-II, participants were administered the autobiographical memory task. Participants then received eight once-weekly, 90-minute sessions of cognitive–behaviour therapy (CBT). This therapy involved one session of education, six sessions of imaginal exposure combined with cognitive restructuring, and one session of relapse prevention (for full details, see Bryant, Moulds, Guthrie, Dang, & Nixon, 2003). Six months after treatment, an independent clinical psychologist who was blind to responses in the initial assessment, readministered the CAPS-2, BDI-II, and the Autobiographical Memory Test.

Results

Preliminary Analyses

Fifteen of the 20 participants who were initially assessed completed the subsequent assessment. There were no differences between those who did and did not complete the second assessment in terms of initial CAPS-2, BDI-II, memory specificity or memory latency. At the 6-month follow-up assessment, 9 participants no longer met criteria for PTSD and 6 participants did meet criteria. As expected, participants who met criteria for PTSD scored higher on the CAPS-2 than participants who no longer met criteria for PTSD, $t(13) = 3.56$, $p < .005$.

Memory Specificity and Latency

Table 3 presents the mean number of specific memories and response latencies for participants who had PTSD and no-PTSD after treatment. A 2 (Participant Group) × 2 (Cue Valence) × 2 (Assessment Point) analysis of variance (ANOVA) of specific memories indicated a main effect for Valence, $F(1, 13) = 14.02$, $p < .005$. There were more specific memories to negative cue words than positive cue words. A 2 (Participant Group) × 2 (Cue Valence) × 2 (Assessment Point) ANOVA of memory latency indicated a main effect for Valence, $F(1, 13) = 20.50$, $p < .001$. Participants were slower to recall positive memories than negative memories.

Relationship Between Pretreatment Memory Retrieval and Treatment Response

To determine the relationship between initial retrieval patterns and treatment response, we calculated change scores (pretreatment minus posttreatment) for CAPS-2 and BDI-II and then conducted Pearson correlations between these change scores and pretreatment autobiographical memory specificity and latency. There were no significant correlations between symptom reduction and pretreatment specific retrieval or latency to retrieve.

Relationship Between Symptom Reduction and Memory Specificity

We calculated change scores for CAPS-2 scores, BDI-II scores and autobiographical memory specificity and latency by subtracting participants' scores at posttreatment from their scores at pretreatment. We then conducted Pearson correlation coefficients between these change scores. There was a significant negative correlation between change in CAPS-2 score and change in retrieval of specific memories to positive cues ($r = -.55$, $p < .05$), and a significant positive correlation between change in CAPS-2 score and latency to retrieve memories to positive cues ($r = .61$, $p < .05$). That is, decreases in PTSD symptoms were associated with increased retrieval of specific memories to positive cues and shorter latencies to retrieve memories to positive cues. There were no significant correlations between changes in BDI-II and memory responses.

Table 3
Participant Characteristics and Memory Responses According
to Posttreatment Diagnostic Group

	PTSD		No-PTSD	
	Time 1	Time 2	Time 1	Time 2
CAPS-2	70.00 (6.60)	56.50 (25.96)	67.00 (16.60)	21.44 (12.08)
BDI-II	28.33 (11.78)	22.80 (13.40)	22.33 (9.61)	12.00 (7.89)
Positive specific memories	3.33 (0.81)	2.40 (1.14)	2.78 (1.20)	3.11 (1.45)
Positive memory) latency	26.14 (11.81)	40.00 (11.00)	30.28 (12.73)	24.92 (12.93
Negative specific memories	3.67 (1.75)	3.33 (0.51)	3.56 (1.01)	4.00 (1.12)
Negative memory latency	28.32 (19.56)	26.73 (5.18)	27.41 (10.63)	16.05 (13.92)

Note: CAPS = Clinician Administered PTSD Scale, BDI-II = Beck Depression Inventory—II.
Standard deviations appear in parentheses.

Discussion

As symptoms reduced after treatment, participants with PTSD retrieved more specific memories in response to positive cues, and participants were faster to retrieve these memories. These findings stand in contrast with evidence that overgeneral retrieval does not appear to be associated with changes in self-reported depressed mood (Brittlebank et al., 1993; Kuyken & Brewin, 1995; Mackinger et al., 2000; Merckelbach et al., 1996; Peeters et al., 2002; Sidley et al., 1997; Williams & Dritschel, 1988).

Williams (1996) proposes that deficits in specific retrieval may be attributed to reduced functioning of working memory. An associated proposition suggests that overgeneral retrieval in PTSD may occur because intrusive symptoms deplete working memory capacity, and this may limit capacity for retrieval search (Kuyken & Brewin, 1995). This interpretation is consistent with evidence that intrusions are strongly associated with overgeneral retrieval (Brewin et al., 1999). It is possible that as our patients' symptoms reduced, their working memory capacity increased and allowed for more effective retrieval search. It is also possible that more specific retrieval of positive memories contributed to recovery. Accessing specific memories of positive experiences may contribute to symptom reduction because it allows for more integration of memories that support safe and successful experiences and these can assist in placing the trauma in a context conducive to recovery. The retrieval of specific memories has also been associated with increased specificity accessing images of the future and enhanced problem-solving skills (Goddard et al., 1996; Williams et al., 1996). Learning to retrieve more specific positive memories may have helped our participants to problem-solve, and this may have contributed to symptom reduction.

Concluding Comment

These data provide initial evidence that difficulties in retrieving specific memories may place people at higher risk for developing PTSD-type reactions after trauma exposure. Moreover, by treating PTSD effectively, we can increase the capacity to retrieve specific memories. Taken together, it is possible that by enhancing specific retrieval we can reduce the likelihood of PTSD development. Although untested, the current findings raise the possibility of preparing people for stressful events by training them to retrieve specific memories, and encouraging this cognitive style before and after trauma exposure.

Acknowledgments

This research was supported by a National Health and Medical Research Council Program Grant (300304).

References

Beck, A.T., & Steer, R.A. (1987). *Manual for the Beck Depression Inventory*. San Antonio, TX: The Psychological Corporation.

Blake, D.D., Weathers, F.W., Nagy, L.M., Kaloupek, D.G., Gusman, F.D., Charney, D.S., et al. (1995). The development of a clinician administered PTSD scale. *Journal of Traumatic Stress, 8*, 75–90.

Brewin, C.R., Reynolds, M., & Tata, P. (1999). Autobiographical memory processes and the course of depression. *Journal of Abnormal Psychology, 108*, 511–517.

Brittlebank, A.D., Scott, J., Williams, J.M.G., & Ferrier, I.N. (1993). Autobiographical memory in depression: State or trait marker. *British Journal of Psychiatry, 162*, 118–121.

Bryant, R.A., Moulds, M.L., Guthrie, R.M., Dang, S.T., & Nixon, R.D.V. (2003). Imaginal exposure alone and imaginal exposure with cognitive restructuring in treatment of posttraumatic stress disorder. *Journal of Consulting and Clinical Psychology, 71*, 706–712.

Carroll, J.B., Davies, P., & Richman, B. (1971). *Word frequency book*. New York: American Heritage.

Dalgleish, T., Spinks, H., Yiend, J., & Kuyken, W. (2001). Autobiographical memory style in seasonal affective disorder and its relationship to future symptom remission. *Journal of Abnormal Psychology, 110,* 335–340.

Evans, J., Williams, J.M.G., O'Laughlin, S., & Howells, K. (1992). Autobiographical memory and problem solving strategies of parasuicide patients. *Psychological Medicine, 22,* 399–405.

Foa, E.B., Cashman, L., Jaycox, L., & Perry, K. (1997). The validation of a self-report measure of posttraumatic stress disorder: The Postraumatic Stress Disorder Scale. *Psychological Assessment, 9,* 445–451.

Goddard, L., Dritschel, B., & Burton, A. (1996). Role of autobiographical memory in social problem solving and depression. *Journal of Abnormal Psychology, 105,* 609–616.

Goddard, L., Dritschel, B., & Burton, A. (2001). The effects of specific retrieval instruction on social problem-solving in depression. *British Journal of Clinical Psychology, 40,* 297–308.

Harvey, A.G., Bryant, R.A., & Dang, S.T. (1998). Autobiographical memory in acute stress disorder. *Journal of Consulting and Clinical Psychology, 66,* 500–506.

Kangas, M., Henry, J.L., & Bryant, R.A. (2005). A prospective study of autobiographical memory and posttraumatic stress disorder following cancer. *Journal of Consulting and Clinical Psychology, 73,* 293–299.

Kuyken, W., & Brewin, C.R. (1995). Autobiographical memory functioning in depression and reports of early abuse. *Journal of Abnormal Psychology, 104,* 585–591.

Mackinger, H.F., Loschin, G.G., & Leibetseder, M.M. (2000). Prediction of postnatal affective changes by autobiographical memories. *European Psychologist, 5,* 52–61.

McNally, R.J., Lasko, N.B., Macklin, M.L., & Pitman, R.K. (1995). Autobiographical memory disturbance in combat-related posttraumatic stress disorder. *Behaviour Research and Therapy, 33,* 619–630.

McNally, R.J., Litz, B.T., Prassas, A., Shin, L.M., & Weathers, F.W. (1994). Emotional priming of autobiographical memory in post-traumatic stress disorder. *Cognition and Emotion, 8,* 351–367.

Merckelbach, H., Muris, P., & Horselenberg, R. (1996). Correlates of overgeneral memories in normal subjects. *Behavioural and Cognitive Psychotherapy, 24,* 109–115.

Peeters, F., Wessel, I., Merckelbach, H., & Boon-Vermeeren, M. (2002). Autobiographical memory specificity and the course of major depressive disorder. *Comprehensive Psychiatry, 43,* 344–350.

Robinson, J.A. (1976). Sampling autobiographical memory. *Cognitive Psychology, 8,* 578–595.

Sidley, G.L., Whitaker, K., Calam, R.M., & Wells, A. (1997). The relationship between problem-solving and autobiographical memory in parasuicide patients. *Behavioural and Cognitive Psychotherapy, 25,* 195–202.

Spitzer R.L., Gibbon M., & Williams J.B.W. (1996). *Structured Clinical Interview for DSM-IV Axis I Disorders.* New York: New York State Psychiatric Institute, Biometrics Research Department.

Sutherland, K., & Bryant, R.A. (2006). *Social problem solving and autobiographical memory in posttraumatic stress disorder.* Manuscript submitted for publication.

van Minnen, A., Wessel, I., Verhaak, C., & Smeenk, J. (2005). The relationship between autobiographical memory specificity and depressed mood following a stressful life event: A prospective study. *British Journal of Clinical Psychology, 44,* 405–415.

Vrana, S., & Lauterbach, D. (1994). Prevalence of traumatic events and post-traumatic psychological symptoms in a nonclinical sample of college students. *Journal of Traumatic Stress, 7,* 289–302.

Williams, J.M.G. (1996). Depression and the specificity of autobiographical memory. In D.C. Rubin (Ed.), *Remembering our past: Studies in autobiographical memory* (pp. 244–267). Cambridge: Cambridge University Press.

Williams, J.M.G., & Broadbent, K. (1986). Autobiographical memory in attempted suicide patients. *Journal of Abnormal Psychology, 95,* 144–149.

Williams, J.M.G., & Dritschel, B.H. (1988). Emotional disturbance and the specificity of autobiographical memory. *Cognition & Emotion, 2,* 221–234.

Williams, J.M.G., Ellis, N.C., Tyers, C., Healy, H., Rose, G., & MacLeod, A.K. (1996). The specificity of autobiographical memory and imageability of the future. *Memory and Cognition, 24,* 116–125.

Williams, J.M.G, & Scott, J. (1988). Autobiographical memory in depression. *Psychological Medicine, 18,* 689–695.

CHAPTER 20

Cognitive and Social Support Factors in the Development of Acute Trauma Response in Children

Alicia A. Ellis, Reginald D.V. Nixon and Paul Williamson

This chapter reports the preliminary findings from an ongoing prospective study that examines cognitive and social factors theorised to influence acute stress disorder (ASD) response, depression, and the development and maintenance of posttraumatic stress disorder (PTSD) in children. Varying estimates of ASD prevalence have been observed in children. For example, Winston et al. (2002) found approximately 16% of inpatients following traffic accidents experienced significant ASD symptoms. Other research has indicated that 28% of children injured in traffic accidents, including pedestrians and bicyclists, experienced ASD symptoms (Winston, Baxt, Kassam-Adams, Elliott, & Kallan, 2005). In terms of PTSD, Fletcher's (1996) meta-analysis estimated that 36% of children exposed to trauma develop PTSD.

Current theories of PTSD in adults are consistent in their emphasis that cognitive processing and the meaning attached to the trauma and subsequent symptoms are important contributors to the aetiology and maintenance of PTSD (Brewin, Dalgleish, & Joseph, 1996; Ehlers & Clark, 2000). It has also been argued that these mechanisms explain posttraumatic stress in children, and that developmental factors and social support may be critical elements of children's posttrauma adjustment (Fletcher, 1996; Meiser-Stedman, 2002; Salmon & Bryant, 2002).

Prospective studies are beginning to investigate the trajectory from ASD to PTSD in children (e.g., Meiser-Stedman, Yule, Smith, Glucksman, & Dalgleish, 2005; Winston et al., 2005); however, research has generally focused on children's responses at the diagnostic level. In addition, when appraisals have been studied in the trauma field, especially in child samples, *negative* appraisals are frequently studied, that is, cognitive mechanisms likely to lead to poor psychological adjustment. More systematic study of the association between appraisals and posttraumatic stress symptoms in children is necessary. A major focus of the present research was to examine whether children manifest *protective* appraisals, even in the weeks following trauma, that buffer them from developing maladaptive responses to traumatic events.

Accordingly, in line with a cognitive and developmental conceptualisation of childhood trauma response, this research is testing the proposal that adaptive and maladaptive appraisals and social support play important roles in determining children's adjustment following trauma. Thus children are being assessed within 4 weeks of their trauma for post-trauma appraisals, ASD and depression symptomatology, and perceived social support. We are also assessing parents' perceptions of their availability and support to their children. Potential correlates (e.g., injury severity) are also being measured. Families are followed up 6 months later, but data will only be reported from the first assessment. In regard to specific hypotheses, we predict that after controlling for potential correlates:

(1) negative trauma appraisals will be positively correlated with elevated ASD symptoms and depression.

(2) adaptive appraisals and children's perception of social support will be negatively correlated with ASD symptoms and depression.

(3) Parent report of availability and support to their child will be negatively correlated with ASD symptoms and depression.

Finally, the relative contribution of negative appraisals, protective appraisals, social support and depression on ASD symptoms will be examined in a series of hierarchical multiple regressions.

Method

Participants and Procedure

Children and adolescents aged between 7 and 17 who have experienced a single-incident trauma (e.g., road traffic accident) and their families are recruited from the emergency department or inpatient ward of two major metropolitan hospitals. The current sample consists of 58 children and adolescents who completed their initial assessment approximately 3 weeks following trauma either by post, telephone, or face-to-face. Table 1 details the sample characteristics.

Measures

Trauma interview. A brief interview with parents was used to collect demographic information, the child's prior trauma history, family history of psychological problems, previous treatment for emotional problems, and length of hospitalisation. Parents also rated the severity of their child's injury on a 4-point scale (0 = *no injury*, 1= *minor*, 2 = *moderate*, 3 = *severe*).

Trauma symptoms and depression. Children completed the Acute Stress Checklist for Children (ASC-Kids; Kassam-Adams, 2006). Items 5–23 from the 29-item measure were utilised to assess ASD symptomatology. Preliminary psychometric properties of the ASC-Kids demonstrate good reliability and validity (Kassam-Adams, 2006). The 17-item Child PTSD Symptom Scale (CPSS; Foa, Johnson, Feeny, & Treadwell, 2001) was also used as a measure of acute stress symptomatology, and depression was measured with the Child Depression Inventory (CDI; Kovacs, 1992).

Appraisals. A 21-item measure, the Adaptive Appraisals Questionnaire (AAQ) was developed to measure potentially protective cognitive appraisals. The questions were guided by theory (Ehlers & Clark, 2000; Meiser-Stedman, 2002), therapy guidelines (Perrin et al., 2004) and previous research (Ehlers, Mayou, & Bryant, 2003). The questions assessed the child's perception about other peoples' reactions to the trauma (e.g., 'Other people think I'm brave'), their beliefs about how well they reacted to the trauma and its consequences (e.g., 'Getting over the event will make/has made me better at coping'), and whether they believed the event to be in the past (e.g., 'I feel like the event is finished/over'). The AAQ is scored with a 4-point Likert-type scale (1 = *'don't agree at all'*, 4 = *'agree a lot'*), and Cronbach's alpha = .78. Children also completed the Child Posttraumatic Cognitions Inventory (cPTCI; Meiser-Stedman, Smith, Yule, & Dalgleish, 2003), a 25-item self-report measure of children's negative appraisals about the trauma and its consequences.

Social support. Children's perception of social support adequacy was assessed using the Multidimensional Scale of Perceived Social Support (MSPSS; Zimet, Dahlem, Zimet, & Farley, 1988). The MSPSS consists of 12 items (scale 1–7) where a higher score reflects more adequate social support. Parents' perception regarding how supported and satisfied they feel in their parenting role and how well they communicate with their child was measured with two subscales of the Parent–Child Relationships Inventory (PCRI; Gerard, 1994). The PCRI-support and PCRI-communicate subscales consist of 9 items each, with a higher score suggesting higher levels of social support.

Results

Preliminary Screening

Descriptive statistics for the variables of interest are reported in Table 1, and relevant correlations are reported in Table 2. The majority of potential correlates (e.g., gender, prior trauma, length of hospitalisation) were unrelated to trauma and depression symptom measures. Older children were more likely to report depressive symptoms, and there was a trend for family history of psychological problems to be associated with depression. Using a clinical cut-off of 11 for the CPSS (Foa et al., 2001) resulted in 36% being in the highly symptomatic range, although it should be recognised that this cut-off is based on a PTSD not ASD sample, thus probably overestimates the prevalence of clinically significant posttraumatic stress.

Table 1
Sample and Trauma Characteristics, Including Means, Standard Deviations, Minimum and Maximum Scores

Variable	M	SD	Min	Max
Child age	12.02	2.89	7	17
Gender[a]	62%M			
Time since trauma (days)	20.33	7.87	7	36
Length of hospitalisation (days)	5.31	8.54	0	28
Injury severity	1.72	0.99	0	3
Child prior trauma[a]	42%			
Child prior psychological treatment[a]	21%			
Family history of psychological problems[a]	23%			
CPSS	10.79	9.09	0	39
ASC-Kids	12.47	7.86	0	33
CDI	8.38	6.22	0	26
cPTCI	39.95	13.79	25	84
AAQ	65.57	8.97	16	80
MSPSS	68.84	12.84	30	84
PCRI-S	20.91	4.62	11	34
PCRI-C	16.05	2.89	10	23

Note: CPSS = Child Posttraumatic Stress Scale; ASC-Kids = Acute Stress Disorder Checklist for Children; CDI = Child Depression Inventory; cPTCI = Child Posttraumatic Cognitions Inventory; AAQ = Adaptive Appraisal Questionnaire; MSPSS = Multidimensional Scale of Perceived Social Support; PCRI-S = Parent–Child Relationships Inventory, Support subscale; PCRI-C = Parent–Child Relationships Inventory, Communication subscale.
[a] Variable coded dichotomously.

Table 2
Correlations Between Symptoms, Appraisals, and Potential Correlates

Variable	ASC-Kids	CPSS	CDI
Symptom measures			
ASC-Kids	—		
CPSS	.81***	—	
CDI	.54***	.70***	—
Appraisals and social support			
cPTCI	.66***	.63***	.66***
AAQ	−.36**	−.52***	−.62***
MSPSS	−.04	−.25†	−.45***
PCRI-S	.04	.06	.15
PCRI-C	−.01	.02	.07
Demographic and potential correlates			
Child age	.05	.20	.32*
Gender[a]	.15	.16	.06
Time since trauma (days)	.03	−.17	−.14
Length of hospitalisation (days)	−.17	−.19	−.14
Injury severity	−.11	−.02	.00
Child prior trauma[a]	.03	.10	.23
Child prior psychological treatment[a]	.06	−.09	.15
Family history of psychological problems[a]	.19	.18	.25†

Note: ASC-Kids = Acute Stress Disorder Checklist for Children; CPSS = Child Posttraumatic Stress Scale; CDI = Child Depression Inventory; cPTCI = Child Posttraumatic Cognitions Inventory; AAQ = Adaptive Appraisal Questionnaire; MSPSS = Multidimensional Scale of Perceived Social Support; PCRI-S = Parent–Child Relationships Inventory, Support subscale; PCRI-C = Parent–Child Relationships Inventory, Communication subscale.
[a] Correlations with dichotomous variables are Spearman rank-order correlations.
† $p < .10$; * $p < .05$; ** $p < .01$; *** $p < .001$.

In terms of depression, 10% of children scored above 17 on the CDI, which approximates to the 85th percentile.

Main Results
As hypothesised, negative trauma appraisals (cPTCI) were strongly correlated with posttrauma symptoms (ASC-Kids, CPSS) and depressive reactions (CDI). Similarly, the more children reported adaptive appraisals (AAQ), the less likely they were to report posttrauma psychopathology. Mixed findings were observed in relation to children's perception of social support (MSPSS). On the one hand, social support was negatively correlated with depression scores, but only showed a trend when posttrauma reactions were measured with the CPSS. The correlation between

social support and acute stress symptoms, as measured by the ASC-Kids, was nonsignificant. Interestingly, and contrary to prediction, *parents'* ratings of their level of support for their children (PCRI) were unrelated to any symptom measure.

Hierarchical multiple regression analyses were conducted to examine the relative contributions of hypothesised predictors on ASD and depression symptomatology. Given that appraisals were the primary area of interest and the cross-sectional nature of the data, order of predictor entry was varied to determine the influence of appraisals on symptomatology. Nonetheless, the theoretical stance that appraisals generally influence traumatic symptom development, not the other way around, was adopted. Since analyses using the ASC-Kids and CPSS replicated one another, in the interest of brevity only regressions with the ASC-Kids are reported.

In the first regression, the unique variance explained by protective appraisals on ASD symptoms was examined after controlling for negative appraisals. As can be seen from Table 3, negative appraisals accounted for 43% of the variance in ASD symptoms, while protective appraisals had no significant effect on ASD symptoms. Entering protective appraisals before negative trauma appraisals explained 13% of the variance; but this was no longer significant once negative appraisals were entered, the latter continuing to predict approximately 31% of the variance in ASD symptom scores (see Table 3).

Protective appraisals accounted for significant variance in depressive scores, even after controlling for child's age, and negative trauma appraisals (Table 4). Protective appraisals uniquely accounted for approximately 10% of the variance in depression scores. In this instance, entering negative

Table 3
Summary of Hierarchical Regression Analysis of Acute Stress Symptoms (ASC-Kids): Negative and Protective Appraisals as Predictor Variables

Predictors	B	SE B	β	ΔR^2	Adjusted R^2	Multiple R	Overall F
Step 1: cPTCI	0.37	0.06	.66***	.43	.42	.66	$F(2, 53) =$ 20.72***
Step 2: AAQ	–.07	0.08	–.10	.01	.42	.66	
Step 1: AAQ	–0.26	0.09	–.36**	.13	.12	.36	$F(2, 53) =$ 20.72***
Step 2: cPTCI	0.35	0.07	.61***	.31	.42	.66	

Note: ASC-Kids = Acute Stress Disorder Checklist for Children; cPTCI = Child Posttraumatic Cognitions Inventory; AAQ = Adaptive Appraisal Questionnaire.
   *$p < .05$; **$p < .01$; ***$p < .001$.

Table 4
Summary of Hierarchical Regression Analysis of Depression Symptoms (CDI):
Child Age, Negative and Protective Appraisals as Predictor Variables

Predictors	B	SE B	β	ΔR²	Adjusted R²	Multiple R	Overall F
Step 1: Age	0.70	0.28	.32*	.11	.09	.32	F(3, 56) = 25.42***
Step 2: cPTCI	0.28	0.05	.63***	.38	.47	.70	
Step 3: AAQ	−0.21	0.06	−.37**	.10	.57	.77	
Step 1: Age	0.70	0.28	.32*	.11	.09	.32	F(3, 56) = 25.42***
Step 2: AAQ	−0.32	0.06	−.57***	.30	.38	.63	
Step 3: cPTCI	0.22	0.04	.48***	.19	.57	.77	

Note: CDI = Child Depression Inventory; cPTCI = Child Posttraumatic Cognitions Inventory;
AAQ = Adaptive Appraisal Questionnaire.
*$p < .05$; **$p < .01$; ***$p < .001$.

Table 5
Summary of Hierarchical Regression Analysis of Depression Symptoms (CDI):
Child Age, Negative and Protective Appraisals, and Child Social Support as
Predictor Variables

Predictors	B	SE B	β	ΔR²	Adjusted R²	Multiple R	Overall F
Step 1: Age	0.70	0.28	.32*	.11	.09	.32	F(4, 52) = 23.42***
Step 2: Appraisals				.49	.57	.77	
AAQ	−0.21	0.06	−.37**				
cPTCI	0.22	0.04	.48***				
Step 3: MSPSS	−0.13	0.05	−.27**	.05	.62	.80	

Note: CDI = Child Depression Inventory; AAQ = Adaptive Appraisal Questionnaire; cPTCI =
Child Posttraumatic Cognitions Inventory; MSPSS = Multidimensional Scale of Perceived
Social Support.
*$p < .05$; **$p < .01$; ***$p < .001$.

trauma appraisals before protective cognitions did not alter the findings, suggesting that both types of appraisals contribute to depressive symptoms (see Table 4).

Finally, after controlling for the child's age, and both negative and protective appraisals, children's perceived availability of social support predicted a small, but significant amount of variance (5%) in depression scores (Table 5). It is worth noting that *all* regression findings held, even when acute stress was entered at Step 1 in regressions predicting depression, and vice versa.

Discussion

Although the present data are preliminary and cross-sectional, they support the notion that appraisals following traumatic events and symptoms of anxiety and mood are strongly linked. Clearly, conclusions about the direction of these relationships cannot be made until our prospective data are analysed, but the findings are consistent with cognitive models of PTSD (e.g., Ehlers & Clark, 2000). It is worth noting that appraisals and child's perception of social support accounted for reasonably large total proportions of variance in ASD and depression symptom scores (adjusted R^2 ranging between 42%–62%). A slightly different pattern of findings using the two appraisal measures suggested that the proposed protective appraisal measure (AAQ) was not simply a positively worded measure of negative trauma cognitions assessed by the cPTCI. Thus, although negative cognitions predicted both ASD and depression symptoms, it appeared that adaptive cognitions were associated with less depression symptoms but not ASD reactions.

Children's perception of social support was associated with less depressive but not ASD symptoms, and this relationship held even when the effects of both protective appraisals and negative appraisals were controlled. It may be that having someone to talk with about problems and to share happy experiences, is protective against depression, but not ASD symptoms. Given the timing of assessment (approximately 3 weeks posttrauma), analysis of follow-up data will allow examination of other explanations (e.g., social support may become more relevant in relation to longer-term posttraumatic stress reactions).

Interestingly, parent report of support and communication with their children did not predict either ASD symptoms or depression, nor was it correlated with child report of availability of social support. It is possible that the two subscales of the PCRI used do not measure the hypothesised constructs; alternatively they may not be related to child symptomatology.

Clinical Implications

Despite the preliminary nature of the data, they have important clinical implications. First, ASD and depression reactions are highly related and relatively common following single-incident trauma, thus children should be screened for both in the acute phase after trauma exposure. Second, many children with relatively minor injuries still reported significant symptoms. This is consistent with other research that has found mixed findings in regard to injury severity predicting psychological symptoms (e.g., Bryant, Mayou, Wiggs, Ehlers, & Stores, 2004; Daviss et al., 2000), and indicates the need to screen for ASD and depression even after minor accidents. Third, although somewhat speculative, children's perceptions of social support may reflect their need for support better than parent report. Nonetheless, parental support is likely to be an integral component of any intervention. Fourth, fostering children's adaptive appraisals of their experience, and targeting negative interpretations is likely to be a useful method of early intervention. Although we are not aware of any controlled treatment trials of cognitive–behaviour therapy (CBT) for childhood ASD, such a cognitive restructuring approach makes sense given that CBT is an empirically supported intervention for childhood PTSD (National Collaborating Centre for Mental Health & National Institute for Clinical Excellence, 2005).

Acknowledgment

This research was supported in part by a grant from the Australian Rotary Health Research Fund.

References

Brewin, C.R., Dalgleish, T., & Joseph, S. (1996). A dual representation theory of posttraumatic stress disorder. *Psychological Review, 103*, 670–686.

Bryant, B., Mayou, R., Wiggs, L., Ehlers, A., & Stores, G. (2004). Psychological consequences of road traffic accidents for children and their mothers. *Psychological Medicine, 34*, 335–346.

Daviss, W.B., Racusin, R., Fleischer, A., Mooney, D., Ford, J.D., & McHugo, G.J. (2000). Acute stress disorder symptomatology during hospitalization for pediatric injury. *Journal of the American Academy of Child and Adolescent Psychiatry, 39*, 569–575.

Ehlers, A., & Clark, D.M. (2000). A cognitive model of posttraumatic stress disorder. *Behaviour Research & Therapy, 38*, 319–345.

Ehlers, A., Mayou, R.A., & Bryant, B. (2003). Cognitive predictors of posttraumatic stress disorder in children: Results of a prospective longitudinal study. *Behaviour Research and Therapy, 41*, 1–10.

Fletcher, K.E. (1996). Childhood posttraumatic stress disorder. In E.J. Marsh & R. Barkley (Eds.), *Child psychopathology* (pp. 242–276). New York: Guildford Press.

Foa, E.B., Johnson, K.M., Feeny, N.C., & Treadwell, K.R.H. (2001). The Child PTSD Symptom Scale: A preliminary examination of its psychometric properties. *Journal of Clinical Child Psychology, 30*, 376–384.

Gerard, A.B. (1994). *Parent–Child Relationship Inventory (PCRI)*. Los Angeles: Western Psychological Services.

Kassam-Adams, N. (2006). The Acute Stress Checklist for Children (ASC-Kids): Development of a child self-report measure. *Journal of Traumatic Stress, 19*, 129–139.

Kovacs, M. (1992). *Children's Depression Inventory (CDI)–Manual*. New York: Multi-Health Systems.

Meiser-Stedman, R. (2002). Towards a cognitive-behavioral model of PTSD in children and adolescents. *Clinical Child & Family Psychology Review, 5,* 217–232.

Meiser-Stedman, R., Smith, P., Yule, W., & Dalgleish, T. (2003, July). *Predictors of chronic PTSD in children and adolescents following road traffic accidents and physical assaults.* Paper presented at the 31st Annual Conference of the British Association of Behavioural and Cognitive Psychotherapy, York, UK.

Meiser-Stedman, R., Yule, W., Smith, P., Glucksman, E., & Dalgleish, T. (2005). Acute stress disorder and posttraumatic stress disorder in children and adolescents involved in assaults or motor vehicle accidents. *American Journal of Psychiatry, 162*(7), 1381–1383.

National Collaborating Centre for Mental Health, & National Institute for Clinical Excellence. (2005). *Post-traumatic stress disorder: The management of PTSD in adults and children in primary and secondary care.* London: Royal College of Psychiatrists and British Psychological Society.

Perrin, S., Smith, P., & Yule, W. (2004). Treatment of PTSD in children and adolescents. In P.M. Barrett & T.H. Ollendick (Eds.), *Handbook of Interventions that work with children and adolescents. Prevention and treatment* (pp. 217–242). Chichester, UK: Wiley.

Salmon, K., & Bryant, R.A. (2002). Posttraumatic stress disorder in children: The influence of developmental factors. *Clinical Psychology Review, 22,* 163–188.

Winston, F.K., Baxt, C., Kassam-Adams, N.L., Elliott, M.R., & Kallan, M.J. (2005). Acute traumatic stress symptoms in child occupants and their parent drivers after crash involvement. *Archives of Pediatrics & Adolescent Medicine, 159*(11), 1074–1079.

Winston, F.K., Kassam-Adams, N., Vivarelli-O'Neill, C., Ford, J., Newman, E., Baxt, C., et al. (2002). Acute stress disorder symptoms in children and their parents after pediatric traffic injury. *Pediatrics, 109,* e90.

Zimet, G.D., Dahlem, N.W., Zimet, S.G., & Farley, G.K. (1988). The multidimensional scale of perceived social support. *Journal of Personality Assessment, 52,* 30–41.

CHAPTER 21

The Role of Therapist Schema in the Training and Supervision of Cognitive Therapists

Beverly Haarhoff

Cognitive therapy (CT) has expanded over the past 15 years and protocols for the treatment of complex and chronic diagnostic presentations such as the personality disorders have been developed (Clark & Fairburn, 1997). This has resulted in longer periods of treatment and a modification of some CT protocols to include an emphasis on interpersonal aspects of the therapeutic relationship as an intervention (Beck, Freeman, & Davis, 2004; Young, Klosko, & Weishaar, 2003). In this chapter the implications of these developments on the training of cognitive therapists are discussed. A number of methods, which can be used in training and supervision to facilitate understanding of the impact of interpersonal processes on the therapeutic relationship in a manner conceptually consistent with the CT model, are suggested. The Therapists' Schema Questionnaire (TSQ; Leahy, 2001) is discussed as a useful method to identify and understand 'therapist' schemas (TS), which if ignored, could potentially derail the therapy process.

Essential CT competencies include (1) the ability to build effective therapeutic relationships, (2) the ability to conceptualise therapeutic issues, (3) awareness of potentially therapy interfering with personal problems and (4) the application of tailored CT interventions (Dobson & Shaw, 1993). It follows that facilitating the development of interpersonal skills relating to understanding and working with the therapeutic relationship in a conceptually coherent manner, is a training priority.

The importance of the therapeutic relationship is widely acknowledged (Bachelor & Horvath, 1999) and has been variously described by clinical writers representing dominant models in psychotherapy. Cognitive–behavioural models emphasise collaborative empiricism and 'coaching' analogies. The interpersonal aspects of the therapeutic relationship per se are seldom a focus. Rogerian principles of accurate empathy and positive regard are recognised as central to a 'good working relationship' but labelled nonspecific and of lesser importance to 'specific' CT interventions. Little attention is given to actively developing these capacities in CT training.

Recently, the idea that the therapeutic relationship is secondary has been challenged by CT therapists working with diagnostic presentations, such as the personality disorders, where maladaptive interpersonal relationships are a defining characteristic of the disorder. Increasingly, the therapeutic relationship is seen as the vehicle through which alternative, more adaptive, interpersonal patterns can be explored. This has resulted in the psychoanalytic concepts of transference, countertransference, and resistance being reconceptualised to fit more comfortably with the CT model (Layden, Newman, Freeman, & Morse, 1993; Leahy, 2001; Linehan, 1993; Rudd & Joiner, 1997; Young et al., 2003). CT rejects the 'unconscious' elements of the psychoanalytic understanding of transference and countertransference. Current influences which highlight the interaction between cognitive, affective, and behavioural reactions of both therapist and patient are instead emphasised. If the therapist ignores, or fails to understand the countertransference, negative therapy interfering consequences can result; for example, technique avoidance, guilt or fear over patient anger, feelings of inferiority, and the inability to set limits (Leahy, 2001).

Introducing the Notion of Countertransference to CT Trainees

Understanding countertransference is complex and requires that the therapist attend to interpersonal process issues in a manner different to that of ordinary daily interpersonal transactions. This entails 'the awareness of the other's (*and own*) behaviour, seeing the other (*and self*) as provocation or elicitor, self (*or other*) as the object of the other's (*self's*) experience, and self-other role-taking' (Leahy, in press). Such awareness should occur within current interactions, other relationships with similar patterns, or past relationships (Leahy, in press). Leahy (2001) suggests some guidelines to help in the understanding of the countertransference. Firstly, acknowledging that the phenomenon exists is important in CT, which traditionally relies on treatment protocols emphasising specific factors at the expense of relationship factors. Secondly, noticing the different levels of arousal triggered by different patients or types of problems can predict particular associated belief patterns and behavioural responses. For example, patients who are dependent may trigger overinvolvement or withdrawal from some therapists, depending on the personal beliefs of the therapist. Thirdly, becoming aware of personal schemas which manifest in the trainees' everyday life situations is helpful as therapy can trigger these habitual responses. For example, a fear of 'abandonment' may make ending therapy difficult. Asking questions such as, 'Which problems concern me most?', 'Are there particular clients that I am drawn to, or would like to avoid?', and 'What are my beliefs about emotional expression?' can reveal therapist beliefs which may impact on the therapeutic process.

Utilising this awareness in a therapeutically helpful way requires that trainees understand their reactions in a manner conceptually consistent with the CT model. Therefore, the trainee should develop an awareness of negative automatic thoughts, underlying assumptions, and core beliefs as triggered by the therapeutic relationship. Introducing trainees to models such as the 'therapeutic belief system' (TBS; Rudd & Joiner, 1997) is one way of alerting them to countertransference processes. The TBS sets out a framework to identify the therapists' and patients' beliefs about *themselves, each other*, and *the course of treatment*, the emotions these beliefs may trigger, and typical behavioural responses. For example, the therapist may see the patient as a 'hostile aggressor', 'helpless victim', or 'collaborator'. These perceptions result in different emotional and behavioural responses. For instance, perceiving the patient as a 'helpless victim' might precipitate an anxious or depressed response in the therapist, resulting in avoidant, overcautious, excessively nurturing behaviour. In these instances, appropriate interventions such as exposure may not be applied.

Practicing CT on oneself and reflecting on the outcome is another helpful way to increase trainees' awareness of their countertransference. Useful interventions include monitoring mood in relation to situational triggers, constructing a personal functional analysis using a five-part model (Padesky & Mooney, 1990), working through a dysfunctional thought record (Beck, 1995), or devising and reflecting on the outcome of behavioural experiments. Other self-practice involves the completion of questionnaires used to identify schemas, and underlying assumptions, for example, the Dysfunctional Attitude Scale (Weissman & Beck, 1978), the Personal Belief Questionnaire (Beck & Beck, 1995), the Young Schema Questionnaire (Young & Brown, 2001), and the TSQ (Leahy, 2001).

The Therapist's Schema Questionnaire

The TSQ is a qualitative measure, consisting of 46 assumptions representing 14 TS. A schema refers to mental structures integrating events mean-ingfully (Beck, Freeman, & Davis, 2004). In CT, schemas are defined as 'A broad, pervasive theme or pattern, comprised of memories, emotions, cognitions, and bodily sensations, regarding oneself and one's relationship with others, developed during childhood and adolescence, elaborated through one's lifetime and dysfunctional to a significant degree' (Young et al., 2003, p. 7). Dysfunctional schemas can be associated with diagnostic presentations, for example, schemas overestimating personal vulnerability and external threat are common in the anxiety disorders (Beck, Emery, & Greenberg, 1985). TS have a similar dysfunctional connotation. Less pervasive and unconditional than described above, TS are triggered in specific, therapy-related contexts and do not usually signal mental health problems. TS are influenced by factors such as supervision, stage and experience of training, clinical experience, peer group, psychotherapy model, and personal experience. Some examples of TS schemas are 'demanding standards' (inflexible or high expectations of compliance), 'abandonment', 'need for approval', 'excessive self-sacrifice' (the inability to set boundaries or act assertively with patients), and 'special superior person' (a grandiose view of one's therapeutic skill).

The TSQ is a simple screening technique used to identify TS. Once identified, TS can be used in training and supervision as a starting point for discussing some of the trainees' potential countertransference processes within the context of the CT model. A recent study tracked the responses to the Leahy TSQ of four groups of trainees enrolled in the Postgraduate Diploma in Cognitive Behaviour Therapy at Massey University, New Zealand (Haarhoff, 2006). Two groups had completed the final theoretical paper in year one of the diploma, and the other two groups were made up of trainees in their practicum year. A total of 64 trainees answered the questionnaire. Analysis of the responses revealed a consistent pattern. The most commonly identified TS were 'demanding standards' (75%–87%), 'special superior person' (62%–87%), and 'excessive self-sacrifice' (57%–62%). The majority of participants identified with the 'demanding standards' schema — signalling a somewhat obsessive, perfectionist, and controlling approach to therapy. The expectation that there is a 'right' way to do things may lead to frustration and insecurity when therapy throws up unexpected issues. This stance may indicate insecurity and a belief that if therapy deviates from the predicted structure one's job is not being done properly and that, at worst, the trainee will be exposed as a 'fraud'. A greater range of responses between groups was noted for the identification of the 'special superior person' schema, with a higher percentage of participants in the practicum group, 85%–87%, identifying with this schema. Those identifying with this schema see the therapy situation as an opportunity to achieve excellent results and have grandiose expectations for their own performance. There may be a tendency to idealise the patient, or conversely, devalue or distance self from a patient who does not improve or comply with treatment. The therapist may lack empathy. Between 57% and 62% of participants identified with the assumptions associated with 'excessive self-sacrifice'. Leahy suggests that therapists with this schema tend to overemphasise the importance of their relationships with patients. They may fear abandonment or feel guilty that they are better off than the patient. Self-defeating behaviours, such as, going 'overboard' to meet the needs of the patient may result from this schema. 'Persecution' (6%–12%), the belief that patients are deliberately trying to undermine or harm the therapist; 'goal inhibition' (0%–12%), a belief that the patient is blocking the therapist's goals; and 'emotional inhibition' (0%–19%), the belief that the therapist has to repress all of his or her emotional responses were the least identified.

It could be hypothesised that the consistent pattern of schema identification across the four groups of participants relates to their stage of development as cognitive therapists. Unfortunately there are, at the time of writing, no comparative data in the form of a group of more experienced therapists' responses to the TSQ to support this hypothesis. In the personal observation of the writer, an experienced supervisor, 'demanding standards' — indicating a need for certainty and a lack of tolerance for ambiguity — is characteristic of novice therapists. The emphasis on structure, and the strong evidence-based reputation of CT, can encourage an expectation that there is always an 'answer' and a 'right way' to proceed. When confronted with patients who do not comply with treatment, fail to improve, or present with complex problems, the novice therapist can lose confidence and attribute difficulties to their own shortcomings, or lose faith in the model. Similarly, 'excessive self-sacrifice' is often observed in novice therapists who find it difficult to be appropriately assertive with patients (this schema is frequently observed in therapists; Young et al., 2003). When this schema is present there may be a tendency to avoid techniques such as exposure for fear of upsetting the patient. The prominence of the 'special superior' TS in the practicum groups appears to contradict the other two prominent schemas, with its connotations of entitlement and narcissism. This schema can be understood as 'schema overcompensation'. Overcompensation is one of three schema processes or coping styles (schema overcompensation, surrender, and avoidance), which can result from schema activation (Young, et al., 2003). The presence of the 'special superior person' TS may be overcompensation in response to the 'demanding standards' and 'excessive self-sacrifice' schema, which have connotations of 'not being good enough'. The experience of the clinical practicum places the trainee in a position where their clinical work is intensely scrutinised in supervision through the evaluation of videotaped therapy sessions. Feeling special and superior may be, in some instances, a way of coping with the feelings of inferiority generated by this experience. It was heartening to observe that the 'persecution' TS was *least* identified. An attitude of mistrust and a mindset which expects the worst from patients could be expected if this schema were present, and this attitude would seriously interfere with 'unconditional positive regard', which is one of the most frequently cited attributes of a therapeutic relationship conducive to positive change in patients.

Using the Leahy TSQ in Training and Supervision

The TSQ can be used (1) as a screening device to increase the personal insight of trainees and therapists, (2) as a teaching aid to extract general themes that may be relevant to stage of training and (3) in clinical supervision to alert trainees to the potential triggers and implications of TS. Each of these applications will be discussed below.

A Screening Device

The TSQ can be used as a screening device to speed up the identification of potential problems that may emerge in the therapeutic relationship. For example, if a trainee has a large number of significant schemas this could signal depression, low self-esteem, an unsupported professional environment, or significant interpersonal issues which may require individual personal therapy. Conversely, a TSQ indicating no significant schemas might point to a lack of personal insight or to the trainee being somewhat complacent about his or her therapeutic skill. The responses to the TSQ could highlight significant schemas or combinations of schemas indicating serious interpersonal difficulties which need to be addressed.

General Themes

Themes relevant to the stage of training can be elicited by the TSQ. It is an engaging way to introduce trainees to the existence of TS about their patients. The particular TS prominent in a group can be made part of class discussions and developmentally contextualised in terms of stage of training. For example, the 'demanding standards' schema can be discussed in terms of unrealistic expectations which may be imposed on

Table 1
Therapist Reactions to Homework Noncompliance When Therapist Schemas 'Demanding Standards' is Activated

Trigger	Homework noncompliance
Beliefs about self	'I'm an incompetent therapist', 'I am responsible/ accountable for this client improving and he/she is not', 'I'm worthless, hopeless as a counsellor'
Beliefs about the patient	'This client is non-compliant/unmotivated/lazy'
Beliefs about the course of treatment	'Things should go to plan', 'CT should work', 'CT won't work if she/he does not complete his/her homework'
Unhelpful behavioural response	Demanding, controlling, technique-driven, avoiding difficult patients
Healthy alternative	*Decreasing control, encouraging client decision-making*

patients, and the importance of tolerating a degree of uncertainty as psychotherapy unfolds, can be highlighted.

Therapeutic Implications of Therapist Schemas

Prominent recurring TS can be conceptualised in supervision using the CT model. For example, TS could be explored using headings adapted from the Rudd and Joiner (1997) TBS model — namely triggers, therapist beliefs about self, the patient, the course of treatment, unhelpful behavioural strategies resulting from the TS, and healthy alternatives. Table 1 illustrates a number of unhelpful reactions which could result for the TS 'demanding standards'.

Schema processes and maladaptive coping styles can be explained and trainees can use this knowledge to become more sensitised to their idiosyncratic triggers in therapy and generate constructive alternative responses. Trainees can be encouraged to practise CT techniques helpful in altering strong beliefs, on themselves. Self-reflection on this process will improve their knowledge of the application of CT interventions and increase their self-awareness (Bennett-Levy et al., 2001).

Conclusion

The contribution of the therapist and the impact of the therapeutic relationship are emphasised as important common factors in therapy outcome (Frank & Frank, 1993; Hubble, Duncan, & Miller, 1999, Wampold, 2001). When this factor is juxtaposed against the fact that therapists perceived by their patients to be nonempathetic and punitive have been shown to have a negative effect on the course of therapy, the importance of training in this area is amplified (Bachelor & Horvath, 1999; Wampold, 2001). Incorporating methods such as the TSQ to encourage focused self-reflection and improve interpersonal understanding is a potentially important addition to CT training programs.

References

Bachelor, A., & Horvath, A. (1999). The therapeutic relationship. In M. Hubble, B.L. Duncan, & S.D. Miller (Eds.), *The heart and soul of change: What works in psychotherapy* (pp. 133–165). Washington DC: American Psychological Association.

Beck, A., & Beck, J. (1995). The personality belief questionnaire. Bala Cynwyd, PA: Beck Institute for Cognitive Therapy and Research.

Beck, A., Freeman, A., & Davis, D. (2004). *Cognitive therapy for personality disorders* (2nd ed.). New York: The Guilford Press.

Beck, A., Emery, G., & Greenberg, R. (1985). *Anxiety disorders and phobias: A cognitive perspective.* New York: Basic Books.

Beck, J. (1995). *Cognitive therapy: Basics and beyond.* New York: The Guilford Press.

Bennett-Levy, J., Turner, F., Beaty, T., Smith, M., Paterson, B., & Farmer, S. (2001). The value of self-practice of cognitive therapy techniques and self-reflection in the training of cognitive therapists. *Behavioural and Cognitive Psychotherapy, 29,* 203–220.

Clark, D., & Fairburn, C. (Eds.). (1997). *The science and practice of cognitive therapy.* Oxford: Oxford University Press.

Dobson, K., & Shaw, B. (1993). The training of cognitive therapists: What we have learnt from treatment manuals. *Psychotherapy, 30,* 573–577.

Frank, J., & Frank, J. (1993). *Persuasion and healing a comparative study of psychotherapy.* Baltimore: The John Hopkins University Press.

Haarhoff, B. (2006). The importance of identifying and understanding therapist schema in training and supervision. *New Zealand Journal of Psychology, 35*(3), 126–131.

Hubble, M., Duncan, B., & Miller, S. (1999). *The heart and soul of change: What works in therapy.* Washington DC: American Psychological Association.

Layden, M.A., Newman, C.F., Freeman, A., & Morse, S.B. (1993). *Cognitive therapy of borderline personality disorder.* Boston: Allyn & Bacon.

Leahy, R.L. (2001). *Overcoming resistance in cognitive therapy.* New York: The Guilford Press.

Leahy, R.L. (in press). Schematic mismatch in the therapeutic relationship. In P. Gilbert & R. Leahy (Eds.), *The therapeutic relationship in the cognitive behavioural psychotherapies.* London: Routledge.

Linehan, M.M. (1993). *Cognitive–behavioural treatment of borderline personality disorder.* New York: Guilford Press.

Padesky, C., & Mooney, K. (1990). Clinical tip: Presenting the cognitive model to clients. *International Cognitive Therapy Newsletter, 6,* 1–2.

Rudd, M., & Joiner, T. (1997). Countertransference and the therapeutic relationship: A cognitive perspective. *Journal of Cognitive Psychotherapy: An International Quarterly, 11*(4), 231–249.

Safran, J., & Segal, Z. (1996). *Interpersonal process in cognitive therapy.* Northvale, NJ: Jason Aronson Inc.

Skovholt, T., & Rønnestad, M. (2003). The hope and promise of career life-span counselor and therapist development. *Journal of Career Development, 30,* 1–3.

Wampold, B. (2001). *The great psychotherapy debate.* Mahwah, NJ: Lawrence Erlbaum Associates.

Weissman, A., & Beck, A. (1978, March 27-31). *Development and validation of the Dysfunctional Attitude Scale: A preliminary investigation.* Paper presented at the Annual Meeting of the American Educational Research Association, Toronto, Canada.

Young, J.E., & Brown, G. (2001). *Young schema questionnaire.* New York: Cognitive Therapy Center.

Young, J.E., Klosko, J.S., & Weishaar, M.E. (2003). *Schema therapy a practitioner's guide.* New York: The Guilford Press.

CHAPTER 22

The Advantage of Accessing Early Maladaptive Schemas in Early Childhood Memories and Empirical Evidence of Their Predictive Worth

Stephen Theiler and Glen Bates

This chapter begins with a summary of a treatment process that we implement in therapy sessions. Some differences between this treatment and pre-existing ones are then highlighted and the findings from two research studies that investigated some core assumptions from our clinical method are described. Our contribution to therapy and research is the integration of Bruhn's (1985, 1990) method of analysing early childhood memories with Young's (1999) conception of maladaptive schemas and their links with adults' current difficulties.

In practice, we incorporate ideas (e.g., from Beck, 1996; Young, Klosko, & Weishaar, 2003) that assume clients have core maladaptive schemas that are not necessarily consciously available. In our experience, once these tacit core beliefs are accessed, and acknowledged by the client, therapy and its outcomes can improve. In particular, we find that certain early maladaptive schemas (Young, 1999) that are uncovered in early childhood memories are intrinsically related to central problems that need to be addressed in therapy. Consequently, we have found that quite early in the counselling process, it is possible to discern clients' deep-seated difficulties and then work towards addressing them.

The links proposed by Young et al. (2003) between noxious early childhood memories and adult self-reported maladaptive schemas (Young, 1999) and psychopathologies were explored in two related studies using two different samples. Our findings support the relevance of themes and maladaptive schemas contained in early memories for distinguishing people with high levels of maladaptive schemas and psychological distress.

The results and implications from these two research projects are outlined after the discussion of treatment.

Background and Description of the Treatment Model

Our focus in the therapy process is related conceptually to McAdams's (2006) model of three levels of personality data. McAdams suggests that people can be understood by knowing their traits, adaptations and life stories. For example, it is helpful to know that a person has traits such as dominance and a tendency towards depression and that they adapt to particular difficulties in ways that demonstrate particular active schemas. However, it is at the level of the life story narrative that the clearest indication is given of internalised current difficulties and developmental issues in childhood that relate to the person's model of self and identity and which are at the core of schemas. In relation to McAdams's model of personality, we endeavour to understand the main themes and dispositions in a person's life, his or her maladaptive schemas and the life story that is constructed to integrate the past, the present and the future.

Beck (1996) and others (e.g., Young et al., 2003) indicate that maladaptive schemas are like prisms through which we view our world. They often comprise dysfunctional lifelong attitudes or assumptions about ourselves, others, and the world. Young's identification of core maladaptive schemas is very comprehensive in this regard. In his model, schemas are grouped into five domains such as the domain of 'disconnection and rejection' that contains the schemas of 'abandonment/instability', 'mistrust/abuse', 'emotional deprivation', 'defectiveness/shame' and 'social isolation/alienation' (see Young et al., 2003). Importantly, in our experience, some maladaptive schemas may be obvious to some clients and not others.

In the cognitive therapy literature, the notion of powerful maladaptive schemas operating outside of conscious awareness is not a new one. Beck (1996), for instance, acknowledged that maladaptive schemas may not be evident to the client but can be activated by unwelcome circumstances. Although recognising the importance of core maladaptive schemas that were outside conscious awareness, Beck (1996), Young (1999), and others (e.g., Epstein, 1994) did not use methodologies that directly accessed these maladaptive schemas. Nevertheless, they all mentioned the potential of revealing these schemas through examining early childhood memories. In this regard, we have adopted Bruhn's (1990) early childhood memory procedure as a vehicle to access these maladaptive schemas that might have a negative influence on clients.

As a contemporary early childhood memory theorist, Bruhn (1990) extended Adler (1956), Mayman (1968) and Bartlett's (1932) ideas to develop a cognitive perceptual theory (CPT). Consistent with McAdams, Bruhn proposes that stable sets of idiosyncratic schemas are stored in memory and new information that does not fit a person's existing schemas is usually discarded. Therefore, rather than memories being analysed as veridical accounts of the past, early childhood memories are viewed as identifying important underlying information about these stored schemas that is related to current difficulties. In our clinical practice we have found this to be the case.

To reveal underlying dysfunctional patterns of viewing the self, others and the world, we ask our clients to complete a number of tasks that may help to clarify areas of difficulty at different levels of personality. These measures include a case history, Young's Schema Questionnaire-Short Form (YSQ-S; Young, 1998) and four early-childhood memories based on the procedure outlined by Bruhn (1990). This comprises writing out two spontaneous earliest memories and also earliest memories of mother and father. The instructions for the spontaneous memories sections begin with 'What is the earliest memory that comes to mind that *you* actually remember'.

These memories, when analysed for their main themes and schematic content, often indicate the main area of underlying concern. The other two memories can also reveal relationship dynamics with parents and authority figures and maladaptive schemas that are operating in relationships with other men and women. For instance, the following is an example of an early memory (slightly changed to protect anonymity) from a person who came to therapy with clinical levels of depression. This memory was brought to the second session.

> When I was in primary school I was bitten on the shoulder by a wasp. I went to the teacher and he asked sarcastically, 'And what's wrong with you? Got a broken arm?' *I was shocked and crushed* and went away without another word. When I went home and told my parents about what happened at school *they did nothing about it.* I wished that they would ring the teacher and admonish him, but they did nothing. *I felt a lack of support and care from them as well.* The strongest feeling was *'despair'.*

Memories such as this one are analysed for Young's maladaptive schemas, negative affect and main themes. In this case, the memory clearly depicts a person who is wounded and who, when asking for help, was not taken seriously by a person with the power to do so. The maladaptive schemas in the memory ('abandonment' and 'emotional deprivation') indicate an overriding sense of disconnection and rejection by others, especially those in authority.

This information was very important to have early in therapy. The client was able to verify that he still experienced similar feelings as an adult. He found it difficult to express his concerns and he felt that others, such as his father, did not acknowledge him or recognise his needs. This information alerted the therapist that this person was in pain and that he may have an underlying sense of abandonment and rejection by others. Therefore, it was important for the therapist to validate this experience of pain and to help the client to explore the relevant underlying schemas as a precursor to change.

Young et al. (2003, p. 182) refer to this aspect of therapy as 'limited reparenting'. The therapist can provide an environment that mirrors good parenting that the client may not have experienced previously. In relation to maladaptive schemas in early memories, we have found a direct correlation between the themes in clients' memories and their current psychological difficulties in life. To reveal these core, maladaptive schemas can by quite transforming for the client.

The next sequence of memories is an example of using memory of mother and father. It is from a person who presented with relationship difficulties with her son and husband (changed to ensure anonymity).

> Memory of mother: I was 2–3 years old. I ran excitedly into my mother's room bursting to tell her something. The room was dark and she was reading a book or newspaper while breastfeeding. She completely ignored me. She then became cross and asked me to leave. *I didn't think she cared about me then.* The strongest feeling was *'rejection, not being important, a crushing feeling'. I felt frustrated that she did not listen to me, I was just ignored.*
>
> Her memory of father: My father took me to kindergarten. He held my hand very tightly and *promised me that he would not leave me. He then left me and I was devastated.* The strongest feeling was that: *'He lied and left me'.*

The memory of mother reveals themes of 'abandonment' and 'emotional deprivation' and the memory of father has elements of 'mistrust'. As it turned out, this client had major issues surrounding trust. Accepting that significant others were trustworthy (including the therapist) was very difficult, and the early memories were able to pinpoint this and other issues that could be addressed in therapy. Being able to access these issues early in therapy deepened the relationship and helped to contain the client.

Our Contribution in Relation to Other Treatments

We concur with Young et al. (2003) when they claim that many clients do not have access to their feelings with brief training. Many clients block, or are out of touch with, some of their feelings for a variety of reasons, such as an inability to consciously express an identifiable problem. In this regard, a number of studies attest to the efficacy of using Bruhn's (1990) early memory procedure (e.g., Bruhn & Davidow, 1983; Bruhn & Schiffman, 1982; Fowler, Hilsenroth, & Handler, 2000; Wheeler, 1987) to reveal underlying difficulties.

Our contribution is the integration of Young's (1999) maladaptive schemas to identify specific salient schemas with Bruhn's early-childhood memory procedure. We also compare the schemas evident in early-childhood memories with clients' self-reported maladaptive schemas (Young, 1999). It is mostly the case that clients feel understood in a very deep sense, when core information about their self is revealed and acknowledged by the therapist. This deeper understanding gives impetus for change and provides a rich source of schema-relevant material that can be addressed in cognitive therapy. A further contribution is empirically testing the ability of Young's schemas that are found in early memories to predict people's current difficulties.

Our Research Studies and Findings

To examine the link between people's maladaptive schemas in early childhood memories and their self-reported difficulties, evidence was obtained from two related studies. These studies incorporated early childhood memories as the method to access the underlying core maladaptive schemas, negative affect and perceptions of self, other and the environment. The participants in Study 1 comprised 249 undergraduate psychology students. There were 198 women and 50 men with a mean age of 22 years who were asked to write down four early childhood memories using Bruhn's (1990) early memory procedure.

The participants then filled out the short form of the YSQ-S. Independent raters coded the memories for Young's early maladaptive schemas, and Last and Bruhn's (1992) object relations categories of 'perceptions of others', 'perceptions of the self', 'perception of environment', and 'degree of interpersonal contact', and 'individual distinctiveness'.

In relation to Study 1, polyserial correlations indicated significant relationships between maladaptive schemas represented in early memories and self-reported maladaptive schemas. However, the maladaptive schemas identified in memories were not linked to the same maladaptive schemas that were being self-reported. This suggested that the schemas represented in memories were most likely tapping into a different source of information than conscious self-reports.

A discriminant function analysis (DFA) was then performed with the sample divided into three groups (low, medium and high YSQ-S scorers). The results showed maladaptive schemas identified in early memories that corresponded to Young's (1999) 'disconnection and rejection' domain and, Last and Bruhn's (1992) object relations theme of 'perceiving the environment as unsafe', were significant predictors of people in the group with high levels of self-reported maladaptive schemas. These variables also differentiated people in the high group from those in the low group at a greater rate than chance (33%). Fifty-six per cent of people were correctly allocated to the high group on the basis of representations of these particular schemas in their memories. When only the low and high groups were analysed, using individual schemas rather than domains, 'mistrust/abuse', 'social isolation', 'emotional deprivation' and 'subjugation' schemas in the first analysis and 'perceptions of the environment as unsafe' in the second analysis were found to be significant predictors. These predictors correctly classified 70% of cross-validated cases in the high groups in both analyses.

For Study 2, a different sample of students was accessed. The participants comprised 278 undergraduate psychology students. There were 65 men and 206 women with a mean age of 22 years who provided accounts of the same four early childhood memories used in Study 1. They also completed the Brief Symptom Inventory (BSI; Derogatis, 1993) to measure levels of psychological distress. As with Study 1, the accounts of the completed early childhood memories were coded by independent raters who examined the memories for Young's (1999) maladaptive schemas and Last and Bruhn's (1992) object relations categories. Additionally, following each memory, the participants rated their memories using Hermans and Hermans-Jansen's (1995) list of affect terms.

The sample was divided into three groups on the basis of the General Severity Index (GSI) scores (*low, medium* and *high* scorers) that were derived from the BSI (Derogatis, 1993). A discriminant function analysis showed that maladaptive schemas identified in the memories that corresponded to Young's (1999) 'disconnection and rejection' domain were significant predictors of people in the group with high levels of self-reported psychological symptoms (Derogatis, 1993). Fifty per cent of people (which is greater than the chance rate of 33%) were correctly predicted as belonging to the high-distress group on the basis of representations of schemas from this domain.

In another DFA analysis that used individual schemas instead of domains, 'abandonment' and 'insufficient self-control', together with 'perceiving the environment to be safe' and 'negative affect', were found to be significant predictors that correctly allocated 58% of people into the high GSI group. Further analysis using only the low and high groups resulted in 83% of people in the high group being correctly identified on the basis of representations of 'abandonment', 'insufficient self-control' and 'perceiving the environment to be safe'. These results endorse the relevance of the relationships among an underlying sense of abandonment and insufficient self-control with high levels of psychological symptoms of distress.

After analysing approximately 2000 early childhood memories in total from both studies, there was clear evidence that negative affect and perceptions of the environment, along with Young's (1999) maladaptive schemas, especially from the 'disconnection and rejection' domain, were able to predict adults with high levels of self-reported maladaptive schemas and psychological distress. The research findings provided evidence that these relationships exist (possibly outside of clients' conscious awareness) and were linked to adults' current self-reported difficulties.

Conclusion

Taken together, the findings from both studies support the theoretical proposition that maladaptive schemas residing outside of conscious awareness have a pervasive link with psychological health and wellbeing. A particularly important discovery was that a relatively small number of schemas aligned with perceptions of 'disconnection and rejection' from others were significantly linked to people in both studies who self-reported a wide range of psychological difficulties. Interestingly, Young et al. (2003, p. 13) mention that in their clinical practices people with schemas from this domain 'are often the most damaged'. Additionally, we found that schemas that were revealed in early memories were at times strongly related to different self-reported schemas. This suggests schemas may be active and affecting current functioning but are not self-reported.

The implications of our findings for therapy are that it is important to investigate themes and maladaptive schemas via early memories that may identify the underlying problems currently influencing the client. Identifying maladaptive schemas in early memories can hone in on the core schemas that underlie the person's problems in a relatively short period of time and is meaningful to the client. Our research findings support our clinical practice. Maladaptive schemas associated with disconnection and rejection represented in clients' early childhood memories can be viewed as very important schemas to examine. This is especially important given that such schemas may not be consciously accessed or easily articulated by clients, and may be intrinsically linked to a range of conscious psychological difficulties.

References

Adler, A. (1956). *The individual psychology of Alfred Adler: A systematic presentation in selection from his writings* (H.L. Ansbacher & R.R. Ansbacher, Eds. & Trans.). New York: Basic Books.

Bartlett, F.C. (1932). *Remembering: A study in experimental and social psychology.* Cambridge, UK: Cambridge University Press.

Beck, A.T. (1996). Beyond belief: A theory of modes, personality, and psychopathology. In P.M. Salkovskis (Ed.), *Frontiers of cognitive therapy* (pp. 1–25). New York: The Guilford Press.

Bruhn, A.R. (1985). Using early memories as a projective technique: The cognitive perceptual method. *Journal of Personality Assessment, 49,* 587–597.

Bruhn, A.R. (1990). *Earliest childhood memories volume 1: Theory and application to clinical practice.* New York: Praeger.

Bruhn, A.R., & Davidow, S. (1983). Earliest memories and the dynamics of delinquency. *Journal of Personality Assessment, 47,* 476–482.

Bruhn, A.R., & Schiffman, H. (1982). Prediction of locus of control stance from the earliest childhood memory. *Journal of Personality Assessment, 46,* 380–395.

Derogatis, L.R. (1993). *BSI: Brief Symptom Inventory* (3rd ed.). Minneapolis, MN, 55440: National Computer Systems.

Epstein, S. (1994). Integration of the cognitive and the psychodynamic unconscious. *American Psychologist, 49,* 709–724.

Fowler, J.C., Hilsenroth, M.J., & Handler, L. (2000). Martin Mayman's early memories technique: Bridging the gap between personality assessment and psychotherapy. *Journal of Personality Assessment, 75,* 18–32.

Hermans, H.J.M., & Hermans-Jansen, E. (1995). *Self-naratives: The construction of meaning in psychotherapy.* New York: The Guilford Press.

Last, J., & Bruhn, A.R. (1992). *Comprehensive Early Memory Scoring System Manual-Revised.* (Available from Arnold Bruhn, 7910 Woodmount Avenue, #1300, Bethesda, MD 20814.)

Mayman, M. (1968). Early memories and character structure. *Journal of Projective Techniques and Personality Assessment, 32,* 303–316.

McAdams, D.P. (2006). *The person: A new introduction to personality psychology* (4th ed.). Brisbane, Australia: John Wiley.

Wheeler, M.S. (1987). Assessing strengths from achievement memories. *Individual Psychology: Journal of Adlerian Theory, Research & Practice, 43,* 144–147.

Young, J.E. (1998). *The Young Schema Questionnaire: Short form* [Web Page]. Retrieved January 16, 2002, from http://www.schematherapy.com

Young, J.E. (1999). *Cognitive therapy for personality disorders: A schema-focused approach.* Sarasota, FL: Professional Resource Press.

Young, J.E., Klosko, J.S., & Weishaar, M.E. (2003). *Schema therapy: A practitioner's guide.* New York: The Guilford Press.

Index

www.ingramcontent.com/pod-product-compliance
Lightning Source LLC
Chambersburg PA
CBHW072100040426
42334CB00041B/1515